Kropotkin, Read, and the Intellectual History of British Anarchism

Kropotkin, Read, and the Intellectual History of British Anarchism

Between Reason and Romanticism

Matthew S. Adams
University of Victoria, Canada

palgrave
macmillan

First published 2015 by
PALGRAVE MACMILLAN

Palgrave Macmillan in the UK is an imprint of Macmillan Publishers Limited, registered in England, company number 785998, of Houndmills, Basingstoke, Hampshire RG21 6XS.

Palgrave Macmillan in the US is a division of St Martin's Press LLC, 175 Fifth Avenue, New York, NY 10010.

Palgrave Macmillan is the global academic imprint of the above companies and has companies and representatives throughout the world.

Palgrave® and Macmillan® are registered trademarks in the United States, the United Kingdom, Europe and other countries.

ISBN 978–1–137–39260–2

This book is printed on paper suitable for recycling and made from fully managed and sustained forest sources. Logging, pulping and manufacturing processes are expected to conform to the environmental regulations of the country of origin.

A catalogue record for this book is available from the British Library.

A catalog record for this book is available from the Library of Congress.

For that which is incapable of change has no history,
and records which state only the invariable need not be written,
and could not be read.

John Ruskin, *Modern Painters,* Volume III (1856)

Contents

Acknowledgements

This book is the product of three cities: Manchester; Washington, DC; and Victoria, British Columbia. It started life at the University of Manchester in 2011, under the guidance of Stuart Jones and Kevin Morgan, and I am indebted to both for their advice and astute criticism. I am also grateful to Ruth Kinna and Michael Sanders for their careful reading and thoughtful comments on earlier versions of this work.

I completed a significant amount of the research for this book whilst I was British Research Fellow in the John W. Kluge Center, at the Library of Congress in Washington, DC. I am grateful to the Fellows of the Kluge Center for making my time in DC so productive.

The opportunity to revise this book for publication was afforded by my appointment as Banting Postdoctoral Fellow at the University of Victoria. Allan Antliff went to great lengths to bring me to Canada, for which I am very appreciative.

I shared my time at Manchester with a wonderful cohort of scholars who each helped in various ways. I'm particularly grateful to Catherine Feely, Vicky Morrisroe, Iain Stewart, Luke Kelly, Ben Anderson, Beck Conway, Tom White, Jason Crowley, and David Woodbridge. Dominique Meithing was foolhardy enough to read early portions of the manuscript and offered a number of thoughtful comments, and thanks go to Timo Schaefer and Huw Wahl for discussing aspects of my research with me. I'm also indebted to Mike Dasher (dascodesign.com) who provided the cover art for this book.

I am thankful to the unflappable librarians and archivists at the following institutions: John Rylands Library, University of Manchester; The British Library of Political and Economic Science, London School of Economics; The British Library, Manuscripts Collection; The British Library, Newspapers Collection; Senate House Library, University of London; McPherson Library, University of Victoria; Brotherton Library, University of Leeds; Salford Working Class Movement Library; McKeldin Library, University of Maryland; City of Westminster Archives Centre; Royal Geographical Society; and the Bishopsgate Institute.

Grants from the Arts and Humanities Research Council (UK) and the Social Sciences and Humanities Research Council of Canada enabled this research, and I acknowledge their support.

My final thanks are to my wife Vinaya, and my mum and dad, who have been unfailing sources of support and encouragement. This book is dedicated to them.

Introduction

Regardless of the difficulties it would cause librarians, Herbert Read insisted in a letter to T.S. Eliot in 1949, that the title 'Reason & Romanticism' was perfect for a fresh edition of his collected essays. Sent to Eliot in his capacity as editor at the publishing house Faber and Faber, Read added that the phrase was 'in a way prophetic'. The confusion for the 'card cataloguers' would stem from the fact that this was a title Read had used before, gracing the frontispiece and spine of his first edition of essays, *Reason and Romanticism: Essays in Literary Criticism* (1926).[1] His return to it hints at a certain circularity, but, as he wrote to Eliot, its true value in 1926 lay in its powers of prophecy, revealing the extent to which the tension between 'reason' and 'romanticism' he had pondered at the dawn of his career, remained vital at its zenith. Returning to this theme at the dénouement of the definitive version of his autobiography, *The Contrary Experience* (1963), he repeated the idea that the expression 'reason and romanticism' was 'at once descriptive and prophetic':

> In this story of the growth of my mind, every advance has been due to the exercise of the faculty of reason; but that advance is not uniform, unimpeded... The very bases of reason, the perceptions of an unclouded intellect, are continually... contradicted by the creative fictions of the imagination... It is the function of art to reconcile the contradictions inherent in our experience... In this fact lies the... inescapable justification of romantic art, and it is to the... illustration of this truth that I have devoted my intellectual energy.

Such an encompassing project must also have a political component, Read judged and, 'led by logic and by history', he adopted anarchism.[2]

Turning to anarchism as the logical counterpart of the aesthetic principles developed in his investigations into literature and the visual arts, Read drew most notably on the work of Peter Kropotkin. For Kropotkin, plunging into the struggle against capitalism and the state in the late nineteenth century, the tools of rational critique similarly supported a decidedly romantic vision of the ideal life. He hoped to show the correspondence between anarchism and the latest scientific research; he looked to unfettered technological innovation empowering those dehumanised by capitalist production; and he trusted that individual rationality made the arbitrating structures of the state redundant. Yet, as much as this made Kropotkin's politics seem a quintessential product of modernity, its grain also revealed a spirited reaction to the forces that had created the modern world. For sustenance he looked to the decision-making arrangements enacted by Russia's peasant communes; he celebrated the virtues of the soil and the enlivening nature of artisanal labour; and at the core of his politics, was the idea that anarchism provided the most fertile ground for the development of the rounded individual. This last, as Isaiah Berlin once noted, was a key component of the romantic temperament, a feeling that personality, 'was to be learned... through effort, through trying, through hurling yourself against some obstacle which made you feel yourself wholly'.[3] Such a sense of productive strife, the energising quality of tension and conflict, would become a cornerstone of Kropotkin's philosophy.

While separated in time, both Kropotkin and Read were engaged in an effort to articulate anarchism for a British audience. For Kropotkin, this often involved both literal and metaphorical translation, attempting to render a politics whose life-giving spark had come from a reaction to continental autocracy, in a language applicable to urban Britain – a polity undertaking unparalleled experiments in mass suffrage and state intervention. At the forefront of his work was therefore an attempt to define anarchism's originality and demonstrate its relevance to the debates animating British intellectual life, while also revealing its fitness to meet the practical problems caused by Britain's particular journey through modernity. While critics might question Kropotkin's success in refining this message for the British, given anarchism's enduringly marginal status in the country, it would be wrong to underestimate the significance of the indigenous anti-statist tradition. This was a broad body of thought, embracing, on the one hand, individualist thinkers decrying the tightening grip of the state on individuals' lives, and, on the other, a communalist strand of anarchism that Kropotkin's arrival helped pull from the shadows of Victorian socialism.[4] For all the seeming irrelevance of anarchism to a political culture intently exploring the potentialities of the state, the composition of the socialist movement in *fin-de-siècle* Britain remained remarkably fluid. Just as the milieu encompassed a range of positions on the applicability of parliamentary methods, so initially groups often shared members, premises, and printing presses.[5] At the same time, British socialism was always pregnant with the potential for factional discord, most obviously concerning the apparently incommensurable divisions over the significance of conquering political rights in the journey to socialism. This issue had been divisive in the past, notably a key source of antipathy between anarchists and Marxists in the First International of the early 1870s, and played out as a clash of personalities in the battle between Karl Marx and Mikhail Bakunin.

In Britain, ideological differences started to solidify with the importation of these antagonisms, as shown by the friction pervading the London congress of the Second International, the International Socialist Workers and Trades Union Congress, in 1896. It was bound to be fraught, the ground for this gathering having been laid in Zürich in 1893, where socialists looking to securing political rights as a necessary step towards socialism had already clashed with their anarchist opponents in the Swiss summer heat. Amidst much acrimony – with even the receptions of the two factions held separately – the London meeting led to the 'absolute' break between the two groups.[6] With the decision taken to exclude the clusters of obstinate anarchists stubbornly opposing the official endorsement of parliamentary activity, the conflict veered towards becoming physical. As the Georgian anarchist Varlam Cherkezishvili noted angrily, 'Will Thorne and Dr. [Edward] Aveling' applied 'themselves to the task of thrusting the anarchists from the doors of the Congress with the help of the agents of the police'.[7] The official report of the conference was naturally unable to ignore the debacle, and pondered both the presence of many leading anarchists at the event and their dramatic expulsion.[8] The sympathies of the authors were, however, clear. Offering a pencil sketch entitled 'A Dejected Libertarian', it showed a sulking anarchist with his eyes fixed on the floor, his hands thrust deeply into his pockets. The text of the proceedings echoed this image of obduracy. Noting the key role of H.M. Hyndman in forcing the ejection of the dissidents, it relayed his declaration that while he 'personally...loved ... the Anarchist' their lack of scruple in disrupting meetings left no alternative.[9]

Despite the animus, anarchism remained both a force in practical political agitation, and, to the occasional frustration of its opponents, a waspish presence in the intellectual conflicts informing British socialism. For Read, coming of age politically as the First World War discredited socialism's internationalist hopes, Kropotkin's message remained an insistent one. Reading Kropotkin during the war, in which Read saw lengthy active service on the Western Front, lit embers in his mind that continued to burn even though political pessimism overcame him in the aftermath of the Versailles settlement.[10] Read's silence in these post-war years is not a mystery. Although the political situation remained volatile, with bloodshed continuing in Ireland, and labour unrest enduring as trade union membership grew and the Communist Party of Great Britain (CPGB) offered a new model in the war against capitalism, Read was weary of fighting.[11] The war had been an interregnum in his life, by turns exciting and terrifying, but if anything, it had shown him the necessity of acting decisively if he wanted to turn his gifts as a writer into a career in letters.

With the Edwardian generation retaining power in the inter-war period, Read's resentment grew, as he rose to prominence as a propagandist for modern art and design. Although it was the Spanish Civil War in 1936 that cemented his conversion to anarchism, the lingering sense of injustice at the Edwardian dinosaurs who plodded on in political life, and the radicalism of the aesthetic values he was championing, were important contributory factors. With Read nailing his colours to the mast of radical design, he soon observed that the same generation that had led Britain to war comprised the cultural establishment so scornful of contemporary aesthetic innovation. This was a potent mix, especially as the late 1920s and early 1930s witnessed fiery debates about the failures of British war policy.[12] With disrespect for authority figures engrained in its core, anarchism presented an appealing set of conceptual resources to understand this situation, just as the ambition to confront 'conventional sensibilities' guiding artistic modernism made anarchist ideas a fertile bed of speculation.[13] But anarchism, as Allan Antliff suggests, offered more than a vocabulary of dogmatic anti-authoritarianism. Enshrining 'individual liberation', the movement informed a melange of ideas and projects, encouraging 'far-flung cultural rebellion encompassing lifestyles, literature, and art as well as politics'. Echoing such fluidity, the very category of anarchism itself remained intellectually contested, with its premises and tactical objectives open to constant revision, dispute, and frequently acrimonious disagreement.[14]

Such a process of contestation is obviously not confined to anarchism, but a characteristic of all political traditions that continue to influence political action beyond the site of their original formulation. As political theorists respond to the problems of their age – those questions, concerns, and feelings of injustice that spark their intervention – the passage of time demands conceptual revision in order to maintain the analytical purchase of the overarching tradition. Political ideologies thus undergo a process of development in their 'internal morphology', as thinkers strive to 'decontest' the essential claims of their tradition against a backdrop of change, including new political problems, the exigencies of particular events, and shifting cultural and intellectual fashions.[15] After all, as a prominent strand in the history of political thought has insisted, the idea of 'timeless' problems confronting political thinkers irrespective of cultural context is perturbingly ahistorical.[16] To appreciate the nuances of past political thinking, sensitivity to the sites of its articulation is imperative, and demands a broad lens. As Quentin Skinner argues:

> It is hard to see how we can ... arrive at ... historical understanding if we continue to focus our main attention on those who discussed the problems of political life at a level of abstraction and intelligence unmatched by their contemporaries. If on the other hand we attempt to surround these classic texts with their appropriate ideological context, we may build ... a more realistic picture of how political thinking in all its various forms was in fact conducted in earlier periods.[17]

Naturally, the same applies to understanding the activity of thinkers working to revise past traditions of thought with an eye to their contemporary relevance. Engaging with the written fragments of the past, these texts are inevitably shaped by their new context, often transforming their significance, and taking on 'meaning only in relation to others in the set of ideas into which they are incorporated.'[18]

The object of this book is to examine this process of revision in the work of Kropotkin and Read, and in turn to cast fresh light on both thinkers as intellectuals plotting new paths for anarchist theory in their different contexts.[19] As both sought to adapt the core precepts of anarchism to fit immediate political circumstances, they helped outline a tradition of political thinking that has remained an underappreciated presence in British intellectual life. The fame they achieved attests to this prominence, thereby complicating the assessment of Anglo-Canadian public intellectual George Woodcock that British anarchism resembled a 'chorus of voices crying in the wilderness'.[20] The unintended impact of

Woodcock's claim, offered in his highly influential history of anarchist thought, was to canalise further the writing of the history of anarchism as an act of recovery. [21] With anarchism marginalised as a political force, the onus was on the historian to convey the thrust of seemingly arcane arguments, to show their enduring interest or to recover lost histories of valiant dissension.[22] While these historians argued that their interest was not 'self-contained texts' but the 'specific historical context' in which anarchists developed their ideas, their gaze tended to be insular: as if pointing to anarchism's multi-coloured threads compensated for its exclusion from the broader history of socialism.[23] Churlish as it is to criticise these efforts, given the fact that they kept interest in the intellectual history of anarchism alive, there is something unrewarding in their essential makeup. Indeed, such works often tend towards the brand of history pioneered by Arthur Lovejoy in his classic *The Great Chain of Being* (1936), with historians pursuing the 'unit idea' and 'study[ing] . . . words and phrases of a period . . . with a view to clearing up their ambiguities' and 'listing various shades of meaning'.[24] The historian has transmogrified into the Linnaean taxonomist, intently cataloguing thinkers, their ideas and works, before the tide of history washes them out to sea.

As with these histories, the focus in this book is certainly on the 'internal economy' of Kropotkin's and Read's texts, but its scope is broader, looking to their defining interactions with contemporary thinkers and intellectual problems beyond the confines of anarchist discourse.[25] In the end, it was this effort to overcome competing political ideologies – to offer what Kropotkin and Read believed were more fitting responses to the issues that confronted them – that defined the boundaries and content of their politics. This lack of sensitivity to contextual issues was a weakness of these histories, and it is one largely repeated in political theory, which currently dominates work on anarchism. Like the historians that cleared a path for them, the political theorists' attention has done much to encourage interest in anarchism and has led to a real renaissance in the study of anarchist ideas. Similarly, the perspective of political theory does not necessarily preclude historical acuity. Just as a number of recent historians have plotted lusher narratives of anarchism's past,[26] so many political theorists write with clear awareness of these diverse histories.[27]

Nevertheless, just as certain anarchist histories have tended to look inwards, recent studies of political theory, particularly those under the sway of poststructuralism, have done little to illuminate its history. While clearly not their principal ambition, such works have often shown disregard for both the complexity of anarchist history and the broader intellectual history that was its crucible, impoverishing their critique of the historic tradition of anarchism.[28] The richness of the dialogue between Kropotkin and Read points to the kinds of nuance lost in these sweeping theoretical studies. The connection between them – encompassing as it did innovation as much as inheritance – also further demonstrates the problem with the existing historiographical periodisation of anarchism they advance.[29] The notion of 'classical anarchism', referring to the nineteenth-century pioneers of the tradition,[30] is especially useful, allowing these commentators to trace 'discontinuity' between the past and present, and dismiss the radical horizon of a past politics that is limited by its historical remoteness.[31] After Karl Popper, how can a politics of emancipation legitimately rest on a scientific foundation? How is Kropotkin's positivism and political rationality any use to the children of Nietzsche and Freud? As this book argues, such popular sketches of the history of ideas fail to convey both the intricacy of European intellectual history and the complexity of past anarchist thinkers' efforts to orientate themselves with one eye on the past and one on the present. Read was, after all, awakened to the joys of philosophy by reading Nietzsche, and became a lifelong devotee of psychoanalysis and a populariser of Carl Jung. Yet, for him, Kropotkin's thought remained vital, and he saw little difficulty in assimilating the insights of thinkers like Nietzsche and Freud with the historic anarchist tradition.

In examining the ways that Kropotkin and Read strived to articulate an anarchism appropriate for their context, the intention is that this study is a step towards understanding the distinctiveness of anarchism's political culture as it developed in Britain. Central then is the idea that their work contributed to a discernible tradition of libertarian thinking that had deeper roots in British intellectual and cultural history than has hitherto been appreciated, a thesis propounded in a number of impressive recent studies.[32] Approaching anarchism as a political culture, defined as the 'identity and boundaries of the community', and the site where numerous political discourses 'overlap', allows the historian to think about the imaginative ways in which thinkers struggled to redefine their politics and extend its borders.[33] Contingency and change are central to the notion of tradition examined here, emphasising both Kropotkin's and Read's innovations within boundaries set by broader British intellectual and cultural life.[34] Guiding the project is thus a concern with 'authorial experience, intention and context' that is now a mainstay in the history of the political thought, but so far something of a marauder on the margins of anarchist history.[35]

The chapters comprising this book offer a thematic analysis of Kropotkin's and Read's thought. Pursuing these threads, an image emerges of Kropotkin's system of ideas at variance with the increasingly dominant view that he advanced a narrowly mechanistic and deterministic social theory.[36] Examining the epistemological and ontological foundations of his theory; his historical repudiation of the state; his perception of revolutionary transition; and his vision of an anarchist utopia, a picture develops of a thinker obsessed with transience, change, and flexibility. As much as he engaged with the founding fathers of sociological theory to develop his social theory, and although he yearned to root anarchism in the language of contemporary science, this research revealed a universe defined by perpetual movement and adaptation. Anarchism, he concluded, must equally embody this ephemerality – an idea that informed his view of history, understanding of revolution, and illustration of an anarchist utopia.

Looking back to Kropotkin for inspiration, Read nevertheless had his eyes fixed on both the radically different political situation that confronted him between 1936 and 1968, and his special interest: the status of culture. Teasing out the aesthetic implications of Kropotkin's work, he offered a reading of anarchism in which the chief objective was to create the social space for a vibrant and organic culture. The artistic politics of William Morris and John Ruskin both played a role in this theory, but Read was acting firmly in Kropotkin's shadow, attempting to marry technological sophistication with the politics of localism and a predilection for the countryside. The foundations of his worldview; his histories of aesthetics emphasising the vitality of the organic community; his call for 'cellular' social change; and his hope for an anarchist utopia permeated with a sophisticated artistic sensibility all grew from a conversation with Kropotkin occurring across the history of modern Britain.

Beyond the specific points of contact in these theoretical matters, uniting these thinkers, and drawing them to anarchism, as Read noted in his letter to Eliot, were the twin demands of intellect and feeling. Such a tension is not unique to anarchism – Edmund Burke's efforts to reconcile the forces of rational inquiry and tradition offer an obvious parallel – but the pressures of both clearly shaped their politics. Kropotkin looked to science for intellectual sustenance and to socialised technology as the route out of the toxic atmosphere fostered by capitalism and the state. While this might imply a certain rationalistic aridity, he hoped the journey to an anarchist future would lead away from the noxious air of Britain's industrial cities to the fields and meadows surrounding them. Yet he was not an agrarian socialist, and longed instead for an elusive amalgamation that fused the boons of modern life with the organic community of the country. Read was the product of Britain's disappearing yeomanry, although early on he was thrown from the land to the industrial heartlands of the North. His personal journey would transport him into the rarefied world of British letters, but despite his cosmopolitanism in literature, philosophy, and art, the siren song of the soil remained enrapturing. Mirroring Kropotkin, his social thought pointed to the vitalising quality of renewed contact with the land, and the ways in which the frictions and oppositions of an anarchist utopia might vivify life. 'I balance anarchism with surrealism, reason with romanticism, the understanding with the imagination, function with freedom,' Read once wrote, adding that 'the world's unhappiness is caused by men[37] who incline so much in one direction that they upset this balance, destroy this synthesis'. Joy 'is only promised to those who strive to achieve it, and who, having achieved it, hold it lightly poised', he concluded. Kropotkin would have agreed.[38]

1
Contexts: Anarchism in British Intellectual History, 1886–1968

In his fulminating manifesto, *Blast 1* (1914), Percy Wyndham Lewis went to great pains to identify the Vorticist aesthetic as quintessentially British. Frequently derided as a pale imitation of continental Futurism, Lewis insisted that given Britain's industrial pre-eminence, the Vorticist celebration of the mechanical found a natural home in the scepter'd isle. 'Machinery, trains, steam-ships, all that distinguishes externally our time, came far more from here than anywhere else', he wrote, adding that natural wonders also found their proxy in the otherwise 'characterless material climate':

> Our industries, and the Will that determined ... the direction of the modern world, has reared up steel trees where the green ones were lacking; has exploded in useful growths, and found wilder intricacies than those of Nature.[1]

While a champion of Vorticism, Herbert Read was more sensitive than Lewis to the essential dualism at the heart of British modernity. These tensions were apparent in the work of the painter Edward Wadsworth, signatory of Lewis' manifesto, and producer of a number of woodcuts examining industrialisation in the North of Britain. One of these, 'The Black Country', appeared in *Arts and Letters: An Illustrated Quarterly*, the journal that Read temporarily edited in the aftermath of the First World War.[2] In thick black ink, Wadsworth's image shows a landscape bisected by a train track leading the viewers' gaze to a cluster of chimneys encased by black hills, spewing white smoke into a dark sky. Wadsworth's earlier work may have celebrated this industrial strength, but this is a foreboding, 'claustrophobic' image, detailing the effacement of the country by the modern industrial city.[3]

Peter Kropotkin and Read were both chroniclers of the potential, and the depredations, of industrial modernity, and the dichotomies it created. Arriving as an exile in London, Kropotkin was not enamoured with his new city. In the Russian edition of his memoirs, in a chapter tactfully expunged from the British version, he commented on the difficulties of émigré life and his first impressions of the nation's capital:

> London is a dreadful city, a monster grown to enormous proportions. The cost of living is... high... for a man to whom the sum of sixpence represents a day's or... two days' sustenance. If work, or simply fate, has cast him to one end of the city, and his acquaintances or comrades live at the other... he must go... weeks... without seeing anyone close to him.[4]

London's poverty, and its contrasting extremes of opulence, also provided Kropotkin with a rich stock of images. He contrasted those 'plush'-wearing 'West End ladies' with the 'workmen... sleeping between two newspapers in the neighbourhood of Trafalgar Square'.[5] Similarly, he decried the 'universalised' antagonism between 'capitalists and labourers' that divided people into 'property-holders and masses living on uncertain wages'. Recent 'revelations' had highlighted this 'pitiless oppression' in the 'sweating system at Whitechapel and Glasgow' as well as 'London pauperism and York unemployment'.[6]

Kropotkin's allusion to Seebohm Rowntree's 1899 investigation into poverty in York is indicative of the growing popular sensitivity to the issue of social deprivation in nineteenth-century Britain. As Alexis de Tocqueville had noted decades earlier though, the problem was that not only was this penury immortalised in bricks and mortar, but that urban poverty existed in tandem with unrivalled prosperity. Manchester, he wrote, encapsulated this cruel symmetry:

> A sort of black smoke covers the city. The sun seen through it is a disc without rays. Under this half daylight 300,000 human beings are ceaselessly at work... From this foul drain the greatest stream of human industry flows out to fertilize the whole world. From this filthy sewer pure gold flows. Here humanity attains its most complete development and its most brutish; here civilisation works its miracles, and civilised man is turned back almost into a savage.

Despite its brutishness, the city's demands were insatiable, and its attraction undiminished. 'We hear in Manchester that crowds of country folk are beginning to arrive', Tocqueville added, 'wages, low though they seem, are nevertheless an improvement on what they have been getting'.[7] Victorian Britain was a society defined by these contrasts: wealth and poverty; opulence and degradation; power and powerlessness.

The industrial cities of the North embodied these contrasts, and in a different era, Read saw lingering echoes of this apparently Victorian problem. Coming of age in pre-First World War Leeds, his instinctive boyhood Toryism faded as his social conscience grew in response to the inequality he saw encapsulated in the city around him. Aside from the inequality, however, Read's distaste for life in the modern city was aesthetic. 'I passed through areas in which factories were only relieved by slums', he wrote in his memoirs, 'slums by factories – a wilderness of stone and brick, with soot falling like black snow'. Deprivation and repulsiveness were tandem aspects of modern life, he added, 'ugliness and poverty, dirt and drabness, were too universal to be ignored'.[8] Confronted with the realities of urban life, Read reassessed his political beliefs and, finding them wanting, looked to the past for more instructive guides. There he found an outcry against the despoliations of capitalism that seemed enduringly relevant, and the skeleton of an aesthetic reaction to industrialism that held hope for the future.

Though forty years of dramatic political change divided them, for both Kropotkin and Read capitalism was a floundering project. Capitalism and the deprivation that they believed greased its wheels was not only dehumanising and inhibitive of meaningful freedom, it also mutilated the landscape. The poverty of the powerless was therefore not only economic and existential, but also aesthetic: memorialised in an environment of slums, slagheaps, and smokestacks. Kropotkin and Read coalesced in seeing anarchism, with its commitment to anti-statism, emphasis on collective action, and belief in the constructive potential of non-hierarchical organisation, as the solution to the crises of capitalism, and an antidote to this aesthetic barbarism. Yet, as much as they were united in this crusade and Read looked back to Kropotkin for inspiration, their politics were decisively shaped by the context of its articulation. For Kropotkin, moving from Russia to France before settling in Britain, this took the form of striving to locate a political vocabulary forged in reaction to continental autocracy, to a society on the path towards representative democracy and state-led social reform. Read, growing politically conscious in the pre-war years, imbibed some of the theoretical openness that had characterised the late-Victorian radical milieu. As his politics matured in the 1930s, as capitalism wallowed in fresh crises and the Spanish Civil War fleetingly presented an alternative to official communism, he explored these lessons afresh. But Read's adoption of the language of Kropotkin's anarchism was itself shaped by its broader intellectual context. Emphasising the constructive aspect of Kropotkin's vision and presenting his politics as contiguous with that of William Morris and John Ruskin, Read diminished the role of violent revolution. A member of the generation thrown into the maelstrom of the First World War, Read's taste for a quietly constructive politics and efforts to rehabilitate romanticism as a vital source of modern art, echoed both a broader thirst for modesty, and a respect for the past as an anchor of stability. For Read the return of war, rather than invalidating these lessons, made this modest, Kropotkinian politics, all the more urgent.

Progress and Poverty: Debating the state

For the American economic thinker Henry George, writing in moments snatched from his precarious career as a gas-meter reader, the kind of urban poverty deplored by nineteenth-century social explorers was a clear product of industrial modernity. As the title of his major work implied, there was absurdity in a political economy that achieved such material progress, but also engendered desperate poverty. As he wrote:

> The 'tramp' comes with the locomotive, and almshouses and prisons are surely the marks of 'material progress' as are costly dwellings, rich warehouses, and magnificent churches. Upon streets lighted with gas and patrolled by uniformed policemen, beggars wait for the passer-by, and in the shadow of college, and library, and museum are gathering the more hideous Huns and fiercer Vandals of whom Macaulay prophesied.[9]

George identified the monopolisation of land as the root of this evil, with rising land values reducing wages and the power of capital, as rents increased. His enemy was therefore the landlord, and his 'radical and simple' corrective the abolition of all taxes and their replacement with a single tax on land. Socialism would arrive and fruit trees would line the streets of previously foetid cities, with government assuming a role of Saint-Simonian 'administration', rather than securing socialism through 'repressive decree'.[10]

Victorian political thought derived its richness from the varied attempts to resolve, or at least ameliorate, the effects of the progress and poverty paradox. When it appeared towards the end of the century, George's book was a fillip for radicals seeking a solution. J. A. Hobson was unconvinced by the 'panaceic simplicity' of George's theory, but noted that his tome nevertheless exerted a real influence, 'stir[ring] the issue up to boiling-point'.[11] Kropotkin concurred, noting that George's book had roused socialist feeling in Britain, but argued that while discontent at landed monopoly was 'ripe', agitation focusing solely on the land issue risked merely enthroning a 'new landed gentry composed of the middle class'.[12] Central to Kropotkin's hesitation was a concern that political methods would dissipate the radicalism of any land reform movement and that authoritarianism would reappear in fresh garb. His position also reflected a broader quandary shared by other late nineteenth-century political thinkers, concerning the state's role as an agent of social and moral improvement. This rethinking of the state's purview engendered a new political language of intervention that political theorists endeavoured to accommodate, even if, like Kropotkin, they were fundamentally antagonistic to the direction in which it pointed.

Herbert Spencer was one of those anxious about this process of increasing regulation. While famous for his irascibility, Spencer's agitated tone in his polemic *The Man Versus the State* (1884) stemmed from a fear that the argument over state involvement was being lost. As an early critic of land monopolisation in *Social Statics* (1851), where he declared that 'equity' does 'not permit property in land', and proposed nationalisation as a corrective, it might be expected that Spencer was sympathetic to Georgist economics.[13] By the time he came to write *The Man Versus the State*, however, Spencer had grown wary of the coercive potential of this notion. 'Pressed by Mr. George', he wrote, the land-nationalisation movement shows 'avowed disregard for the just claims of existing owners', and is a 'scheme going more than half-way to State-socialism'. Animating Spencer was a concern that intervention had moved from the margins of political thinking to the heart of political action. After detailing a number of acts introduced by William Gladstone's second administration, he observed wearily that these 'measures of coercive rule' were the 'doings of the party which claims the name of Liberal'.[14] Spencer's fear that liberals had abandoned their shibboleth of contractual freedom hints at an intellectual struggle that had characterised the recent history of British liberalism. As the 'hegemonic' political tradition in Britain, liberalism had deep and varied roots, which informed its essentially protean character.[15] Nevertheless, a characteristic feature of liberal political thinking in the second half of the nineteenth century was a more conciliatory position on state intervention. The Oxford intellectual T.H. Green, who, despite his early death, exercised a 'compelling' influence on his generation, adopted a language of contractualism familiar to Spencer when offering a revised theory of the bounds of state intervention.[16] 'Freedom of contract' and 'freedom in all the forms of doing what one will with one's own', he wrote, 'is valuable only as a means to an end'. This 'end' was 'freedom in the positive sense', the 'liberation of the powers of all men equally for contributions to a common good'. State action could therefore be beneficial, not in 'directly' promoting 'moral goodness', but in maintaining 'the conditions without which a free exercise of the human faculties is impossible'.[17]

Whilst it is tempting to situate Green's thought in a narrative that sees a fundamental shift in Victorian political thought from individualism to collectivism, the reality is more complex.[18] Rather than an 'emphatic movement from one mutually exclusive position to another', the intellectual history of the period is more fruitfully seen as a time in which the central concepts of key political traditions underwent decontestation against a background of 'changing scientific fashion, new sets of ethico-cultural beliefs, and specific events that made their mark on ideological assumptions'.[19] Pioneers like Green were not committing apostasy, but sought to retain the central precepts of a liberal political identity whilst keeping the tradition in tune with changing political circumstances. Stronger connections exist between a thinker like Green and older liberals like John Stuart Mill than the characterisation of a shift to collectivism in Victorian liberalism might imply. Indeed, it is not true to characterise mid-Victorian intellectuals as unswervingly attached to a laissez-faire ideal.[20] These debates, and the conflicts over the nature of state involvement, contributed to a rich intellectual backdrop before which all political traditions had to perform.

For traditions other than liberalism, the developing appreciation of state power might seemingly have involved less soul searching. The idea that the conciliatory attitude towards intervention that characterised 'new liberalism' stemmed from a closing of the gap between liberalism and socialism, assumes that British socialism held a more beneficent view of the state.[21] While socialism, 'one of the most elusive, vague, and diverse concepts of English social and political thought', was always a heterodox movement in Britain, towards the end of the century there was increasing weight behind the notion that social emancipation would be achieved under the aegis of state action.[22] In part, this conclusion emerged from an assessment of the history of socialism in

Britain, and a sense of frustration at a history of wasted opportunity and whimsicality. Speaking of Robert Owen, the socialist John Gray, an advocate of centralised economic planning, hinted at an air of gentlemanly dilettantism pervading many of these schemes for renewal: 'we are much at a loss for a systematic treatise... which can be analysed, objected to, or improved'.[23] Owen, whose 'schemes of communist villages' Kropotkin deemed a formative step on the path to anarchism, was ambiguous on state involvement, maintaining a paradoxical commitment to state centralisation as a prerequisite for his 'decentralised communitarian millennium'.[24] As Owenite communal ventures faltered and collapsed – debacles at New Harmony, Indiana, and Queenwood Farm in Hampshire followed Owen's initial success at New Lanark – the value of these schemes came under increasing scrutiny. Writing in his exposé of urban poverty in Manchester, Friedrich Engels noted that Owen exercised an enduring, and baleful, influence:

> English socialism arose with Owen, a manufacturer, and proceeds therefore with great consideration towards the bourgeoisie and great injustice towards the proletariat... The Socialists are thoroughly tame and peaceable... They acknowledge no historic development, and wish to place the nation in a state of Communism... overnight... They preach... a philanthropy and universal love far more unfruitful for the present state of England... Hence they are too abstract, too metaphysical, and accomplish little.[25]

The charge of failing to heed the trajectory of historical development would later underpin Marx and Engels' considered rejection of 'utopian' socialism, but, more broadly, a sense that only state-led action could secure socialism began to gain traction as the lure of Owenism declined.[26]

To later British socialists acting self-consciously in the spirit of Marxism, the centrality of the state to social renewal was axiomatic. For H.M. Hyndman, who sought to popularise his idiosyncratic brand of Marxism through the Democratic Federation, later Social Democratic Federation (SDF), which he established in 1881, the state had the potential to prevent the domination of a privileged social group. 'The State, as the organized common-sense of public opinion', he urged in *England for All* (1881), 'must step in, regardless of greed or prejudice, to regulate the nominal individual freedom which simply strengthens the domination of the few.' While for Spencer the role of the state was that of an umpire adjudicating between contesting parties, for Hyndman, who had excelled at cricket while at Cambridge, it was the means of reshaping the social fabric. As he wrote, contra Spencer, the recent record of increasing state involvement was in fact a bright note of optimism in the stygian darkness: 'Where the State has interfered to control and change the baleful conditions of life for the mass of our countrymen, there, and there alone, has some little good been done.'[27]

As the title of his book implied, Hyndman's was a socialism built on a notion of English exceptionalism. Indeed, Engels, writing to German socialist August Bebel, noted the peculiarity of Hyndman's political potion and his penchant for self-aggrandisement: 'Hyndman, is an arch-conservative and an arrantly chauvinistic but not stupid careerist'.[28] Imperialism did not therefore pose a problem for Hyndman, and while advocating a 'direct voice in her own administration' for India, he coupled this with a belief in the primacy of the 'Anglo-Saxon race' and their necessary 'slight supervision'.[29] Given that this period was characterised by a peak in popular imperialism, a development lamented by both Kropotkin and Spencer, it is not surprising to find some socialist theoreticians seduced by imperialist rhetoric. This was especially the case when this socialism was 'not only popular but populist', as with the founder of the influential organ *Clarion*, Robert Blatchford.[30] Socialism was Blatchford's solution to the problem that Britain 'does not belong to the British', and he argued that it could be achieved simply: 'As a matter of fact *Socialism* is only a method of extending State management... until State and Municipal management becomes universal all through the kingdom.'[31]

Manchester's poverty was again crucial, with Blatchford's observation of it inspiring his municipal vision, but equally important was his involvement with an influential group of socialists that looked with confidence to the ineluctable expansion of socialism through state agency.[32] Writing in *Fabian Essays in Socialism* (1889), Sidney Webb noted the increasing 'unconscious abandonment of individualism', and characterised Spencer's outcry against this process as a plaintively lonely one. Even 'younger Conservatives' like Joseph Chamberlain 'advocate far reaching projects of social reform through State and municipal agency', he continued, and the 'immediately practicable demands of the most exacting socialists' were already being met by state action. With the broadening of democracy, Webb predicted that socialism, 'its economic obverse', would become increasingly entrenched.[33] While Fabianism became synonymous with this 'gradual and institutional approach' to social reform, the group, founded in January 1884, had heretical origins.[34] In his history of the Society, Edward Pease betrayed as much when he noted that they emerged after an amicable division from The Fellowship of the New Life, a group to which he had been drawn on account of his interests in 'Spiritualism and subsequently in Psychical Research'.[35] The early temper of the Fabians was similarly unpartisan. Of the varied lectures organised by the group, contributions came from the *anarchistant* J.H. Levy, offering 'An Individualist View of Capital and Interest', and the founder of the secularist periodical *The Freethinker*, G.W. Foote, examining 'The Case Against the Eight Hours Bill'.[36] Membership of the group was also mixed. The anarchist Charlotte Wilson, who would later found *Freedom* with Kropotkin, was involved from the outset, and served two terms on the group's executive committee. Sydney Oliver, later Colonial Secretary of Jamaica, and Annie Besant, 'then notorious as an advocate of Atheism and Malthusianism' joined in 1885 and 1886 respectively.[37] Fabianism also held an appeal for intellectuals, with both George Bernard Shaw and the artist Walter Crane active in the group, while later, and more transiently, H.G. Wells would be a member.

The intellectualism of the Fabians has led to accusations that their influence on British political history has been overstated.[38] Whatever the case, Blatchford grew disenchanted with their emphasis on securing policy change through permeation and persuasion, and threw his weight behind organising a new socialist party to push the interests of labour. A conference at Bradford in January 1893 led to the creation of the national Independent Labour Party (ILP), although its genesis was 'from the bottom upwards, with independent parties emerging in several places well before the national meeting'.[39] This fact perhaps explains Blatchford's confused reminiscence that the party 'was founded, I think, in 1892' and that it was created by 'seven men ... I believe I was one of the seven; but I am not sure'.[40] Despite the confusion over its origins, and despite its modest electoral success, the formation of the ILP increasingly canalised labour politics in Britain down a parliamentary route. Disappointing results in its first general election in 1895, and growing concerns amongst trade unionists over their legal status, contributed to the formation of the Labour Representation Committee (LRC) in 1900, later shortened to the Labour Party after successes in the 1906 general election.[41] For James Keir Hardie, leading figure in the ILP, Member of Parliament (MP) for West Ham South in 1892, and future Labour Party parliamentarian, the emergence of socialism as a force in British politics belied the decline of individualism of a Spencerian form. Writing in his 1907 work *From Serfdom to Socialism*, Hardie nevertheless suggested that the distance between their respective positions was modest:

> [Spencer] and the school of Individualists ... which still has its representatives ... differ ... from the Socialist only in the method by which he sought to achieve the end which both have in common, the freedom of the individual. To Spencer any interference with the freedom of individual action seemed baneful. He conceived society as a collection of units, each one struggling to make the best of his ... life.

Noting the 'great attractions' of this view, Hardie added that its weakness lay in its assumption of 'conditions which do not exist', and that the 'judge, the soldier, and the policeman' were 'violations' of Spencer's rule. If state protection of the poor was injurious to freedom, then the same must logically apply to these guarantors of bourgeois wealth. Indeed, Hardie concluded that this entire argument rested on a faulty understanding of the role of the state, and that the desideratum was the elevation of 'the people' to responsible political participation, which would extend socialist 'brotherhood'.[42]

Hardie's sympathetic critique of Spencer also highlights the remarkable fluidity of radical political thinking in the late-Victorian and early-Edwardian period. As already seen in the discussion of the Fabians' diverse origins, although groups on the left were often fissiparous, they inhabited an intellectual field that encouraged cooperation and cross-pollination as well as disagreement and dispute. And while divisions risked entrenching ideological differences, many key theoreticians remained remarkably nondoctrinaire. Frustrated by Hyndman's heavy handedness and his overtures to conventional political action, William Morris left the SDF and helped establish the Socialist League (SL) in 1885. *The Manifesto of the Socialist League,* ratified at the very end of 1884, railed against the 'state of economical slavery' that trapped the vast majority, and reiterated the revolutionary nature of the League's socialism. With their recent experiences in the SDF in mind, the *Manifesto* also rejected conventional solutions:

> As to mere politics, Absolutism, Constitutionalism, Republicanism, have all been tried ... and all have alike failed in dealing with the real evils of life ... No better solution would be that State Socialism ... whose aim it would be to make concessions to the working class while leaving the present system of capital ... in operation: no number of merely administrative changes ... would make any real approach to Socialism.

More pointedly, the pamphlet closed by calling for 'equality and brotherhood' to be the eternal watchwords of the movement, lest the 'selfish ambition of leadership' lead 'the workers' down another dead end.[43] Despite its earnest rejection of authoritarianism, the *Manifesto* left the route to socialism unclear, an indication of the competing elements within the League. Equally repulsed by Hyndman's domineering methods, anarchists like Frank Kitz and Joseph Lane, members of the SDF-allied Labour Emancipation League, sided with Morris and the Socialist League after its secession. While Morris borrowed widely in formulating his socialism, and was therefore sympathetic to anarchist ideas, the League encompassed a range of attitudes, some more hostile to anarchism.[44] Ernest Belfort Bax, for instance, coupled his Marxian socialism with a preference for Jacobinist tactics, hoping that the League would imitate the federal structure of the Jacobin Club.[45] Edward Aveling and Eleanor Marx were also key protagonists in the split from the SDF, but their willingness to countenance parliamentary activity as a weapon in the struggle against capitalism frustrated libertarians in the League. Aveling, and then Bax, resigned co-editorship of the League's organ *Commonweal* as the anarchists grew more powerful, and in 1889 Morris was deprived of his position as editor, leaving the organisation the following year.[46]

The development of new liberalism, Hardie's sympathetic reading of Spencer, and the machinations inside the SDF and SL, demonstrate the heat generated around debates about state involvement at the end of the nineteenth century. As the case of Hardie shows though, while he was critical of Spencer, he was at pains to unite the languages of 'brotherhood' and individualism, rather than simply renounce the latter. This further supports the idea that the most useful way to understand the political changes in the period is in terms of developing political vocabularies and shifting fashions, rather than a decisive move from one defining attitude to another. The vitality of the era's political thought was a product of this contestation, debate, and search for synthesis, while thinkers pondered fresh ways to deal with the progress and poverty paradox at the heart of British modernity.

Memoirs of a Revolutionist: Kropotkin and anarchism

Kropotkin entered this febrile intellectual atmosphere in 1886. He had spent time in London before, passing a frustrating year in the capital at the end of 1881 after fleeing France to escape a death sentence imposed on him by the reactionary Russian secret society the Holy League. It was,

Kropotkin noted in his memoirs, 'a year of real exile' for 'one who held advanced socialist opinions'. '[John] Burns, [Henry Hyde] Champion, Hardie, and the other labour leaders were not yet heard of', he continued:

> The Fabians did not exist; Morris had not declared himself a socialist; and the trade unions ... were hostile to socialism. The only active ... representatives of the socialist movement were Mr and Mrs Hyndman ... They had held in the autumn of 1881 a small congress, and we used to say jokingly – but it was ... nearly true – that Mrs Hyndman had received all the congress in her house.[47]

Kropotkin's frustration with phlegmatic British radicals, and the Holy League's desire to assassinate him, demonstrates that by this time Kropotkin had already risen to prominence as a radical. His origins as a scion of the Russian nobility accentuate the remarkable nature of this journey to anarchism. Born Prince Peter Kropotkin in Moscow, 1842, Kropotkin had a privileged childhood, but the death of his mother while he was in his infancy, and the aloofness of his father, meant that it was a lonely one. Finding solace in the companionship of his older brother Alexander and his father's serfs, Kropotkin left for an elite military school in St. Petersburg, the Corps de Pages, in 1857. Despite finding the petty restrictions of this military life irksome, and possessing a proclivity to defiance, Kropotkin excelled in his studies, and, as the highest-achieving student, served as *pages de chambre* to the Tsar, Alexander II.

Rather than assimilation into the Russian establishment, Kropotkin's experiences shaped his increasing radicalisation. Intellectual self-improvement became a particular concern, and with the benefits of a diverse and multilingual education, he read voraciously and widely. Science held especial enticements and even though he would later achieve fame as a geographer, he viewed all knowledge as an essential patchwork. In a revealing panegyric, he noted, for instance, how even basic tuition in astronomy opened new vistas:

> The never ceasing life of the universe, which I conceived as *life* and evolution, became for me an inexhaustible source of higher poetical thought, and gradually the sense of man's oneness with nature, both animate and inanimate – the poetry of nature – became the philosophy of my life.[48]

Admitting to initial reverence for Alexander II, 'the liberator of the serfs', this, and the glamour of court life, ultimately gave way to disenchantment. Completing his education, Kropotkin had the pick of elite Russian regiments to join, but opted instead, much to everyone's consternation, for the remote 'Cossacks of the Amur'.[49] Filled with ambition to participate in the reform of this remote Siberian province, he later wrote that these 'five years' were 'a genuine education in life and character'. Despite his disciplined work, the 'wave of reaction' that swept across Russia following the Polish revolt against Russian rule in 1863, frustrated hopes of meaningful reform. Disappointed, Kropotkin instead channelled his energy into an exploration of Siberia's isolated regions; a survey that broadened his knowledge of the diverse people of this region, but also informed an original geological theory concerning the formation of the Siberian landscape that would constitute his 'chief contribution to science', later published by the Russian Geographical Society.[50]

The intellectual pleasures of a desk-bound life lay before Kropotkin, but his growing familiarity with the true state of Russia, and the failure of social reform in Siberia led to an epiphany. Vladimir Lenin may have made it famous years later, but the question posed by Nikolay Chernyshevsky's influential novel *What Is to Be Done?* (1863) was on the lips of many young Russians. Offered the lucrative post of Secretary to the Geographical Society, Kropotkin declined:

> What right had I to these higher joys [of scientific research], when all round me was nothing but misery and struggle for a mouldy bit of bread; when whatsoever I should spend to enable me to live in that world of higher emotions must... be taken from the... mouths of those who grew the wheat and had not bread enough for their children?... Knowledge is an immense power... What if knowledge should become the possession of all?[51]

Kropotkin's 'conscience-stricken' desire to abandon privilege and live amongst the peasantry was an expression of a broader theme in Russian intellectual history during this period, with the end of the 1860s witnessing the growth of a populist, or *narodnik*, movement that 'wanted to work in the villages in the name of the authentic ideals of the peasantry'.[52] Echoing the generational conflict of Ivan Turgenev's *Fathers and Sons* (1862), Kropotkin highlighted the radical divide in Russia between representatives of tradition, and the new mood of the young whose 'watchword was, *V narod!* (To the people; be the people).'[53]

But at this point, he looked west. Travelling across Europe to Switzerland in 1872, Kropotkin spent time in the Russian émigré community in Zürich, turning his insatiable curiosity to learning about modern socialism, especially the International Workingmen's Association. Thirsty for more information on the International, he ventured to Geneva, 'then the great centre of the international movement', but grew disenchanted by its leaders' desire for political respectability.[54] Despairing at their timidity, he sought an introduction to the 'Bakuninist' section in Geneva, before visiting Neuchâtel, home of 'that famous Jura Federation' in which the 'no-government, or anarchist, tendency' was paramount.[55] Kropotkin's Swiss sojourn occurred in the year that the divisions which had caused tensions in the International finally split it, as the Marxist and Bakuninist factions irreconcilably divided at the Hague Congress of 1872.[56] While apparently not privy to these machinations, Kropotkin's immersion in the ferment of the Jura Federation, then articulating a distinctively anarchist position in reaction to 'State socialism', was decisive. Returning to St. Petersburg later that year, Kropotkin hoped to realise the revolutionary ideas he had encountered in Switzerland, joining the influential 'circle of Chaikovsky' that devoted itself to the discussion of radical ideas, and, assuming the pseudonym Borodin, propagandised amongst the peasantry.[57] With the Russian state striving to contain dissent, it was not long before Kropotkin came to the notice of the authorities. Arrested in 1874, he was incarcerated in the Peter and Paul Fortress, formerly home to the Decembrists, Dostoevsky, and Bakunin, whose health was shattered by the harsh conditions.[58] Kropotkin suffered too, and spending two years in prison without facing formal charges, his health deteriorated rapidly. The intervention of influential relatives led to his transfer to a prison hospital, from where in June 1876, with the help of fellow radicals he audaciously escaped.[59]

This would not be Kropotkin's only experience of prison life, but as he fled Russia through Sweden, and boarded a ship at Christiania bound for Hull, he expected his time away from his homeland to be brief.[60] In fact, he began an exile that lasted over forty years, but while he would spend most of it in Britain, he soon repaired to Switzerland wishing to throw himself once more into political agitation.[61] Here he became acquainted with a number of figures who cemented his anarchist sympathies into real conviction, notably Bakunin's friend James Guillaume, the French geographer Élisée Reclus, and the Italians Carlo Cafiero and Errico Malatesta.[62] Kropotkin also helped establish, and largely wrote, the influential anarchist newspaper, *Le Révolté* in 1879, and would contribute to its successors *La Révolte* and *Les Temps Nouveaux*. His peripatetic life continued, however, and after another brief stay in London and a journey around Spain, the assassination of Alexander II in 1881 led to renewed suppression of radical activities. In August, under pressure from Russia, Switzerland expelled Kropotkin, who then proceeded to France before spending his frustrating year in Britain. Escaping British torpor in 1882, he returned to Thonon in France, but increasing labour unrest meant that the authorities kept him under close observation. In December, the gendarmes arrested Kropotkin and transferred him to Lyon, the scene of two recent dynamite attacks by disgruntled socialists. As he wrote in his memoirs, the French police could not link these incidents to the activities of the anarchists, so instead 'the government adopted the Machiavellian course of prosecuting us for having belonged to the International', resurrecting a law passed in the wake of the Paris Commune outlawing membership of that organisation.[63] Given that the International had ceased to exist following its dissolution in Philadelphia in 1876, many saw this charge as a cynical attempt to crack down on troublesome dissent. Despite an eloquent speech from the dock outlining his principles, Kropotkin received a sentence of five years, and was removed to Clairvaux prison in northern France.

The Lyon trial received modest attention in the British press, but Kropotkin's reputation, and the sense that an injustice had occurred, grew. One reporter, discussing the early days in court, noted that even though there were good grounds for indicting several of the anarchists on trial, the case against Kropotkin was flimsy. He added that Kropotkin cut an impressive figure before the bench:

> When his name was called ... he advanced from the body of the room where he was sitting with the other prisoners, between two gendarmes, and stood cool and self-possessed ... For a few seconds the President and he looked each other full in the face like intellectual gladiators ... [One barrister noted that] ... in all his experience ... he has never been present at a more interesting interrogation ... in which a prisoner has shown so much ability.[64]

The incongruity of Kropotkin's princely status and intemperate political views were the reason for much of this attention, even if the exact nature of his politics eluded most commentators. As a correspondent for *The Times* noted, the prosecution built a case on establishing his position as 'chief of the Nihilist party', while observing that a Lyonnaise newspaper had confirmed that 'Prince Krapotkine [sic] ... was the chief of the Anarchist movement'.[65] Whilst his social status made Kropotkin a beguiling figure, his developing prominence as an intellectual was also important. During his brief visits to Britain, Kropotkin had already begun to cultivate a scholarly network to provide much-needed work writing articles and reviews. He had met Belfort Bax and Hyndman in 1882, and the MP Joseph Cowen who introduced him to James Knowles, editor of the periodical *The Nineteenth Century*, which would be the future vehicle for many of Kropotkin's key works.[66] He had also met John Scott Keltie, sub-editor of the journal *Nature* and future secretary of the Royal Geographical Society, and begun to write for that publication, and short pieces for *The Times* on geographical explorations in Russia.[67] Based in Thonon, Kropotkin prepared articles on geographical matters for the *Encyclopaedia Britannica*, and pieces for Cowen's newspaper the *Newcastle Daily Chronicle*.

Interned at Clairvaux, he continued to write while his health permitted. The children's periodical *Chatterbox* noted that Kropotkin, ever the empiricist, had contributed from his prison cell a piece to a French newspaper confirming that cats could indeed see their reflection. The prisoner also suggested that, judging by the feline companion sharing his confinement, cats were 'susceptible to music', his own being particularly taken by 'the waltz from Faust'.[68] With the small garden that he tended to supplement his prison diet with fresh vegetables, and the daily 'pint of claret', Clairvaux was a considerable improvement on the Peter and Paul Fortress, but Kropotkin suffered from both scurvy and malaria.[69] Calls for clemency continued, and Victor Hugo presented the French Minister of Justice with a petition signed by a phalanx of Victorian intellectuals, including Leslie Stephen, William Morris, Alfred Russel Wallace, and A.C. Swinburne.[70] Finally released in January 1886, Kropotkin recovered in Paris, then the site of a 'very animated socialist and anarchist movement', and lectured on anarchism. Expecting expulsion, he fled to London that year.[71]

Kropotkin was feted on his arrival in the capital. Writing to a friend in March 1886, Morris pointed out that Kropotkin had already thrown himself into action: 'Kropotkine new come [sic] from prison spoke, and I made his acquaintance...I like him very much.'[72] This appraisal was a common one, shared by thinkers less sympathetic to his politics than Morris, and by some commentators actively hostile to Kropotkin's views. Hyndman, while perplexed by Kropotkin's politics, championed his release, admitting to being 'captivated by the charm of his manner and the unaffected sincerity of his tone', a view echoed by Belfort Bax who, similarly unimpressed by anarchism, nevertheless phrenologically complemented his 'picturesque and benevolent-looking head'.[73] Others were struck more by the content of this capacious dome. Morris' protégé Walter Crane, who contributed artwork to *Commonweal*, noted the 'universal respect and sympathy' that greeted Kropotkin, and praised his 'disinterested enthusiasm for the cause of humanity, and ... his valuable sociological writings'.[74] The journalist Henry Nevinson, also noting Kropotkin's impressive head, and a face ravaged by 'prison-scurvy', echoed the sense of his personal magnetism, opining that 'eternal youth suffused his speech and stature', and that 'he knew so much, thought so much, felt so much'.[75] The popular press carried similar descriptions. One article from a Parisian 'sympathizer' commented on his 'mild' manner and 'absolute freedom from crotchetiness'. 'Intensely intellectual', he added that 'Krapotkin [sic] and Shelley would have understood each other'.[76] Given the prominence of anarchism in the popular imagination as a creed of violence and villainy, journalists liked to stress the apparent contradiction between Kropotkin's personal charm, intellectual prowess, and politics. As one purported interviewer made clear at the outset of his article 'whatever may be his peculiar views, and we have nothing to do with them' Kropotkin 'is, as his rank denotes, an accomplished gentleman and scholar', and 'one of the most kindhearted men'.[77]

Kropotkin's growing stature as an intellectual is important in understanding his activity in Britain. While observing in his autobiography that the domestic radical scene had improved since his last visit, it is evident that he was predisposed to treat British socialism with some disdain. In a letter to Morris' daughter May, in February 1889, he let slip that he was rather unenthused by the indigenous socialist movement. 'It seems so hard to get audiences for anarchist subjects', he complained, 'in London, just now ... people are to [sic] much [concerned] with [the] petty home affairs of politics'.[78] The real source of his frustration was anarchism's weakness in Britain compared to its continental cousins, but the anarchist movement's modest size had an important effect on Kropotkin's career path. One consequence was that Kropotkin and a small group that included Charlotte Wilson established the anarchist newspaper *Freedom*, of which Wilson was the first editor, with the first issue appearing in October 1886.[79] The other result was that, hampered by increasingly insecure health, Kropotkin channelled his energy into the articulation of anarchism as a distinctive social philosophy. As he wrote to William Morris, establishing 'the principles of Anarchist philosophy' was a burdensome but necessary task for a fledgling 'system of thought'.[80] Drawing on contacts nurtured during his earlier forays across the Channel, he pursued this mission, producing a series of works seeking to establish the relevance of anarchist ideas to contemporary political debates. Crucially, therefore, while Kropotkin's political thought germinated in response to Russian autocracy, grew in the Swiss hills, and flowered after contact with the tradition of French socialism, his British context was central to the mature elaboration of this politics. Freshly rooted in British soil, Kropotkin turned his attention to translating the concepts of continental anarchism for a new audience, and attempted to locate anarchism as a politics of critique in the context of ongoing debates over the role of the state in British life.

Versed in the systematic philosophy of Spencer and Auguste Comte, Kropotkin aimed to produce a synthesis in the elucidation of this 'new' philosophy. His first two books, *Words of a Rebel* (1885) and *The Conquest of Bread* (1892), were composed of articles contributed to *Le Révolté* and *La Révolte*. Central to these texts was a desire to distinguish anarchist communism as a distinctive variety of anarchist thought, and demonstrate the practicality of its core assumptions: the viability of communal life and consensual decision-making; the redundancy of centralised authority; and the necessary communisation of both production *and* distribution. These themes defined Kropotkin's thought, but in Britain he strived to place them on a sounder theoretical footing, in accord with current scientific and sociological thinking. The chief product of this was *Mutual Aid: a Factor of Evolution*, collected as a book in 1902 from articles appearing in *The Nineteenth Century* between 1890 and 1896. This work challenged what he saw as the increasing tendency to read Darwinian evolutionary theory through the lens of an aggressive individualism. Looking beyond animal societies, Kropotkin argued that the cooperation central to survival in nature also influenced early human societies, underpinning the subsequent development of ethical thought. He concurrently explored these themes in a number of pamphlets, including *Anarchist Morality* (1892); *The State: Its Historic Role* (1896); and *Anarchism: Its Philosophy and Ideal* (1897). *Fields, Factories and Workshops* (1898), again adapted from lengthy articles contributed to *The Nineteenth Century*, examined the possibility of regional self-sufficiency in Britain, secured through an integration of agriculture and industry, and overcoming the division between 'brain work and manual work'.[81] Alongside regular articles for *Freedom* newspaper, Kropotkin's next major work was the monumental historical study *The Great French Revolution* (1909), the culmination of a lifelong fascination with revolutionary France. His final, unfinished project was the product of another abiding interest. *Ethics*, which appeared in 1925, four years after his death, attempted a history of ethical thinking, leading on to an unfinished analysis of a distinctively anarchist system of ethics.

It is a popular conception that the Edwardian summers of garden parties and 'long afternoons bathed in lost sunlight' ended as the thunderclouds of war rolled across Europe in 1914.[82] This narrative is, of course, problematic. As much as this was the era of E.M. Forster's sun-dappled Italian novels, it also saw Robert Tressell complete the manuscript of *The Ragged Trousered Philanthropists* (1914). Labour unrest reached a crescendo during this period, and the rise of syndicalism suggested that anarchism, dismissed as an irrelevance 'outside [of] Spain' by 1900, retained importance.[83] As Kropotkin entered his twilight years, however, his position on the First World War caused serious dispute in the anarchist movement. Throughout his life, Kropotkin had associated Germany with militarism and political centralisation: the country of Marx and Bismarck, as much as Goethe. His attachment to French culture in contrast, nurtured by the Russian predilection for France in the nineteenth century and his affinity with the French socialist tradition, drew Kropotkin to the allied cause. For both his friends and enemies, this decision to support the war effort was confounding. The Italian anarchist Errico Malatesta, for instance, sharing his British exile, commented that Kropotkin seemed to have forgotten that he was a socialist, an anarchist, and an internationalist.[84] Already retired to Brighton in the hope that the sea air would be a tonic for his ailing health, Kropotkin became increasingly isolated from the mainstream of the anarchist movement, as his wife Sophie occupied her time 'mak[ing] Dressings [sic] and splints for the wounded'.[85]

While the failure of international solidarity to prevent war in 1914 dismayed many socialists, events in 1917 shook them from their inertia. Kropotkin had always had his gaze fixed on his homeland, hoping that bubbling discontent would eventually unleash a revolution effervescent enough to topple Russian autocracy. That this might allow his return home was an added boon, and when Tsarism tottered in 1905 Kropotkin avidly followed the events that changed every day 'as in a Kaleidoscope', plotting his return 'after Christmas'.[86] The failure of this revolution depressed him, as did the subsequent treatment of the vanquished revolutionaries, but when discontent stirred again in 1917 his exuberance returned.[87] Writing to May Morris, he presented the revolution in anarchist terms, seeing 'the old-regime' swept away 'in the villages and provincial towns', and 'Democratic self-government' emerging, with the 'soldier becoming a citizen'.[88] Kropotkin left Britain on 4 June 1917, but arriving home his optimism waned as conditions in Russia worsened, and the October Revolution, in anarchist eyes at least, produced a '"statization" of economic authority' that curtailed local independence.[89] Hopeful of contributing something to the revolution, Kropotkin was ultimately marginalised. His insistence that Russia must first defeat German militarism displayed an obvious ignorance of conditions on the Eastern Front and the suffering of the Russian people during the long years of grinding warfare, and for many radicals, the practical achievements of Bolshevism proved seductive. 'The superannuated anarchist Kropotkin', Leon Trotsky sarcastically wrote, 'made use of the war to disavow everything he had been teaching for almost half a century'.[90] He died in Dmitrov, a small town north of Moscow, in early February 1921. A month later, the suppression of the Kronstadt Rebellion by the Red Army seemed, for many anarchists, depressing proof of the new civilization that had been created.

The socialist movement that Kropotkin encountered in Britain in the last quarter of the nineteenth century was striving to orient itself in a fresh language of intervention. Comparatively open ideological boundaries began to harden, in part a response to increasing confidence in state-led action. The 1867 Reform Act, which extended the franchise to urban property owners and furthered the appeal of parliamentary action, was one such step, transforming 'England into a democracy' in the rather teleological words of one historian by enshrining the inevitability of further reform in 1884, 1918, and 1928.[91] The role that befell Kropotkin was to translate anarchism to this fresh context and expound his political principles in a language that chimed with vogue appeals to municipal socialism, but retained the core critique of statism that defined his position. Attempting to sell anarchism to the British was therefore pressing, and Kropotkin advanced a unique vision of anarchism as a meeting of elements of old and new. Ruminating on the organisational acumen of peasant communes might lack purchase in Britain's industrial heartlands, but appeals to the patina of modernity ('Museums, free libraries, and free public schools; parks and pleasure grounds; paved and lighted streets') were attempts to explain the relevance of his politics to the urban working-class.[92] Though the closing acts of his life were played out in his homeland, Kropotkin's British exile was formative.

This Torch of Freedom: War, culture, and politics

Stanley Baldwin spent much time thinking, writing, and speaking about what Britain meant. Central to his vision of the country was a sense that British history was an organic continuum, and that British freedoms were the product of innate virtues of modesty and tolerance. 'English parliament has had no one man for its maker', he said in a speech of 1935:

> No man made it, for it grew. It was the natural outcome, through long centuries, of common sense and the good nature of the English people, who had always preferred committees to dictators, elections to street-fighting, and Talking Shops to revolutionary tribunals.[93]

Against the dark clouds gathering on the world-stage, Baldwin added that 'this torch of freedom' cast a comforting light, and that the duty of Britain and its colonies was to keep this glow 'alive, until other nations come to see our ways'. But Baldwin also thought these liberties imperilled; assailed from both left and right. 'There are those on the right who demand first and foremost efficiency', he wrote, 'they put it above liberty'. Against the 'slow and cumbrous methods of parliamentary government' they juxtapose the 'dictatorship of the strongman' and want 'Caesarism, not democracy'. While on the left were those angry at 'too little democracy... despite all our electoral machinery the people, they say, are impotent'. Pursuing the 'paradise of Communism' they countenance 'dictatorship of the proletariat', seeking to 'enthrone in power' the 'People, with a capital P.' For all the threat that these forces posed, Baldwin remained confident that Britons' intrinsic capacity for self-control would guide them through this tumultuous age. While these currents 'overwhelm democracy in some European countries', he looked to Walter Bagehot's description of 'animated moderation' for support.[94] As Bagehot suggested in *Physics and Politics* (1872), 'the English... excel all other nations' in this quality of engaged restraint, and Baldwin concurred that it was the envy of 'our continental neighbours'.[95]

Baldwin's conservatism was rooted in the soil. In one of his most famous speeches, delivered in 1924, he pronounced that the heart of Britain was the country: 'the anvil in the country smithy, the corncrake on a dewy morning, the sound of the scythe against the whetstone, and the sight of a plough team coming over the brow of a hill'.[96] These earthy appeals clearly struck a chord, for Baldwin served three terms as prime minister between 1923 and 1937. This is perhaps surprising because his bucolic language looked to the past rather than the present, for as early as 1881 England's agriculture-dominated counties, on which his rhetoric drew, possessed just 29 per cent of the national population.[97] Moreover, his predilection for voluntarism over state intervention, resting on a prediction of a 'reaction from bureaucracy', is seemingly out of tune with the perceived political spirit of the age.[98] As the conventional narrative describes, the demands of total war in 1914–1918 heightened the already steadily increasing tendency towards intervention, with the '[nation's life] as a whole, [coming] in one way or another under public supervision'.[99] In A.J.P. Taylor's memorable words, describing the triumph of collectivism over the discredited language of Asquithian non-intervention in wartime, the 'sensible, law-abiding Englishman' living peaceably before 1914, could go through life and 'hardly notice the existence of the state'. In the post-war world it could not be missed.[100]

In this context, while Kropotkin's campaign against the state in the late nineteenth century may have seemed ambitious, seen against the backdrop of Britain's war-ridden twentieth century, hopes for the state's abolition might look even more fantastic. Taylor overstated the case in assuming the hegemony of collectivism and the role of the war in cementing change, but the language of planning in post-war radical politics was certainly in fashion. In part though, this emphasis on 'planful control' was a reaction to the apparent failure of the main political parties to recognise the urgent need for central action to meet the challenges of inter-war economic strife.[101] With centralism being explored afresh on the left in the wake of the war and the apparent successes of Bolshevism, the duty of those antipathetic to this process was to 'decontest' again the core principles of their politics against this new intellectual backdrop.[102] The war might have entrenched collectivist attitudes, but significant spaces of dissent endured, even if many of the dissidents hoped simply to smooth the despotic implications of some of these popular trends. A new reading of anarchism would be a strand of this resistance; a politics looking back to the pre-war tradition that Kropotkin helped articulate, but in Herbert Read's hands, a philosophy pushed in new directions.

Those returning home from war in 1918 faced a quandary. With the Edwardian homilies of heroism and duty discredited by the experience of modern warfare, and as regimes tottered on the continent, the time looked ripe for radical renewal. Yet, the privation and suffering of war had also created a thirst for homelier diversions. Baldwin's home and hearth conservatism tapped into this spirit, offering an antidote to the trauma of mechanised war with its vision of an ancient and stable national history, and espousal of the values of caution.[103] His 1929 election slogan 'safety first', a riposte to the imagined recklessness of the Liberals' Keynesian dictum 'we can conquer unemployment', might have been unsuccessful but the mood of moderation captured in the motto was pervasive.[104] Even Labour's first dalliances with political power adhered to the safety first maxim, with Ramsey MacDonald's minority government of 1923 making 'respectability and reassurance' the order of the day.[105] MacDonald's keenness to demonstrate the responsibility of a Labour government, and the fact that he was premier at the forbearance of Asquith's Liberals helps to explain this timidity, but as he and Baldwin exchanged power in the inter-war years, intervention remained unpopular. Caution continued to reign when economic depression followed on the heels of the Wall Street Crash in 1929, confronting a vulnerable MacDonald at the head of a hung parliament. With his party torn over swingeing spending cuts, a national government replaced Labour who haemorrhaged votes at the polls in 1931, and MacDonald appalled many former Labour colleagues by assuming the premiership in a mixed cabinet.[106] For the historian and socialist R.H. Tawney, Labour's failure to deal with the economic crisis was the product of a 'pernicious anaemia producing general futility' betraying a lack of 'clear convictions'. Labour 'frets out of office and fumbles in it', he wrote, throwing 'themselves into the role of The Obsequious Apprentice... bent on proving that... His Majesty's Labour government could rival the most respectable of them in cautious conventionality'.[107]

For those sharing Tawney's irritation at Labour's apparent toothlessness, radical alternatives existed. The success of the Russian Revolution meant that for many the Russian path to socialism offered 'the magic formula that would transform the leaden dross of the old order into the rich gold of the new'.[108] In 1920, a number of small factions coalesced into the Communist Party of Great Britain. Alongside the Communist Unity Group (CUG), the British Socialist Party (BSP; heir of Hyndman's SDF) was the largest organisation behind the formation – so much so, in fact, that in its early days the CPGB was 'the BSP writ a little larger'.[109] While the 'peculiarly English' nature of the discussions that led to the founding of the CPGB suggested that, at this stage, Russian influence was light, financial support from Moscow helped 're-emphasise the pre-eminence' of the BSP.[110] At its foundational 'unity convention' in 1920, while the dictatorship of the proletariat was quickly endorsed, the hoary issue of parliamentary participation soon arose.[111] Sylvia Pankhurst's Workers' Socialist Federation (WSF) had already reneged on a decision to attend the conference, objecting that any concessions to parliamentarianism were self-defeating, while the Labour Party rebuffed the CPGB's overtures and the ILP similarly rejected affiliation in 1921.[112]

The early history of the CPGB is one of its increasing professionalization, often under Russian tutelage, and an ongoing effort to make an impact in British politics. Opting for electoral activity, 1922 saw two communist candidates, Walton Newbold and Shapurji Saklatvala, returned to parliament. But hindered by official repression and unspectacular membership figures, the CPGB struggled to make a serious impression.[113] Under pressure from Moscow, and inspired by Lenin's characteristically astringent *'Left-Wing' Communism: An Infantile Disorder* (1920), the party abandoned the policy of broad-based cooperation with other labour groups, in favour of the 'class against class' line championed by Joseph Stalin at the end of 1927.[114] Reflecting the Comintern's view that the current 'third period' was one of 'economic catastrophe and revolutionary opportunity', the new policy demanded the denunciation of collaborationists like Labour and those 'who abjured their insurrectionary aims'.[115] Later, as fascism menaced Europe, and the incompetence of the German left showed the dangers of sectarianism, a fresh desire for defensive cooperation emerged – albeit with the aim of winning further recruits in the heat of the struggle.[116]

The potential tortuousness of the Soviet tether became more obvious in the tumultuous years at the end of the 1930s. Initially, as civil war erupted in Spain, Labour's acquiescence to the Baldwinian position of staying aloof from the conflict with the hope of containing it, made the CPGB's demand for action seem, at least for those identifying with the Republican cause, all the more heroic.[117] Yet, as the show trials in Moscow mounted, and this paranoia crept into Spanish affairs – recorded most memorably by George Orwell in *Homage to Catalonia* (1938) – the CPGB's position was undermined. As European war again seemed likely, the CPGB continually tried to adapt its position to meet these changing priorities. Having consistently asserted the threat of fascism, the Nazi–Soviet Non-Aggression Pact forced a change in tack, but their ambitious claims that it showed Soviet tactical nous sat uneasily with the previous line of denouncing Neville Chamberlain and the 'pro-Fascist Men of Munich'. As German tanks rolled across the Russian steppe in 1941, this line was revised too, and what had been viewed in Leninist terms as a renewed war of European imperialism, became a 'people's war, pure and simple'.[118] Despite the twists and turns, CPGB membership in fact rose to around 60,000 in 1942, before collapsing again after the war. While the language of planning grew in popularity in these years, the beneficiaries were not the CPGB, but a renewed Labour Party. 'War breeds national unity', concluded William Beveridge in his momentous governmental report of 1942, deeming the time ripe for change. 'If the united democracies… can show strength and courage and imagination equal to their manifest desire', he added, they 'can plan for a better peace even while waging total war'.[119]

To fixate on membership figures or the doctrinal dexterity displayed in debates with Moscow can obscure the significance of the CPGB as an influential arena of cultural critique. The appeal of radical politics to the literati was partly a 'belated' reaction to the experience of the First World War. One of the potent 'myths' of that conflict, as its poetry made clear, was that the older generation was to blame for its tragic waste and the failure to rebuild in the rubble.[120] This context is central to Read's own politicisation, and the CPGB attracted its share of intellectuals disgusted by the failure to deliver a New Jerusalem. The poet Hugh MacDiarmid is a typical example. As his familiarity with Bolshevism developed in the wake of 1917 he grew more disenchanted with military life, although the three bouts of malaria he suffered in Salonika probably contributed to this.[121] Under the tutelage of 'Marx and Lenin and Stalin', MacDiarmid later became an opponent of 'English ascendency' and an apostle of Scottish independence.[122] The title of his collection *Second Hymn to Lenin and Other Poems* (1935) made his debts explicit, and contained a caustic rebuttal of A.E. Houseman's 'Epitaph for an Army of Mercenaries', dismissing the British Expeditionary Force as 'professional murderers' motivated by 'blood money'.[123] The popular science writer J.B.S. Haldane had a different journey to Communism. Enrolling in the Black Watch at the outbreak of war, Haldane in fact thoroughly enjoyed his war experiences, even, to his surprise, the act of killing. Nevertheless, the ineptitude of military command vexed him, and appalled by the limp reaction of the British government to the threat of fascism in the 1930s he moved towards Communism, joining the CPGB in 1942.[124]

For those, like Haldane, armed with a scientific imagination, the impending decline of capitalism was no longer a matter of conjecture. The USSR, embodying a commitment to central planning, offered a tantalising example of a form of organisation superior to the seemingly perennial instability of capitalism – even though onlookers tended to overlook the extent to which the rhetoric of planning masked massive inefficiency and waste.[125] Given the potency of this new model, for communists and fellow travellers, mainstream political parties seemed terminally out of touch. After all, not only did David Lloyd George linger on in public life, diminishing his reputation in the eyes of many as an appeaser of Hitler, even Herbert Asquith saw out most of the 1920s. Pondering the 'next thirty-three' years in 1933, Haldane predicted the ineluctable rise of the USSR and its advance towards 'the organization of leisure', while diagnosing the 'general decay of our economic system' punctuated by war and revolution. Burdened with an ageing population, he also suggested that by '1966 Britain will be a second-rate power, full of old men and women'.[126] Another populariser of science, Lancelot Hogben, was equally concerned by the rate of population growth in capitalist societies. While avoiding proposing the USSR as a model worthy of emulation, he did suggest that its egalitarianism was an important counterweight to the patent 'biological failure of the Acquisitive Society', seizing on the famous title of Tawney's 1920 book, and that planning was the answer.[127] To Sidney Webb, contemplating what the future held, the 'Land of Hope' was not that celebrated in Edward Elgar and A.C. Benson's hymn to British supremacy, but the USSR. Not only had the country disproved prognostications of its imminent collapse, but it was, Webb surprisingly concluded, on a path to securing an individual freedom grander than that of 'Great Britain or the United States'.[128]

In the context of the seeming senility of capitalism in the late 1930s, the language of planning had a clear political appeal, especially for scientifically inclined theorists like Haldane and Hogben.[129] Although the idea of rational organisation as a solution to the volatility of capitalism has a long history in socialist thought, the apparent success of the Soviet model lent weight to these calls. Yet, despite the temptations of Marxism, the leviathan state was not for everyone, and Britain possessed a rich vein of more heterodox thinking. One political strand attempting to negotiate the Charybdis of planning and Scylla of anarchy were the Guild Socialists, a group occupying a political space increasingly suffocated by the emergence of official Communism, but who had an enduring influence on dissentient intellectuals like Read.[130] Given its original impetus by A.J. Penty in his book *The Restoration of the Gild System* (1906), the movement was rooted in nineteenth-century socialism and its neo-Gothic veneration of craft labour. Indeed, at the outset, Penty stated that the idea of the 'Gild system as a solution' to the evils of industrialism was present in Ruskin, but that Ruskin had failed to develop it into a scheme for social renewal. Citing Morris and Kropotkin, Penty rejected collectivism, adding that nationalisation reduced competition, producing a wasteful 'State Commercialism' that lowered 'labour to the level of drudgery', and produced shoddy goods.[131]

Leeds, the city that awoke Read's social conscience, played an important part in the development of Guild Socialism.[132] While working in the city as an architect, Penty developed a friendship with A.R. Orage who, with Holbrook Jackson, established the Leeds Art Club in 1903.[133] A circle for the discussion of radical political and artistic ideas, Read would also later attend the Club. In 1906, Jackson and Orage followed Penty to London, and in 1907, with financial assistance from George Bernard

Shaw, purchased the journal *The New Age*. Hitherto politically diverse, *The New Age* under Jackson and Orage's editorship, and solely under Orage's guidance from 1908, became an influential and eclectic literary journal and a vehicle for Guild Socialism, bringing a number of thinkers dissatisfied with collectivism into its orbit.[134] G.D.H. Cole, for instance, who had misgivings over the failure of *The New Age* to elaborate the 'democracy' at the heart of Guild Socialism, was nonetheless attracted to its 'lucid and coherent' politics.[135] Contributing a series of three articles on French syndicalism to the journal in 1914, he deemed Guild Socialism a more practicable sibling of this movement.[136] While hostile to the overweening state, these socialists remained committed to it in a refined capacity as an organising body. Repudiating 'state socialism' as a solution to capitalistic avarice, S.G. Hobson suggested that the key was to renegotiate the state's role. Identifying the continuance of the wage system as the cornerstone of enslavement in *National Guilds: An Inquiry into the Wage System and the Way Out* (1914), Hobson confirmed that the state 'must be the final arbiter' nonetheless, and continue to assume 'certain functions'.[137] As Cole put it, 'the Guildsman' stood on the fault-line between the 'State Socialist and Co-operative idealist' pointing to a solution: the 'management and control' of each industry by the workers 'engaged in it', matched by the 'full... representation and safeguarding of the consumers' point of view'. A 'new co-ordinating body' was necessary, one historically discontinuous in having renounced its role as an 'instrument of coercion', and one with such a circumscribed remit it would probably 'wither away' through 'atrophy'.[138]

Other political solutions to capitalism's inherent instability similarly couched their panaceas in the language of rational planning, while traducing the modern state. Sharing the pages of *The New Age* with Cole, Hilaire Belloc asserted the apparent truism that 'mere Capitalist anarchy cannot endure', and predicted a movement towards a 'servile state': security and subsistence for the proletariat at the price of their political freedom, while 'the Owners' became secure in their profits.[139] Collaborating with Cecil Chesterton in the settling 'heat and dust' of the 1911 general election, they prophesied the imminent demise of a 'degraded Parliament', and a party system no longer fit for purpose.[140] Multifarious co-operative bodies 'binding men of the same craft or of the same village', like those comprising the 'DISTRUBITVE STATE' of the Middle Ages were the answer, halcyon days lost to the 'moral anarchy... which goes by the name of *Capitalism*'.[141]

Historians of anarchism have long lamented the impact of the First World War and the Russian Revolution on the anarchist movement.

Radical circles previously pullulating with libertarian ideas contracted as anarchists swooned before resurgent nationalism, or, like Victor Serge, were persuaded by the practical achievements of Bolshevism.[142] Others resisted these sirens, but as various national Communist parties colonised the left, they still found themselves manoeuvred into obsolescence. Despite the appeal of this narrative, however, the political history of the post-war period demonstrates the continuing attraction of radical critique and its enduringly hydra-like manifestations. While mainstream political actors adopted a mollifying language of consensus and radical statists looked to the remedy of central planning, for dissenters like Cole, Hobson, and Belloc planning did not necessarily imply central direction. Anarchism played a quiet role here too, evinced by the occasional invocations of Kropotkin's creative solutions. But this subterranean politics would flare once again, as the Spanish Revolution showed that the anarchist torch of freedom still had fuel to burn. For Read, growing politically aware as the debates between collectivists and decentralists continued, this flame cast a pellucid light on Britain and its history.

The Truth of a Few Simple Ideas: Herbert Read and anarchism

Read came of age intellectually in this era of radical solutions, as doomsayers continued to forecast the demise of capitalism and rushed to define what would replace it. A member of the Leeds Art Club, avid reader of, and eventual contributor to, *The New Age*, Read's ideas grew in a matrix in which challenging the authority of conventional political action and centrally directed solutions remained prominent. His journey to anarchism, however, was not a foregone conclusion, and initially his political ideas remained inchoate. Like Kropotkin a son of the soil, Read's early life on a farm on the North York Moors left an abiding delight in the English countryside. The early chapters of his autobiography, *Annals of Innocence and Experience* (1940), considered by George Orwell to be Read's finest work, traced the rustic pleasures of his early life, offering ethereal reflections on the orchard, cow pasture, and mill.[143] These earthy attachments informed Read's early political attitudes; a commitment to Conservatism he deemed instinctual, sustained by a diet of Edmund Burke, Viscount Bolingbroke, and Benjamin Disraeli. With its tradition of agitational politics, Leeds would lead him to sunder the connection with his conservative past, but his 'age of unearthly bliss' ended much sooner when the death of his father meant

Read was dispatched to the Crossley and Porter Orphan Home in Halifax to live a 'Spartan' existence ruled by strict discipline.[144]

The school's Dickensian detachment did not suit Read, and, while developing a passion for the Victorian romances of Walter Scott and Henry Rider Haggard, he left school at fifteen after modest achievements. Reunited with his mother in Leeds, he worked in a bank while 'evening schools and the public library provided me with the means of continuing my education' in anticipation of enrolling at university when he reached eighteen.[145] Read's pedestrian educational journey would be important to his future life and set him apart from the almost uniformly elite backgrounds of his key collaborators and competitors in London's literary milieu of the 1930s. Virginia Woolf's characteristically unkind estimation of 'little Read' resembling 'a shop assistant' when he was trying to establish himself, is indicative of the kind of snobbery pervading these bohemian circles.[146] In turn, Read developed a hostility to elite universities that later informed his educational theory. These institutions, he argued, tended to foist a carapace of learning onto their students that masked any real appreciation or intellectual daring. This was recognisable in the habit of graduates selling their 'classics to the second-hand bookseller before they "come down" from Oxford or Cambridge; or... stor[ing] them in a glazed bookcase... with a college shield on the wall above'.[147]

Read's own university career was brief but intellectually fecund. Enrolling at the University of Leeds in 1912, the utilitarian aspirations of his fellow students troubled him, and with vague ambitions of a literary career, his approach to formal education was more open than that of his peers. He hankered after a 'liberal' education, but ensconced in the library *poring over volumes of forgotten lore*, other books caught his interest:

> With Dostoevsky and Ibsen I was... partly acquainted, but Nietzsche was a new world, and since my discovery of Blake the most cataclysmic. It was Nietzsche who first introduced me to philosophy... from Nietzsche I passed to Schopenhauer, to Kant, Hegel, Hume, Pascal, Plato – in very indiscriminate order.[148]

The untutored nature of these intellectual meanderings would find echoes in Read's subsequent literary life, in which he maintained a 'bricolage' approach to philosophical speculation, drawing on diverse sources for sustenance, and littering his texts with abundant, frequently decontextualized, quotations.[149] For all his despair at Leeds' grimy industrialism and the mediocrity of his fellow students, the city was also home to a small, but vibrant, modern art scene. Penty, Orage, and Jackson had departed for London, but their Art Club endured under the tutelage of Frank Rutter, then also curator of the city's art gallery. Belloc, Shaw, and Edward Carpenter had all passed through the doors of the Club, and in Read's time, it would champion the work of avant-gardists like Wassily Kandinsky.[150]

In mixing dissident forms of socialism, anti-state political ideas, and heightened aesthetic sensibility, the Leeds Art Club was a clear crucible for the development of Read's philosophy. Yet, his association with the Club, and his University education, came to a premature end in 1914. While Read would later tie together his wartime experiences with his turn to pacifism and argue that the basis of his socialism was in place at the outbreak of war, 4 August 1914 already found him in a military camp. Driven 'to some extent' by his 'patriotic past', Read had joined the Officers Training Corps while a student, with the main goal of adding variety to his sedentary intellectual pursuits. 'There, happily at play,' he wrote, 'I was caught by the war.'[151] The final meaning of his wartime experiences always eluded Read, even though he endeavoured to examine these memories in a variety of forms: poetry, autobiographical prose, and political polemic. To the end he was torn between seeing his experiences as in one sense empowering, finally shaking off the parochialism already under attack from his awakening intellect, and on the other, profoundly disabling, inducing a 'pathetic longing for security'.[152] Whatever its emotional cost, Read's long and distinguished service on the Western Front certainly imparted a desire to pursue the budding literary career that began in earnest in 1915, with his first collection of poetry *Songs of Chaos*. The title, gleaned from *Thus Spake Zarathustra* (1883), showed the enduring significance Orage's efforts to popularise Nietzsche through the Leeds Art Club, and Read evidently imbibed the Nietzschean *will*, remaining undeterred when his book sold just twenty-two copies before being pulped.[153]

Its unspectacular reception aside, *Songs of Chaos* shows that despite his disinterment from the University library, Read's period under colours continued to be a time of intellectual growth. Joining his local regiment, the Green Howards, extended periods in training camps before dispatch for France gave ample opportunity for reading. The 'War Diary' that he inserted into the final version of his autobiography, *The Contrary Experience*, detailed his rigorous and catholic reading as he moved between Kent, Staffordshire, and Flanders.[154] He wrote of receiving 'the *New Age* every week', of the authors that inspired him (Thomas Hardy, Henry

James, and Penty), and of those 'landmarks of Philistia' he abhorred, notably H.G. Wells and Rudyard Kipling.[155] Reflecting his interest in Guild Socialism, Read published his first two political articles in *The Guildsman* in 1917, where he rejected the 'mere negative reality of anarchist philosophy' in favour of a Cole-esque guild-led reconstitution of the relationship between the individual and the state.[156]

Rising to the rank of captain, and awarded both the Military Cross and Distinguished Service Order, Read had a successful military career, but the end of the war left him with a predicament. By this time, his vague ambitions of making a living by the pen had crystallised into a zeal. Enthusiastically rallying to the cause of Imagist poetry, Read cleaved to the principles articulated in the 1915 collection *Some Imagist Poets*, adopting their insistence on *exact* over decorative phrasing and preference for poetry that is 'hard and clear, never blurred nor indefinite'.[157] On leave from the Front, Read trudged around the bookshops of Charing Cross Road with Richard Aldington, and met key Imagists including F.S. Flint and Ezra Pound, as well as Orage and Wyndham Lewis.[158] Most significantly, he dined with T.S. Eliot, persuading Eliot to contribute to the new periodical he had founded with Rutter, *Arts and Letters*, which was intended as an antidote to the increasingly pedestrian *The New Age*.[159] Forbidden by army regulations from being named as one the editors of the organ, Read's presence was evident as a regular reviewer and essayist, while the first issue of *Arts and Letters* carried two of his poems.[160] The publication was also visually striking, with early issues bearing thickly lined sketches from Walter Sickert, post-impressionist pointillist contributions from Harold Gilman, studies by Henri Gaudier-Brzeska, and angular sketches and woodcuts from notable British modernists including Christopher Nevinson and Paul Nash.[161] Osbert Sitwell, who would also soon become an editor of *Arts and Letters*, paints a characteristic picture of a determined and rather taciturn Read in this period. Commenting on their regular literary dinners in Piccadilly Circus with Eliot, Pound, and Wyndham Lewis, he described his attraction to Read as one of opposites: 'like a Roundhead, he is extravagant only in the lengths to which art-austerity carries him: whereas I am extravagant in all else'.[162]

For all its literary connections, the Roundhead's new life in modernist London, 'the very heart of it', did not pay well.[163] Adamant that he must write, he contemplated staying in the army, reflecting that Coleridge had seen 'three hours of leisure' as sufficient to pursue literary ambitions. Concluding though that peace would mean a return to the 'discipline and snobbery' of the parade ground, rather than the 'fidelity' of the trenches, he rejected this idea, instead accepting a post in the Ministry of Labour, under his former tutor at Leeds, Arthur Greenwood.[164] Whitehall was not the 'sinecure' that Read had hoped, but he maintained a disciplined writing schedule on returning home, tying himself to his 'desk... from ten o'clock to midnight, night after night, year after year'.[165] Despite the frustrations, in 1919 Read published two well-received editions of poetry *Eclogues*, and a collection of war-verse *Naked Warriors*. Siegfried Sassoon wrote to Read complementing his 'fine book' *Naked Warriors*, and confessing that whilst his own method was 'old fashioned', Read's Imagistic 'stuff absolutely gets me'.[166]

In 1922 Read escaped to a position in the Department of Ceramics at the Victoria and Albert Museum (V&A). His new role reawakened his interest in visual aesthetics dormant since his association with the Leeds Art Club, with the added bonus that he now had more time to write. Believing that art criticism had been fallow 'since the time of Ruskin', and coupled with his newfound commitment to the critical essay, the path was open for Read to unite his interest in the 'history and criticism of art' with the 'history and criticism of literature' in a 'general conception of culture'.[167] These years saw a number of his critical articles collected as volumes, notably *Reason and Romanticism: Essays in Literary Criticism*, which John Middleton Murry deemed the work of 'a true humanist', and *The Sense of Glory* (1929).[168] Read also edited two works that freshened his philosophical appreciation of aesthetics. At the behest of Orage he assembled a collection of the critical writings of war-casualty T.E. Hulme, *Speculations* (1924), and Wilhelm Worringer's *Form in Gothic* (1927), which he also translated from the German. *English Prose Style*, a book commended in *The Spectator*, though it also declared that it had a frustrating habit of treating modern 'fashions with... disproportionate seriousness', appeared in 1928, along with *Phases of English Poetry*.[169] In recognition of Read's growing reputation, Eliot put his name forward to deliver the Clark Lectures at Trinity College, Cambridge. *Wordsworth* (1930), the product of his time at the lectern, was a work that showed his interest in psychology as a tool in comprehending literary subjects, although the critic John Cann Bailey was unconvinced. Although it had a surfeit of 'cleverness', he added that the book 'is too abstract and theoretical, and is fuller of theories about life and philosophy... than it is of Wordsworth'.[170]

Following his lectures at Cambridge, Read assumed the Watson Gordon Chair of Fine Art at the University of Edinburgh in 1931. With his activities at the V&A increasingly humdrum, the assurance of regular sabbaticals for writing presented an appealing change. Edinburgh, however, was a disappointment, and his tenure a brief one, after the scandal of an extra-marital affair hastened Read's return to London in 1933. Edinburgh may not have marked the beginning of a new life as an academic, but his period in Scotland gave Read time to edit articles he had contributed to the BBC's *Listener* magazine. Published as the aphoristic *The Meaning of Modern Art* (1931), it closed with a panegyric on modern artists including Paul Klee, Max Ernst, and Henry Moore, that befitted Read's position as a champion of the avant-garde.[171] The following decades would consolidate this status, and he emerged as both a philosopher of modern art and a leading polemicist for modernism, although not everyone was convinced by the range of his enthusiasms. As early as 1934, the surrealist poet David Gascoyne questioned whether Read might be exaggerating the value of Klee's work, while some years later, Wyndham Lewis bitingly rejected him as a 'Mister Abreast-of-the-Times for Everyman ... trumpet[ing] ... any movement in painting ... hurrying along a path as opposite as possible from what had appealed to civilized man through the ages'.[172] *Art Now* (1933) extended Read's defence of modernism, aiming to uncover the 'gradual change in the general philosophy of art' that paved the way for a modern art that was 'transformative' and had an 'independent cognitive status'.[173] *Art and Society* (1937) followed, examining the ubiquity of the 'aesthetic impulse' in human history, and stressing that the most significant works were organic expressions of this instinct. This idea led on to a critique of Socialist Realism, which Read thought perverted this innate capacity through 'the imposition of an intellectual predetermined conception of what art should be'.[174] Individual studies of Paul Nash, Klee, Ben Nicholson, Naum Gabo, Kandinsky, and Hans Arp, written and edited by Read betrayed the aesthetics he favoured, and further exegeses on the theory of art attempted to address the origin of the unique artistic vision, a focus that encouraged a turn to the work of Carl Jung and Sigmund Freud.

Such fascination with the inner-life of the artist explains Read's attraction to Surrealism. In 1936, he threw his energies into organising the International Surrealist Exhibition in London, which included contributions from André Breton, Man Ray, and Salvador Dali, and home-grown trendsetters like Moore, Nash, and Roland Penrose. The lure of Surrealism marked a significant liminal point in Read's intellectual history, leading him to sharpen the political edge of his work and openly commit himself to the defence of the romantic implied in his critical writing on literature, in contrast to his previously astringent defence of Imagist detachment. In the volume *Surrealism* (1936), which emerged from the Exhibition and boasted contributions from Breton and Paul Éluard, Read opined that Surrealism had resolved the antagonism between romanticism and classicism by 'liquidating' the latter. Later retitling his essay 'Surrealism and the Romantic Principle', Read stressed the uplifting qualities of the romantic against the classical, where one was 'a principle of life, of creation, of liberation' and the other 'a principle of order, of control, of repression'.[175] The political resonance of this was patent, but Read's articulation of it was decidedly unanarchist. Chiding the 'stupid... aesthetic intolerance' of Russian Communism, he nevertheless concluded that:

> In a world of competing tyrannies, the artist can have only one allegiance: to that dictatorship which claims to end all... tyranny and promises, however indefinitely, the complete liberation of man: the dictatorship of the proletariat.[176]

This was a timorous endorsement of Communism, and once the Spanish Civil War raised awareness of anarchism's past, it was one that Read jettisoned. Indeed, he was soon asked to pick a side in that conflict. Writing in *Authors Take Sides on the Spanish War* (1936), sandwiched between the Soviet-apologist and sometime Labour Party MP Denis Pritt and CPGB member Edgell Rickword, Read struck an anti-state stance:

> In Spain... there still lives a spirit to resist the bureaucratic tyranny of the State and the intellectual intolerance of all doctrinaires. For that reason all poets must follow the course of this struggle with open and passionate partisanship.[177]

The deadening effect of bureaucratic rationalism was a theme in Read's only work of fiction, the richly elusive novella *The Green Child* (1935). His first sustained political polemic, *Essential Communism*, also appeared in 1935 and presented a parallel case, calling for socialists to be sensitive to the uniqueness of the 'artist's approach' in politics. It was not, however, an anarchist tract, but published in the 'Pamphlets on The New Economics' series of the Social Credit movement, and in it Read explicitly endorsed the 'economic analysis of [Major C.H.] Douglas and Orage'.[178]

Read's commitment to Social Credit was a brief one, and showed the enduring influence of Orage on his social theory. Indeed, in 1935 Read also coedited an edition of Orage's collected essays, primarily dealing with art and literature.[179] The popularity of Major Douglas' ideas more broadly demonstrates the intensity of the search for a solution to the anarchy of capitalism in the 1930s, with Social Credit's emphasis on leisure appealing to the artistically minded: Ezra Pound, Edwin Muir, and Storm Jameson would all contribute pamphlets to the New Economics initiative. With his interest in politics reawakened, Read's writing on cultural matters strove to emphasise the necessary interrelation of cultural and political theory. Another collection appeared in 1936, *In Defence of Shelley,* in which Read railed against British art after John Constable and William Turner deeming its 'ugliness and vulgarity' a product of Britain's industrial triumph: 'They are the expression of the taste of the age, and they are appalling and shameful.'[180]

As Read's identification with anarchism strengthened, and his formal association with the movement developed through his writing for *Freedom,* he tied these ideas more directly to his politics.[181] *Poetry and Anarchism* (1938), *The Philosophy of Anarchism* (1940), *To Hell With Culture* (1941) and *The Politics of the Unpolitical* (1943) all pondered the 'fate' of the artist in the 'industrial age', and the debasement of culture at the hands of market logic.[182] Anarchism informed a counter vision of vibrant art flowering in a rich soil of direct democracy, mutual aid, and the removal of the division between the city and country borrowed directly from Kropotkin.[183] In acknowledgement of this debt, he edited a detailed reader of Kropotkin's works for Freedom Press in 1942.[184] Wartime also saw Read's first sustained intervention in the field of educational theory, with *Education Through Art* (1943), a work he later described as the most 'influential book I have written', but one whose libertarian message was often overlooked.[185] The radical potential of aesthetically led education became a central concern, and he endeavoured to condense the densely abstract *Education Through Art* into pithier offerings. *The Education of Free Men* followed in 1944, published by Freedom Press, as did *Education for Peace* (1950) and *The Redemption of the Robot* in 1966, along with a number of shorter pieces. A series of temporary academic appointments led to further adumbrations of his aesthetic philosophy. *The Grass Roots of Art* (1947) emerged from a series of lectures at Yale, *Icon & Idea* (1955) from the Charles Eliot Norton Lectures at Harvard, and *The Origins of Form in Art* (1965) from a period at Wesleyan. The pinnacle of his mature aesthetics, *The Forms of Things Unknown* (1960) originated from the spiritually inflected Eranos conference on Lake Maggiore in Switzerland, where Read met Jung once again.

Ink was not his only contribution to the cause of modern art and literature in Britain, or the sum of his political activity. He began acting as a literary advisor to Routledge and Heinemann in 1937, becoming a partner of the former in 1939, and published books by nonconformist intellectuals including Samuel Beckett, Martin Buber, and Simone Weil, as well as Jung's collected works.[186] Keen on creating a gallery of modern art in Britain, Read followed a foundering collaboration with Peggy Guggenheim in 1939 with the successful foundation of the Institute of Contemporary Arts in London in 1946. The year before, Read helped establish and chaired the Freedom Defence Committee, an organisation set up to aid the defence of Vernon Richards, John Hewetson, Philip Sansom, and Marie-Louise Berneri, editors of the anarchist publication *War Commentary*. While Berneri was acquitted on a technicality, the other defendants were imprisoned for encouraging soldiers to desert, and the Defence Committee transmogrified into a broader campaign group assisting those 'penalised for exercising their rights to freedom of speech, writing and action', before it fizzled out in 1949.[187] As the spectre of nuclear confrontation came to centre stage, Read was drawn to the peace movement, joining the Committee of 100 when it launched in 1960.[188] Reflecting the strengthening of his commitment to Gandhian direct action, Read would nevertheless leave the organisation the following year in protest at what he saw as its increasingly confrontational activities.

In recognition of Read's status as a public intellectual, in 1953 he was awarded a knighthood. Few failed to see the irony of his decision to accept the honour and it marked the end of his brief association with the mainstream anarchist movement in Britain. The philosopher Maurice Cranston, whose own route into the aristocracy was through marriage, captured the general temper in a scathing review of Read's collected political essays *Anarchy and Order* (1954):

> All the best anarchists are men of title, and since the Honours List of 1953 Sir Herbert Read has occupied his rightful place among them...Anarchists of lower rank are dangerous men; when they proclaim rebellion they mean rebellion.[189]

Given that Read must have been aware that his acceptance of a knighthood would lead to ridicule, historians have generally been at a loss to explain his decision, variously noting pressure from his wife, vanity and, curiously, an abiding penchant for the myths of chivalry.[190] All probably influenced Read, but also significant is the elitism of the intellectual world he inhabited, one that made his inauspicious education and failure to live absolutely independently as a writer a source of frustration and embarrassment. With this Cranston, himself tormented by the fact that he had not attended a public school, might have had some sympathy.[191]

Read's remaining years may not have involved much active politics, but he continued to identify as an anarchist and propound the aesthetic-politics developed over his career. Remaining a prolific writer until his death in 1968, he kept abreast of developments in the world of modern art, but the former trendsetter was less than enamoured with some contemporary styles. Always holding American culture in some disdain, in his elegiac 1962 article 'What Is There Left to Say?', Read bemoaned 'the beatniks and the drug-addicts... the "pop"-artists and the Californian buddhists', for failing to appreciate the productive power of meaningful art. The revised version of *Concise History of Modern Painting*, published in the year of his death, reiterated this scornful assessment. Dismissing the 'solipsism' of abstract expressionism, he concluded that Jackson Pollock's art was distinctly un-expressive:

> We, the spectators, react to its 'pure harmony' with appropriate feelings, but the painting does not 'express' these feelings – it merely provokes them, and in this sense is an object of the world, as impersonal as an apple or a mountain.[192]

All this, it seemed for Read, was some distance from the real value of art, that being the pursuit of 'self-knowledge', and the reconciliation of the fragmented personality in the act of creation. 'We must become whole men', he wrote, shortly before his death, deeming this 'the present and urgent necessity' in the face of global instability. And to do this, all that was necessary was to recognise the integrative capacity of artistic creation, the vitality of community, and the functional importance of mutual aid to a vibrant society. In short, he concluded: 'it is a question of having faith in a few simple ideas'.[193]

Kropotkin and Read in context

The denizens of Casterbridge, according to Thomas Hardy, were not perturbed when accidentally unearthing the skeletal remains of the Roman soldiers lying buried in the soil of their town. Their historical remoteness had a balming effect: 'They had lived so long ago, their time was so unlike the present... that between them and the living there seemed to stretch a gulf too wide for even a spirit to pass.'[194] The distance that separated Kropotkin and Read was by no means as great, but they still inhabited radically different ages. Yet, for Read, disinterring the bones of Kropotkin's anarchism, it remained an intellectual achievement freighted with possibility. Confronting the political challenges of the world around them, both thinkers clung to a set of ideas: the rejection of authority encapsulated in the modern state, trust in the constructive abilities of free individuals, faith in the unitary potential of communalist ethics, and belief in the equity of communised distribution.

For political traditions to endure innovation must also occur. Ideas must be decontested afresh, to meet new intellectual challenges and mirror the political discourses that enable meaningful dialogue. In striving to maintain the pertinacity of these ideas, their simple reapplication was insufficient. Rather, the articulation of these values changed, as contextual pressures demanded rephrasing, rethinking, and repurposing. Fundamental was the effort to translate these ideas into a language appropriate to the broader intellectual climate. For Kropotkin, this involved justifying anarchist claims in a socialist movement that, following a wider political trend in late nineteenth-century society, increasingly saw the state as a solution to capitalism's failure to achieve both technological mastery and general prosperity. When Read looked back from a time facing the same problems of disparity and deprivation, he believed Kropotkin's resistance to state-led solutions remained relevant in an age when centralised planning was especially popular. But in adopting these Kropotkinian precepts, Read also adapted. An attachment to the dignity of purposeful labour and belief that the built environment must be pleasant, was transformed into a conviction that creativity was at the heart or everything; it was, the 'index of social vitality'.[195]

2
Foundations: System-Building Philosophy

At the age of twenty John Stuart Mill was enveloped by a 'cloud' that would not 'pass away of itself'. Calling this period 'a crisis in my mental history', Mill blamed it on a realisation that his ambition to promote social reform was no longer a guarantor of happiness. The Benthamite utilitarianism that had given his life purpose, acquired in part through the unyielding educational experiment endured at the hands of his father James Mill, suddenly seemed insufficient. Mill's tonic would be poetry, notably that of William Wordsworth, but in his *Autobiography* (1873), he framed this disenchantment with the strenuous logicism of Benthamism in an interesting way:

> If I am asked what system of political philosophy I substitute for that which . . . I had abandoned, I answer, no system: only a conviction, that the true system was something much more complex and many sided than I had previously had any idea of.[1]

What is striking is that while abjuring systematic philosophy, Mill nevertheless continued to see his intellectual project in terms of a quest for system. In this, as one biographer has noted, Mill's mission mirrored that of *the* quintessential system-building philosopher: Auguste Comte. For both thinkers an 'adequate conception of the human sciences' that could 'serve as a basis for social reform' was paramount, underpinned by a specific reading of the Enlightenment tradition, and advancing a durable philosophy of history.[2] And, as Mill noted a few sentences after detailing his qualified ambition for system, Comte's contribution was a grand one, even if he had arrived at similar conclusions independently: 'I already regarded the methods of physical science as the proper models for political.'[3]

Dominant perceptions of the period imply that Kropotkin was theorising at the nadir of this intellectual self-confidence. Depicted as an age defined by a 'collapse of the absolute', and marked by the rise of a new generation of thinkers 'less confident and optimistic' than their forebears, the temper of the period was apparently one of disquiet with the arrogant certainties of the past.[4] From Henri Bergson placing the purity of scientific reasoning under the microscope to William James questioning the validity of causal laws, the logic of using models borrowed from science to inform social thought was under attack. As Sigmund Freud diagnosed the irrational impulses lurking behind the veil of civility, and Gustave Le Bon saw the triumph of irrationality in crowd behaviour, political theories resting on appeals to reason also seemed to possess precarious foundations. It is Friedrich Nietzsche though, who stands tallest in historical accounts as the chief anatomist of the platitudes of the age. The irony being that the year that Nietzsche suffered his catastrophic breakdown – 1889 – was when his explosive writings were finally beginning to be taken seriously. Rather than the vainglorious pursuit of some spurious notion of truth, for Nietzsche, the object of philosophy should be to discover that which 'is life-advancing, life-preserving, species-preserving'.[5] Unimpressed by Charles Darwin's characteristically English empiricism, Darwinism had at least shown the ubiquity of struggle, and the metaphysical importance of power.

If *fin-de-siècle* European culture was characterised by numerous anxieties concerning the shape of the future, and the philosophy of the time similarly enshrined crisis, decline, and irrationality, many would see anarchism as a logical product of this paranoid mentality. Indeed, anarchism has frequently found itself incorporated into this narrative of the twilight of European rationalism. Most often, it is Bakunin's legacy that is invoked, reducing his political thought to the irrationalist epithets of 'violence, destruction, incendiarism', or deeming his ideas the product of an aberrant, 'pathological', mind.[6] So too the focus on the era of 'propaganda by the deed' reinforces the image of the anarchist as 'half delinquent, half fanatic', yoking anarchism and irrationalism.[7] Yet, as the best histories have shown, such tidy conceptions offer an unduly stable appreciation of the intellectual history of the period. Freud may have exposed the uncomfortable realities of human motivation, but he did so while proclaiming the scientific credentials of psychoanalysis. And, as H. Stuart Hughes noted long ago, rather than distaste for the values of the Enlightenment, it was their crude rewriting by positivists that motivated Nietzsche, Freud, Georges Sorel, and their ilk.[8]

As Kropotkin's work shows, amidst the flight from rationality and systematic thought, theorists remained who held fast to the principles of reason, science, and composite philosophy. For post-anarchists, shaped by the rejection of the 'grand narrative' popularised by post-structuralism, Kropotkin's adoption of a 'rationalist semiotics' is troubling, ultimately undermining his attempt to 'articulate a truly radical politics'.[9] In turn, this scepticism has led contemporary accounts to downplay the extent to which Kropotkin was acting within the tradition of system-building philosophy. Read was similarly prone to greet the claims of systematic philosophy with cynicism, reflecting his intellectual growth in an era when the projects of thinkers like Comte seemed hopelessly passé. Yet, despite his protestations at the inadequacies of holistic thinking, Read presented a coherent, aesthetically nuanced anarchist theory that formed the bedrock of his intellectual pursuits. It is therefore necessary to understand both men in terms of their complex relation to the search for a systematic philosophy. Far from reducing the social actor to the product of mechanical laws, in a clear debt to romanticism, their analyses revealed individuals that were the locus of limitless potential. Their pursuit of reason uncovered a universe of wonder.

Modern Science and Anarchism: Kropotkin's synthetic philosophy

In terms of his overarching methodology, Kropotkin appears to the modern reader as a quintessentially Victorian thinker. He placed great faith in science and, writing in the midst of its most profound discoveries, regarded its potential for continual advancement as practically endless. He also saw the translation of scientific concepts from natural to social philosophy as, broadly speaking, an unproblematic exercise. In turn, he regularly framed his anarchism in terms of scientific theories that had revolutionised various branches of scientific enquiry: the atheistic astronomy of Pierre-Simon Laplace, for instance, or James Joule's physics.[10] By far the strongest presence in Kropotkin's work, however, was Darwin. For Kropotkin, Darwin had provided the strongest scientific evidence that an anarchist community was a viable proposition; that humanity, and indeed animal societies, was underpinned by an ethos of mutual aid counterbalancing the propensity to individual competitiveness.

The self-consciously scientific nature of Kropotkin's social thought has raised concerns. It is not only modern critics, cognisant that projects of emancipation resting on supposedly rational foundations often led to more sinister places than Arcadia, that have questioned the similarity he saw between the methods of science and those of anarchism.[11] Transposing ideas gleaned from evolutionary theory to a revolutionary political tradition could also be problematic. If the light of scientific truth was conquering ever more completely the obscurantism and superstition that legitimised authoritarian politics, did revolution remain necessary?[12] Partly in response to issues like this, others have sought to downplay Kropotkin's commitment to the kinds of nineteenth-century social science that borrowed most promiscuously from the natural sciences.[13] For the accurate appreciation of Kropotkin's thought, such ahistoricism is unhelpful, particularly with this formative relationship in mind. In addition, focused attention casts a probing light on how his historical sociology grew from a particular reading of the history of social thought, and the uniqueness of his vision that presented an ontology defined by plasticity. To trace the transmission of these ideas through to Read and his appropriation of this approach in a very different context, the architecture of Kropotkin's social philosophy is a crucial starting point.

Throughout his life, Kropotkin displayed a deep affinity to France. His early education was at the hands of one of the 'debris of Napoleon's Grande Armée', and like many wealthy but disenchanted Russians, he devoured the prohibited books of the French Enlightenment.[14] This apprenticeship in rationalist philosophy would be a recurrent, if usually unacknowledged, source of inspiration throughout his intellectual career. That does not mean he was uncritical of many of the political conclusions of the *philosophes*, but faith in science; an understanding of history as a comprehensible process; an idea that humanity could be in some sense improved; and a conviction that rational organisation could correct the irrationality of the present, were key aspects of his political theory. Overarching these beliefs was a quest for a synthetic philosophy that might unite knowledge in a useful whole, and Kropotkin made it clear that his awakening to science had led him to this conclusion. 'Whatever one's subsequent studies might be', he wrote rather sententiously, 'a thorough knowledge of the natural sciences and familiarity with their methods must lie at the foundation.'[15]

A similar attachment to a conception of scientific knowledge that was translatable to social criticism was common currency amongst the French thinkers associated with that problematic category of 'the Enlightenment'. Voltaire's *Lettres philosophiques* (1734) waxed lyrical on the achievements of Isaac Newton, who 'gave us the thread by which we may find our way' through 'the labyrinth and the abyss of the infinite'.[16] Another 'first generation' *philosophe*, Montesquieu, reached for a social theory that was both scientific and holistic. Noting at the outset of *De l'esprit des lois* (1748) that he had 'not drawn my principles from my prejudices, but from the nature of things', he cautioned the blithe reader that a 'great many truths' will not appear 'until we have seen the chain which connects them'.[17] If Voltaire and Montesquieu stand as the key thinkers of the first of the three generations that developed social science in France, Nicolas de Condorcet is the primary representative of the second.[18] Given Kropotkin's fascination with the French Revolution, Condorcet is a more prominent presence in his writings as an historical actor. Indeed, he deemed him one of the few 'sincere republicans', alongside Thomas Paine, who avoided the tendency of bourgeois intellectuals to settle for 'constitutional royalty'.[19] Aside from this reference, he did not mention Condorcet again until his final unfinished work *Ethics*:

> Condorcet...gave a further development to the idea of progress in his famous work, 'Tableau de progress de l'esprit humain.' He not only endeavoured to prove the existence of the law of progress, but also attempted to derive the laws of future social development from the past history of mankind.[20]

Despite infrequent direct citation, such references demonstrate that Kropotkin was versed in the ideas of the notable forerunners of sociological theory.[21] It is not surprising that this tradition of social thought was a source of intellectual sustenance, given the popularity of French liberal theorists and the first sociologists amongst dissident Russians, Kropotkin's fluency in French, and his immersion in French history from his earliest education. But more significantly, it shows that what attracted him to their work was their quest for an encompassing explanation of social development: the pursuit of the 'laws' that shaped the nature of social life, underpinned by an acute sense of history as a process, and a belief that appreciating the past was crucial to comprehending the present.

Kropotkin's quest for a synthetic philosophy comes into sharper focus once attention shifts to the 'third' generation of social thought in France, personified in the work of Comte. Like the Enlightenment philosophers preceding him, and his mentor Henri de Saint-Simon, Comte's desire was to forge the natural and social sciences into a whole that could cast light on all of humanity's political and moral problems. Kropotkin shared this ambition, and devoted lengthy sections of his pamphlet *Modern Science and Anarchism* (1901) to an appreciative dissection of Comte's approach. Although critical of the political conclusions in Comte's 'Positive Politics', it is indicative that Kropotkin attributed this weakness to Comte's failure to abide by his own rigorous methodological precepts. Mentioning Mill's dismissal of this work, Kropotkin charged that its particular weakness lay in the discussion of the origin of moral feeling.[22] Crucially, he argued that Comte's move away from the conclusions that a truly 'positivist' analysis would have reached was a result of the infancy of biology, predating as it did the revolution in knowledge inaugurated by Darwin's *On the Origin of Species* (1859). Unable to appreciate fully the nature of sociability amongst animals, Comte slipped unwittingly into deist thinking, thereby reconstituting a hierarchical politics:

> He took *God*, the divinity of all the positive religions, which man is requested to worship and to pray to in order to remain moral, and in his stead he put *Humanity* with a capital letter. He invited us to prostrate ourselves before this new divinity, and to address our prayers to it in order to develop our moral feelings.

To Kropotkin's mind, Comte was reaching for, but falling short of the essential truth, that human morality had a *'pre-human origin'*.[23] This was an argument he fleshed out in *Ethics*, but significantly, here too Kropotkin praised Comte's synthetic aspirations:

> Comte realized the necessity of unifying all these new acquisitions and conquests of scientific thought. He decided to unify all the sciences into a single orderly system and to demonstrate the close interdependence of all the phenomena of nature, their sequence, their common basis, and the laws of development.[24]

As Kropotkin was suggesting, echoes of the *philosophes* rang in Comte's work. A notion of progress; the desire for composite knowledge; belief in human perfectibility; and a certainty that a rational system could cure the social malaise, were present. These ideas have their place in Kropotkin's oeuvre too, although he added important qualifications to hubristic concepts like progress. Nevertheless, if Comte was by inclination 'a searcher after system', the same applies to Kropotkin.[25]

Kropotkin only mentioned Montesquieu, Voltaire, and Condorcet in passing; he spilt more ink examining Comte, but by far the most discussed thinker in the context of this sociological tradition was Herbert Spencer. For several reasons this should be no surprise.

Despite censorship, Spencer's work was popular amongst Russia's liberal intelligentsia, and Kropotkin encountered his work at an early age.[26] Indeed, in his memoirs, he reminisced about the difficulties of ordering tea in Scotland equipped only with a grasp of English from translating Spencer's *Principles of Biology* (1864, 1867).[27] Historical circumstance also meant that Comte was isolated from the Darwinian revolution, whereas Spencer, like Kropotkin, tied his philosophy closely to a notion of evolution. So much so, in fact, that when attempting to fathom the exact nature of evolutionary inheritance beyond the pages of *Mutual Aid*, it was Spencer's Lamarckian defence of the inheritability of acquired characteristics to which he turned.[28]

Like Comte, Spencer wrote dense tracts that sought a synthesis of knowledge. But whereas Comte's political conclusions seemed too tainted with authoritarianism, for Kropotkin, Spencer's critique of Gladstone's fervour for intervention, *The Man Versus the State*, was an essentially libertarian text. Getting rather carried away, Kropotkin wrote that the title alone represented 'in itself a whole revolutionary programme', and in its first issue following Spencer's death in 1903, *Freedom* repeated this line, deeming Spencer 'the greatest philosopher of the nineteenth century'.[29] For his part, the nineteenth-century's greatest philosopher, always keen to promote his profundity, denied that there was any relationship between his grand synthesis and that of Comte.[30] Kropotkin disagreed, and saw Spencer's intellectual mission as a broad continuation of the Frenchman's, albeit shorn of the 'new divinity' that betrayed the 'Christian education' Comte was unable to lose. Yet, even if he sidestepped this abstraction, Kropotkin still believed that Spencer's system was riddled with 'fallacies', and diagnosed a similar hesitancy in pursuing the uncomfortable conclusions revealed by his scientific methodology.[31] In other words, while Spencer's exploration of the 'physical sciences, biology and psychology' were revolutionary, impeded by the weight of the ideas of 'middle class radicalism' that had ignited his political imagination in the first place, 'he had not the courage to accept' the political implications of his studies.[32]

As a testament to his influence, and by way of marking his death, Kropotkin devoted a series of lengthy articles to Spencer in *Freedom* between February and September 1904. Behind this interest in Spencer, there was also a tactical element. For a fledgling political movement, association with the *grand homme* of British radical liberalism added a modicum of political respectability. Kropotkin's policy of praising the work of those whose politics he thought lay close to his – Jeremy

Bentham and John Stuart Mill are other examples – was not then a reflection of his benevolence, but the product of a calculated attempt to translate anarchism into English.[33] Kropotkin was not obsequious though, and while praising Spencer's iconoclasm in freeing the scientific epistemology from metaphysics, he remained frustrated by his timidity:

> What Spencer lacks is the spirit of attack, the fighting spirit. He builds his system of the universe without a creator, but we should like him to directly demolish the superstitions that encumber the minds of people, preventing them from accepting his system.[34]

The assault on God was an important project for Kropotkin, reflecting a deeper view that throughout history religion had always acted as an ally of authoritarian politics. But this passage also shows his belief that systematic philosophy had the potential to persistently revolutionise thought. Fond of quoting Georges Danton's famous encouragement for 'audacity', this necessarily had an intellectual component too, and Kropotkin was therefore disappointed when Spencer conceded that some phenomena were 'unknowable'. Following the positivist Frederic Harrison, he argued that this entailed a 'flagrant' contradiction, for to know that something could not be known, meant that 'we must be sure it differs from all that we have learnt to know so far', implying that, actually, 'a good deal' was known about this unknowable.[35]

More important than this bludgeoning exercise in logic is the fact that Kropotkin thought that by limiting the purview of scientific knowledge, Spencer opened the door to a pernicious mysticism. 'Nothing *need* remain unknown forever', he concluded, 'nothing is incapable of being represented in our brain'.[36] While intellectual hesitancy allowed the forces of political reaction to regroup, he argued that staying attuned to a scientific epistemology revealed the veracity of revolutionary politics. This was a view that Kropotkin formulated early on, as seen in his first work *Words of a Rebel*, in a chapter reprinted in a range of formats by British socialists:

> Lover of pure science, if you have opened your minds to the principles of socialism and understand the full significance of the approaching revolution, do you not recognize that the whole of science must be reorganized to suit the new principles; that we will have to carry out... a revolution whose importance will vastly surpass that accomplished in science during the eighteenth century?[37]

Later, musing on Spencer's work, he propounded this belief again, albeit with greater sophistication:

> As soon as we try to construct a synthetic philosophy of the universe, including the life of societies, it is necessary to come, not only to the denial of a creative God governing the universe, not only to the denial of the immortal soul or any special vital force, but we come to the overthrow of that remaining idol – the state, the government of man over man.[38]

Regarding both Comte and Spencer then, Kropotkin's objection was essentially the same. He praised and pursued their method, arguing that just as the Enlightenment had denuded superstition now it was time to exhibit this élan in the rational reordering of social affairs. Committed to their methodology, Kropotkin explained his divergence from their politics by diagnosing a failure in both Comte's and Spencer's translation of this methodology from the natural to social sciences. Both failed to grasp the truths of Darwinism, Comte because he predated it, and Spencer because he failed to notice the kernel of mutuality at the heart of the struggle for existence.[39]

Kropotkin's efforts to position himself in relation to the intellectual lineage of French and, through Spencer, British social thought demonstrate that he attached great value to the project of systematic philosophy. As he argued, any system of ideas worthy of the name must renounce all metaphysical abstractions – the charge of metaphysicality is a reoccurring, rather haphazardly applied, one in Kropotkin's texts – and pursue a holistic course, uniting all phenomena under a complex of generalisations. Anarchism, he suggested, was a necessary component of this explanatory framework:

> Anarchism is a conception of the Universe based on the mechanical interpretation of phenomena, which comprises the whole of Nature, including... human societies and their economic, political and moral problems. Its method is that of the natural sciences, and every conclusion it comes to must be verified by this method if it pretends to be scientific.[40]

On the surface, all of this makes Kropotkin sound like a prototypical proponent of the kind of uninspiring positivism that motivated the flight from rationalism in late nineteenth-century thinking. For those modern commentators inspired by poststructuralist philosophy this, indeed, is a fruitful frame for understanding his work. Important as he may have been in the history of anarchism, the weight of Kropotkin's attachment to 'innate' tendencies, 'essences', and 'inexorable' trajectories, vitiates the constructive power of his politics.[41] In turn, those seeking to protect his political legacy often divorce Kropotkin from this historical context:

> It is fashionable these days to dismiss Kropotkin as a crude positivist and an ardent follower of... Comte... He has even, along with Darwin, been interpreted – quite falsely – as an advocate of mechanistic science.[42]

This kind of ahistoricism is unhelpful. Given his ready praise for both Comte and Spencer, it is clearly wholly legitimate to place him in this context. Nonetheless, the idea that Kropotkin is too readily charged with adopting a naively mechanistic brand of social science is valid. The solution to this quandary is an important one for Kropotkin's theoretical edifice, for as a number of scholars have noted, subscribing to the idea of the inevitable, scientifically verified, triumph of anarchism has disquieting implications for his belief in the necessity of revolutionary transformation.[43] Rather than distancing Kropotkin's thought from this social-scientific crucible, however, the subtleties of his contribution become clearer when seen in this intellectual context.

Although steeped in the language of positivism, a sense of flux, an emphasis on the temporary nature of stability, and a broad anti-essentialism, were central to Kropotkin's philosophy. Characteristically Victorian in being unfazed by disciplinary boundaries, this sense of ontological plasticity was one that informed his various specific studies. *Modern Science and Anarchism* endeavoured to root this vision in European intellectual history, but its most explicit statement came in the pamphlet *Anarchism: Its Philosophy and Ideal* (1897). Crucially, he qualified at the outset the idea of any simple application of the scientific methodology to the analysis of social phenomena. 'I begin by taking... elementary observations borrowed from the natural sciences', he wrote, 'not for the purpose of deducing our social ideas from them', but because they offer illustrative examples of 'certain relations'.[44] Despite this effort to address pre-emptively accusations of determinism, Kropotkin followed this by tracing a bolder connection between anarchism and modern science:

> Under the name of Anarchy, a new interpretation of the past and present life of society arises, giving at the same time a

> forecast as regards its future, both conceived in the same spirit as the . . . interpretation in natural sciences. Anarchy...appears as a constituent part of the new philosophy, and that is why Anarchists come into contact on so many points with the greatest thinkers...of the present day.[45]

The source of tension in Kropotkin's work is his effort to place anarchism under the aegis of contemporary science, while distancing it from competing political traditions claiming the mantle of scientific truth. As with his treatment of Comte and Spencer, he usually achieved this by questioning the purity of their scientific method, and diagnosing its faulty application when attention shifted to the study of societies. The most pressing competition in this sphere was Marxism, and the scientific posturing of 'Scientific Socialism', irked Kropotkin, who often placed the term in knowing quotation marks.[46] That key component of Marx's analytic arsenal, the dialectic, also failed to impress. He dismissed Hegel's 'sonorous phrases' as obfuscating abstractions, and suggested, without explaining, that 'Marxists have lately fallen' into 'economic errors...owing to their predilection for the dialectic method and economic metaphysics'.[47] As the attachment to Hegel apparently betrayed, the scientific ideas that informed Marxism were in fact translations (into 'bad metaphysical German') of the ideas of French socialists like Victor Considerant, and epigones of Charles Fourier and Saint-Simon.[48]

The charge of metaphysical speciousness levelled at the followers of Marx informed Kropotkin's counter-vision of an anarchism attentive to the possibilities of modern science. Where Marx allegedly pursued the 'halo of scientific infallibility' in order to dominate the workers' movement, Kropotkin recommended 'the naturalist' as an instructive guide.[49] With this model in mind, the scientific method was a means of testing theories and sifting evidence, rather than transposing the conclusions of natural philosophy into sociology. In preaching the values of objective investigation free from the contaminants of vogue philosophies, Kropotkin therefore advanced a parallel argument to Émile Durkheim, who was concurrently attempting to codify *The Rules of Sociological Method* (1895). The irony is, of course, that while preaching analytical disinterestedness both inevitably bore the imprint of current intellectual fashions, namely a shared positivism, and for Kropotkin, Darwinism.[50]

Modern science was a source of sustenance for his politics, but at the heart of this project was an attempt to eschew the kind of crude determinism expounded by fellow late nineteenth-century positivists.

Kropotkin's reading of Darwinian theory, for instance, always emphasised Darwin's role in disproving the 'immutability' of species sanctioned by religious orthodoxy. In this vein, he also reached for Spencer, always a peptic in his digestion of the debates dealing with Darwin's legacy at the turn of the century, and adopted his Lamarckian position on species' direct adaptation to their environment.[51] While this mechanism of evolution is now discredited, the important point is that Kropotkin saw change as the fundamental aspect of phenomena. Looking from the earth to the heavens, he traced a similar process of disintegration in astronomy:

> There was a time when man imagined ... earth in the centre of the universe. Sun, moon, planets and stars seemed to roll around our globe; and this globe ... represented ... the centre of creation ... [But] take any work on astronomy of the last century. You will no longer find in it our tiny planet placed in the centre of the universe. But you meet at every step the ideal of a central luminary ... which ... governs our planetary world.

Such was the pace of scientific discovery, he added, that this heliocentric model was also becoming inadequate. As greater knowledge of the universe revealed more planets, astronomers discovered 'that interplanetary and interstellar spaces are peopled and crossed in all imaginable directions by little swarms of matter, invisible, infinitely small ... but all-powerful in their numbers'. This matter too is in constant agitation, dashing through 'space in giddy swiftness'. What this foray into astronomy revealed was that our conception of the universe rested on an increasing disintegration of power, from the earth to the sun as the defining centre, to the collapse of any notion of centre: 'It is everywhere and nowhere'. With perpetual motion the reigning principle of this materialist conception, order and stability appear as a temporary aspect of this dynamic. 'Harmony thus appears', Kropotkin reflected, 'as a temporary adjustment', and an enclave of stability that 'will only last under one condition: that of being continually modified.'[52]

In discussing these moments of stability amidst the chaos, Kropotkin invoked the work of Charles Fourier. The 'harmony that Fourier caught glimpse of' refers to a quotation that Kropotkin had used before, in a speech delivered in Paris just before he fled to Britain, in February 1886:

> 'Take pebbles,' said Fourrier [sic], 'Put them into a box and shake them, and they will arrange themselves in a mosaic that you could

> never get by entrusting to anyone the work of arranging them harmoniously'.[53]

Given that Fourier spent much of his time pondering just how to construct such a social mosaic his position might seem problematic, but for Kropotkin it reflected a truth confirmed by contemporary science, that instability ruled phenomena in the natural world, but when seen in a broader context, moments of cohesion appeared. Although Kropotkin drew on Fourier to make this point, his position hints at a similarity with a figure who would probably have been less palatable for his audience of Parisian socialists: Adam Smith.

Indeed Kropotkin actually mentioned Smith quite often. Echoing the reading of Smith as an unabashed defender of free-market economics that became particularly dominant in the nineteenth century, this was usually in the context of a denunciation of the laissez-faire ideal. Parallel to this reading, however, Kropotkin also confessed to admiring Smith's 'very brilliant and bold' moral theory.[54] It is the former characterisation that tends to dominate comparisons of Kropotkin and Smith, tempting as it is to paint past conflicts as the product of distinct ideological camps: capitalism versus communism; the individual versus the community; and egoism versus altruism.[55] Yet, Kropotkin's praise for Smith cautions against hasty compartmentalisation, and thinking about the common ground between these figures clarifies their differences. There is, for instance, a clear epistemological thread. Smith, in the vanguard of the Scottish Enlightenment, pursued a social theory underpinned by the rigours of a sound scientific method. Displaying an obvious debt to Montesquieu that Kropotkin shared, Smith even met Voltaire and the key physiocrats while touring Europe working as a tutor for the son of a nobleman.[56]

Most striking is the ontological parallel between Kropotkin's notion of order as the consequence of the actions of individual components of a system – be it the universe, the body, or individuals – and Smith's influential belief that the pursuit of individual self-interest promoted the common good. Such a comparison is not unknown, and usually stems from the right of the axis of anarchist political thought, which looks to the unfettered market as a key mechanism in any future non-hierarchical society.[57] Despite the common ground, however, there are important differences between Kropotkin's conception of spontaneous order and Smith's 'invisible hand' – a metaphor he first used in *The Theory of Moral Sentiments* (1759) before popularising it in *An Inquiry into the Nature and Causes of the Wealth of Nations* (1776).[58] The key distinction is that while Kropotkin saw this tendency to moments of stability as an inherently self-regulating system, Smith, despite his place at the apex of free-market ideology, introduced important qualifications. Thus, Smith proposed the necessity of state intervention to secure those needs that market forces might fail to realise: defence against external enemies; prevention of individuals impinging on the freedom of others; and provision of necessary 'public works'.[59] Kropotkin contrarily held a faith in public initiative to recognise and meet these problems. Nevertheless, Smith did trust in this 'invisible hand to make nearly the same distribution of the necessaries of life' as would have occurred if 'the earth been divided into equal portions amongst all its inhabitants', and he added that 'real happiness' did not lie in the material realm alone:

> In ease of body and peace of mind all the different ranks of life are nearly upon a level, and the beggar, who suns himself by the side of the highway, possess the security which Kings are fighting for.

For Smith this may have amounted to a 'beauty of order', but for Kropotkin this signified a far more egregious kind of stability.[60] Rather, this 'order is poverty', he charged; it is 'the Irish peasant dying of hunger... the peasant of Russia dying of diphtheria... Order is a woman selling herself to feed her children'.[61] If Thomas Carlyle had found political economy dismal, Kropotkin believed it much more odious.

To insist upon the differences between Smith and Kropotkin, although valid, misses a broader point. Like Marx righting Hegel, Kropotkin could be critical of a thinker while taking significant insights from their intellectual legacy. In the elucidation of his own system, Kropotkin was necessarily engaged in a conversation with the past, both slaying giants, but also standing on their shoulders in the hope of seeing distant horizons. Pursuing a theoretical synthesis that was rooted in a durable scientific methodology, Kropotkin exposed his debts to the tradition of social science: from its earliest days in the eighteenth century, through to contemporary popularisers like Comte and Spencer. Yet while many found this vogue positivism a pallid affair, rather than reducing life to the operation of basic laws, it uncovered a world of complexity and conflict. Smith saw complex individuals producing stability in the course of their independent action, and for Kropotkin this echoed a deeper truth, revealed by our expanding knowledge of the universe that uncovered the mutually shaping activity of matter. This was the foundation of his anarchism.

Towards an Aesthetic Philosophy: The reluctant system builder

If Kropotkin's intellectual debts made him an archetypal system builder, Read's did not. While Kropotkin's thought was galvanised by contact with the systematic sociology of thinkers like Comte and Spencer, Read's early inspirations were eidoloclasts, pricking the hubris of the systematisers. For Nietzsche, this pursuit of system was a noticeably English disease. 'Respectable but mediocre Englishmen – I may mention Darwin, John Stuart Mill, and Herbert Spencer' had their place as fact-grubbers, but, he acidly noted, 'let it not be forgotten that the English, with their profound mediocrity, brought about once before a general depression of European intelligence'.[62]

Read would concur that Spencer was an apostle of mediocrity, but he was deeply indebted to Kropotkin's anarchism and recognised an intellectual pliability at its heart that ensured its continued relevance. While modern theorists baulk at the implications of Kropotkin's scientific enthusiasms, for Read, similarly sceptical of nineteenth-century social science, naïve determinism was not one of his faults. Kropotkinian anarchism was a deep vein in Read's thought, and in a sense he was an unlikely inheritor of the quest for a composite philosophy that defined the project of his progenitor. Naturally though, this was, at least temperamentally, a very different intellectual task from the elucidation of a durable science of society. Although he did not renounce science, and was in fact an engaged devotee of psychoanalysis, Read was more aware than Kropotkin could have been about the oppressive potentials of the quest for totalising philosophy, and its habit of neutering radical politics. Antonio Gramsci may have complained that Marx was not 'some Messiah' and did not write 'some neat little doctrine', but this objection itself was a response to the 'sterilization of Marx's doctrines at the hands of Positivist Socialists'.[63] If Kropotkin was not convinced by the scientific veracity of the dialectical method, let it not be forgotten that Read was politicised in an era when this was codified in the USSR, with, in Stalin's words, 'socialism . . . converted from a dream . . . into a science'.[64]

For those unpersuaded by the omniscience of Marxism it was clearly an inauspicious time to be a searcher after system. Read was sensitive to this problem, and as a vocal opponent of Socialist Realism, and hostile to the increasing prominence of Marxism in British cultural criticism, he was more aware of these crudities than most. 'It is far from my intention to suggest the rigid system of a universal philosophy on the lines of Comte or Herbert Spencer', he wrote in *Freedom* in 1947, seeing their synthetic ambitions as an exercise in deadening aridity. Instead he offered a Kropotkinian axiom, which also owed something to his reading of Bergson: 'humanity is diverse; evolution is creative'.[65] There is though a desire for synthetism at the heart of Read's thought that commentators have tended to neglect.[66] Preceding his vision of dynamic evolution was an image of the necessary future of anarchism based on an increasing knowledge of various branches of enquiry: history, anthropology, sociology, psychology, and ethics. This was a resonant echo of Kropotkin's aspirations, and while Read usually dressed his holistic ambition in a different garb to the effort to understand anarchism in the light of physics and biology, the 'philosophy of life' that he chased across the page over six decades pointed to a parallel conclusion. Life and nature were dynamic and creative; art was a vital form of existential expression; and anarchism was the only political ideology to recognise these truths.

The fact remains, however, that Read's thought had an eclectic base. Untangling the diverse threads comprising his philosophy is complicated by the fact that Read was ready with praise, and had a tendency to invoke diverse authorities to support his arguments with few contextual scruples. As one contemporary noted, perhaps with a hint of cynicism, 'one cannot but admire his felicitous gift for hitting upon the right text'.[67] Detailing his intellectual growth in his autobiography, Read tells of an early interest in Nietzsche, admitted to 'traces' of William James, Benedetto Croce, Leone Vivante, and Max Scheler in his own philosophy, and confessed an 'emotional' attachment to Thomas Traherne, Søren Kierkegaard, and George Santayana.[68] He augmented this list with a number of political and social critics: Benjamin Disraeli, Carlyle, and John Ruskin were early inspirations, and William Morris, Kropotkin, and Edward Carpenter solidified his politics.[69] Of Morris, Read once noted that while his argument that a new culture could not emerge without a 'transformation of society' had been advanced 'in the year I was born', he stood before the modern reader 'as a disciple' repeating 'this warning'.[70] Similarly, of Ruskin, he once declared that his work 'is always by my side', and his ideas are 'almost as various as Shakespeare'.[71] The unlikely pairing of Georges Sorel and Mohandas Gandhi were also influential, as was the egoist Max Stirner.[72] To George Woodcock, he wrote that T.S. Eliot had 'meant more than anyone else to me in my literary life', and similarly he told Woodcock that he felt 'nearer' to George Orwell 'than any other English writer of our time'.[73] Freud was also a vital formative influence, shaping both his cultural and political writing, before growing familiarity with the work of Carl Jung led to a shift of allegiances.

While this magpie tendency seemingly undermines any claim for Read as a pursuer of philosophical synthesis, his technique of decontextualized quotation in fact underlays the search for a unified critique. In other words, while Read ranged widely, his cherry picking meant that he summoned particular thinkers to support certain points. He was then something of a 'bricoleur', adept 'at performing a large number of diverse tasks' and making use of 'whatever is at hand', remaining unencumbered by the formality of selecting the tools demanded by the immediate project.[74] As an apostle of modernism and friend of Eliot there is something wholly fitting about this patchwork approach, but this tendency to collage had another origin, lying in Read's unusual journey to his career as a public intellectual and his untutored meanderings in the history of philosophy. His occasionally ostentatious displays of erudition had a paradoxical effect: staking out his claim as a serious scholar in a world of letters dominated by the products of elite institutions, whilst simultaneously highlighting his haphazard exposure to the philosophical canon.

Of all the figures praised by Read, the most illustrative is Nietzsche, especially given Nietzsche's mordant hostility to the system-builders, and Read's defence of Kropotkin's philosophy. In recognition of this influence, Read's first collection of poetry, *Songs of Chaos*, borrowed its title and epigraph from *Thus Spake Zarathustra*. This aphorism – 'one must have chaos within one to give birth to a dancing star' – contemplated the necessity of turmoil for creativity, and Read later portrayed his exposure to Nietzsche's philosophy as a period of ferment:

> I cannot remember which volume I read first – I think it was the one I should have read last, his masterpiece, *Thus Spake Zarathustra*. But I read them all ... Two volumes ... produced the deepest effect ... – the one already mentioned ... and ... *Beyond Good and Evil*. These two volumes contain the essence of Nietzsche's philosophy and the reading of them produced a decisive crisis in my intellectual development.[75]

Nietzsche's words, he explained, enlivened his critical faculties. 'What I found', he continued, 'was the complete destruction of my ancestral gods, the deriding of all my cherished illusions, an iconoclasm verging on blasphemy.' Extending this idea, Read noted that the 'priggish morality' and 'Sunday-school piety' inculcated in his early life were 'consumed' in the 'mental conflagration' that followed his exposure to Nietzsche's 'prophetic fire'.[76]

Read's dramatization of his reading of Nietzsche could give the wrong impression about the nature of this influence. Rejoicing in the liberating glow, Read was adamant that this was a specific kind of attachment. 'My early enthusiasm for Nietzsche', he wrote in his memoirs, 'was purely intellectual: my life was unaffected – I never became a Nietzschean'. He followed this sober appraisal with similar treatments of Plato, Baruch Spinoza, Immanuel Kant, Gottfried Wilhelm Leibniz, Bergson, and Alfred North Whitehead, in which Read confessed to reading them with 'absorption and sympathy' but adding that they 'have never been part of my intimate experience'.[77] This was the voice of experience, but it is possible to trace Read's cooling enthusiasm for Nietzsche through the 'war diary' he inserted in the definitive version of his autobiography. In 1915, while garrisoned at Wareham in Dorset, he reflected that his present surroundings made 'Nietzsche and all the divine heretics seem like a dream', and concluded that 'I am beginning to suspect that Nietzsche's appeal... is largely poetical. Nevertheless... he is a fine stimulus'. Haughtily confessing that he was not 'satisfied with the tendency of modern Democracy', he suggested that he did not see any real solution in Nietzsche. On ground that prefigured his future anarchist understanding of freedom, however, he sketched his rejection of conventional democracy with a discernibly Nietzschean hue:

> Though it is a fine ideal in that it strives for the Utilitarian principle... it offers no encouragement to the development of the personality... It will ensure happiness, but scarcely nobility. It will be fatal to even a spiritual superman... Perhaps my dissatisfaction arises from the fact that, though in economics I am a communist, in ethics I think I am an individualist. Are these... creeds compatible?[78]

Read's rhetorical question must wait, but what this passage reveals is that Nietzsche's primary influence lay in providing a rich stock of phrases and images, rather than the contours of the 'philosophy of life' that he sought. When he wrote that the 'seeds of my philosophy of anarchism' could be seen in *Zarathustra's* rebuttal of the 'coldest of all cold monsters', the state, he added that 'at the same time I was reading Tolstoy, William Morris, Kropotkin and Edward Carpenter'.[79] Seductive as the fiery language was, quoting Nietzsche primarily served to enliven his political writing, and it was these other thinkers that truly succoured his attempt to articulate a distinctive aesthetic politics. For the young Read though, declaiming verses from *Zarathustra* into the shadows of the attic that was his refuge from the world, Nietzsche pointed to broader horizons than Leeds afforded.

Read's praise for Nietzsche, the arch-system destroyer, therefore, does not necessarily invalidate attempts to see him in the context of systematic social thought. Yet, Read himself was inconsistent when making claims for the constancy of his project. Engaging in an act of prolepsis in the introduction to one collection of essays, he wrote that he did not 'claim the virtue of consistency', and conceded that the 'logician' would 'have fine intellectual sport in exposing my contradictions'. Reaching back into literary history for an example to buttress this approach, he noted that the essayists he most admired – Francis Bacon, William Hazlitt, and Walter Bagehot – were similarly 'eclectic'.[80] Despite these protestations, Read repeatedly made the opposite claim. Writing to Francis Berry to congratulate him on his rather fawning pamphlet on Read for the British Council in 1953, he noted with pleasure that Berry had stressed the 'unity' of the various aspects of his work. 'It is the first time anyone has made this point – obvious to me', he wrote, 'and indeed I have often been charged with the inconsistency of my work in various fields'.[81] Similarly, the collection of his political essays *Anarchy and Order* (1954) began with a bold insistence on the centrality of his anarchism to his diverse projects:

> This volume assembles all the various essays that I have written specifically on the subject of Anarchism. There is no categorical separation, however, between what I have written on this subject and what I have written on social problems generally . . . or on the social aspects of art . . . or on the social aspects of education. The same philosophy reappears in my literary criticism and in my poetry.[82]

Closing his autobiography, Read also anticipated the observation that the narrative of his intellectual development gave the impression of an inchoate mind. He rejected this objection, stating:

> I am only interested in facts that feed an interest which is total, directed to the universe and to life as an existing whole; and it is my intuition of the nature of that wholeness, my desire to hold it within my mind as a coherent conception, which drives me on to the discovery of facts and their reconciliation in a philosophy of life.

Spying a parallel between the laws that govern nature and the rules of rhythm and proportion that informed aesthetic experiences, Read added that he discovered anarchism as the 'practical' aspect of this philosophy. The only problem, he lamented, was finding the 'time or leisure to elaborate them even into the outline of a philosophical system'.[83]

Read was perhaps overcautious, for he offered a richly suggestive reading of the anarchist tradition that teased out its aesthetic implications. At the heart of this philosophy was an argument that the artistic impulse – the 'will to form' – was essentially biological.[84] As has been noted, given the dominance of Marxism in contemporary radical cultural criticism, Read's insistence on the biological origins of artistic creativity was a political act.[85] But as much as this approach stressed the primacy of the individual in the face of stress on the material conditions informing artistic creation, Read aimed for a certain synthesis. In an early article on literature and psychoanalysis, he argued that 'what happens individually must also happen collectively', and hinted at his later full-blooded endorsement of Jungian archetypes.[86] Returning to this theme later in life, and admitting that his previous article was published 'with more enthusiasm than discretion', Read developed this position, insisting that psychoanalysis had shown the importance of art in fathoming the 'hidden' symbols of the unconscious.[87] It followed that art, inasmuch as it is the product of 'acuter points of consciousness', also speaks to the community at large, revealing 'the universal in the particular'.[88] For all his sniping at the crudities and 'hasty generalizations' of Marxist cultural commentators, Read was willing to travel some distance with them, admitting that the idea that 'prevailing methods of economic production' shaped art was a sound proposition.[89] However, he qualified, this was not a sufficient explanation, and failed to explain why certain works appeared to possess a timeless beauty. This perplexed Marx too, he noted, as he did not recognise that art was 'a basic human need' giving 'plastic... expression... to our inner intuitions and emotions', and was therefore a universal impulse.[90]

Read explored the subtleties implied in these broad contours across his oeuvre, and while he disavowed the ambitions of systematic philosophy he persistently strived to develop these principles into an encompassing critique. Usually, the specific remit of the book he was writing influenced which aspects of this constellation were at the forefront. A text like *Art and Industry* (1934), for instance, set out its object clearly. The aesthetic values paramount in the machine age are a hangover from 'handicraft methods of production', and while Ruskin and Morris may have favoured a 'return', the real necessity was to establish 'new aesthetic standards for new methods of production'.[91] This was a specific argument, and one that Read offered before his public conversion to anarchism, but it is apparent that the seeds of his looming conversion were germinating. He takes the primacy of art and the necessity of creating an aesthetically satisfying existence to be self-evident. Indeed, he objects that currently only the rich enjoy these luxuries, importing goods from 'countries where a solution of the problem has already been affected', while the ordinary Briton inhabits a world of shoddiness: 'clumsy cutlery, crude textiles, ugly furniture and uglier houses'. This 'solution' had been a temporary one though, as Walter Gropius' Bauhaus, which Read held up as a model of this aesthetic reimagining, closed in the face of Nazi pressure the year before his book appeared. Still, the ephemeral success of the Bauhaus augured well, and he suggested that the 'problem is primarily educational'. As Gropius had recognised, Read surmised we must accept that 'art is a biological function', and on this basis mount 'a complete revision of our educational system'. In turn, the freshly laurelled 'abstract artist... must be given a place in all industries in which he is not already established'.[92]

Art and Industry might have tackled the inadequacy of British spoons head on, but its overall message was far more radical. Aside from Read's confident assertion of the supremacy of modernist design, his book demanded that attention shift to the nature of the lived environment, and insisted on the necessity of unflinching change. As his anarchism became a stronger attachment in the late-1930s, these principles were invested with a more noticeably libertarian edge. *Education Through Art* (1943), composed during the Blitz and in many ways Read's magnum opus, echoed his earlier call but with a more decidedly anti-authoritarian metre:

> The most a democratic philosopher can hope to do is inspire a sufficient number... with his idealism... If at first a revolution can only be guaranteed by force, by means of education it can in ten years be founded on conviction, and in twenty... become unconscious tradition. It follows that a democratic method of education is the only guarantee of a democratic revolution: indeed, to introduce a democratic method of education is the only necessary revolution.[93]

Aesthetic education is at the centre of both texts, but what Read is actually demanding is a reorientation of everyday life with aesthetic values placed at its core. It always frustrated him, he wrote in his last years, that the anarchist import of *Education Through Art* had largely been missed; it was in fact 'humiliating', as it had proved to be 'by far the most influential book I have written'.[94] One contemporary who did not overlook this fact was Woodcock, who noted in a review of the book that to 'recognize the anarchist direction of *Education Through Art*' did not 'minimize its other importance in giving shape to Read's aesthetic philosophy'. Rather, it reinforced the idea that all these writings were 'manifestations of a unified activist philosophy'.[95]

The centrality of Read's anarchism to his world-view comes to the forefront when attention turns away from his major projects to consider those works that have only a seemingly tangential relationship to his political interests. Living off the fruits of his pen, Read was a frequent essay writer and reviewer, and this ephemera reveals that it was not only in his polemics that anarchism was central. The burdens of this lifestyle occasionally came to the surface, particularly in his fractious correspondence with Edward Dahlberg, as they hammered out the details of their joint publishing project *Truth Is More Sacred: A Critical Exchange on Modern Literature* (1961). Initially meeting Read in the early 1920s for lunch in a Chelsea pub with Eliot and F.S. Flint, Dahlberg renewed contact later in life, and grew impatient with Read's tardy responses to his letters. Irritated by this impetuosity, Read snapped. 'Is there any wonder I occasionally get a little rattled', he thumped into his typewriter, 'especially as I am always working under tremendous pressure, a fact you never seem to realize, and largely devoting myself to other people, with no thought of my own genius or my own fame.'[96]

Read's anger, and arrogance, is revealing. Dahlberg was a particularly prickly correspondent, but his outburst reveals the extent of Read's frustration at the time he devoted to writing on the visual arts, over poetry. No doubt one of these distractions was an eccentric reader that he published in 1939, entitled *The Knapsack: A Pocket-Book of Prose and Verse*. A small but thick book, complete with a flap covering the fore edge that could be fixed to a button on the front cover, *The Knapsack* emerged from Read's own experiences of serving in the First World War. Noting the impracticability of the soldier on active duty carrying a 'library' with them, Read's book sought to draw together a diverse range of material to assuage boredom, but also suit a variety of tastes and moods.[97] The authors collected ranged from Jonathan Swift to William Cobbett via Plutarch and Hegel, but two selections towards the end of the book are revealing. One is a moving final letter from Nicola Sacco to his son from Charlestown State Prison, Boston, shortly before his execution in 1927. Another is 'Credo', a short-piece by Italian anarchist Camillo Berneri, father of Read's friend Louise-Marie, who was married to Vernon Richards, both key figures in the resurgence of *Freedom* newspaper in the aftermath of the Spanish Revolution.

Kropotkin was absent from *The Knapsack*, perhaps deemed to offer little relaxation in the lulls between fighting, but references to anarchism in such obscure places affirm the depth of this commitment. Conscious of the isolation that being an anarchist in mid-century British letters afforded, Read was also keen to project his politics onto others. Articles on D.H. Lawrence and Edwin Muir found both shuffled into Read's political orbit. Repudiating accusations that Lawrence's rejection of democracy made him a fascist, Read instead implied that this betrayed the poverty of most commentators' political vocabularies. Instead, he proposed that Lawrence's 'deep loathing' of the state and attachment to the simple way of life of the Etruscans, showed that he was a 'kind of anarchist – not my kind, but somewhere between Tolstoy and Berdyaev'.[98] Similarly, Read's anarchism made its presence felt in other marginal writings. Occasional essays on Naum Gabo could contain references to the barbarism of the Russian 'Thermidorians' and a critique of the baseness of Socialist Realism, while a piece on Frank Lloyd Wright might include a plea for decentralisation.[99]

Lengthier commentaries also abound in his review work, and a striking example appeared in his dissection of Eliot's 1948 book, *Notes Towards the Definition of Culture*. Eliot was both a profound influence on Read's early career, and a close friend, but a peculiar dining companion at the Garrick Club given the contrast in their political attachments. Read admitted as much, observing:

> When he announced in the preface to *For Lancelot Andrews* (1928) that he was a classicist in literature, a royalist in politics and an anglo-catholic in religion, I could only retort that I was a romanticist in literature, an anarchist in politics and an agnostic in religion.[100]

Their friendship notwithstanding, Read's review of Eliot's foray into 'what would usually be called "sociology" ' was biting, and drew directly on his anarchism. Despite the diligent elaboration of the central argument, Read observed that a 'note of fervent apologetics' for Christianity pervaded Eliot's book, informing his assertion that culture develops in tandem with religion. Endorsing Eliot's view that culture was 'never wholly conscious' and is the 'unconscious background of all our planning', Read denied the purity of the connection with religion, asking 'how often has a corrupted church been responsible for the disruption of a culture'? More than this though, Read objected to the latent cultural aristocratism in Eliot's argument, and closed with a philosophically dense articulation of his politics. 'Levels of culture are inevitable;

specialization of culture is desirable; but I am not convinced these depend on an aristocratic organization of society', Read expanded:

> Eliot is contemptuous of the doctrine of egalitarianism . . . I do not think he has given due consideration to what might be called the *mystique* of the doctrine . . . I take my evidence from biology and history, and this evidence suggests . . . that the highest achievements of man, moral and material, are due to the impulse of mutual aid. There is . . . an individual one-way expression of this impulse . . . sympathy or charity. But the higher form of its expression is mutual, an 'I-Thou' dialogue, a sinking of differences an exercise of humility.[101]

Such expressions demonstrate the imprint of Kropotkin's thought on Read's conception of human history, but this passage also hints at his growing familiarity with the work of Austrian-born philosopher Martin Buber. Read had already played a significant role in publishing Buber's work in English, and he increasingly sought to synthesise his 'philosophy of mutuality' and Kropotkin's idea of community.[102] Aside from offering Read a creative and abstract terminology absent in Kropotkin's quest for precision, Buber also imparted a stronger perception of the mutually defining nature of the relationship between the multifaceted individual, and the community:

> Buber . . . points out that the originator, the creator, is by nature and necessity solitary, and that he must reach out to his fellow-creatures lost in the world, to be his friends or comrades beyond the arts. Only in this way does he have an awareness and a share of mutuality.[103]

Eliot apparently missed this subtlety in his theory of egalitarianism, and it is an awareness of culture as the organic emanation of a vibrant society, rather than the product of a religion or an elite, that supported Read's anarchism.

It is clear that Read's politics acted as a touchstone for his diverse intellectual activities, but central to Kropotkin's systemising mentality was a perception of the supremacy of scientific reasoning. Read's relationship to science was more equivocal, in part because he was more willing to invest his anarchism with a spiritual side. In this, Read is a potent example of the dualism at the core of British modernism, torn between the Poundian mandate to 'make it new', and the more soothing 'journey home' to a countryside that was forever England.[104] For those scarred by war, the choice was often not difficult, a poignant example being Arthur

Conan Doyle. Creator of a literary character who exemplified the power of rational thought, Doyle turned to spiritualism to commune with the son, brother, and brother-in-law he lost to the fighting.[105] Read bore the scars too, similarly losing his brother in the closing acts of the war. Modernist abstraction did not necessarily offer much comfort in this context, and Read, for all his trumpeting of this radical aesthetic, helped smooth its edges by stressing its under-acknowledged affinities with the past.[106] Accordingly, his anarchism placed a greater stress on spiritual unity, even looking favourably to the 'communion' of groups like the Hutterites, and rejecting the scientific pretentions of logical positivism and historical materialism. Both of these, he stated, 'find themselves in a state of arid logomachy, their 'poverty... explained by their denial of instinctive modes of thought, or super-rational intuitions'.[107]

Historical distance and changing intellectual fashions posed some limits to Read's reading of Kropotkin, therefore, but while he pointed to the power of the numinous, he did not renounce the claims of science. In fact, he explicitly recognised the contribution of Kropotkin in giving 'coherence to a doctrine' which 'lacked a formulation in the terms of modern scientific thought'.[108] Even in art, an arena where he might be expected to oppose the encroachment of science most vociferously – especially with contemporary Marxisms in mind – this was not the case. In both *Art and Society* and *Art Now* he pursued a 'science of art', and described 'scientific criticism' as the empyrean ideal 'of all criticism' in literature.[109] While Kropotkin was theorising at a time when the influence of Darwinism upon philosophy reached its apotheosis, a different science warmed Read's intellectual climate: psychoanalysis. Just as evolutionary theory provided a rich stock of terms for social thinkers to appropriate and misuse, psychoanalysis was a similarly procrustean discipline, and one that Read turned to with alacrity. In 1926, he had proclaimed its value to literary criticism in Eliot's *The Criterion*, and Jung was an important presence in his major writings on aesthetic philosophy, art education, and anarchism.[110] When Alex Comfort, poet, anarchist, and sexologist, weighed into the debate in 1950 with his book *Authority and Delinquency: A Study in the Psychology of Power*, he hoped to add the weight of scientific analysis to anarchism's rejection of conventional political action, hypothesising that 'delinquent and potentially delinquent persons' often occupied 'office' in 'democratic societies'.[111] Read, feeling that scientific opinion had backed up his distaste for the structures of modern democracy, was less cautious in conveying Comfort's thesis: 'Modern élites... tend to be recruited from various types of psychopaths'.[112]

Even by the turn of the twentieth century, systematic philosophy had become passé. Marking the death of Spencer in 1903, *The Times* implied that his contribution was that of a fading epoch, the 'last… of the brilliant group which must make the Victorian age memorable'.[113] The rapidity of this sunset was dramatic, and soon Spencer, a giant of the nineteenth-century intellectual cosmos, was eclipsed. While Kropotkin sought to attach his philosophy to the Spencerian tradition but also accentuate its divergences, Read was solely acting in the spirit of critical divergence. But for all his efforts to present his philosophy as an antidote to the barrenness of nineteenth-century social science, in following Kropotkin, he cleaved to the system-building mentality in surprising ways. Behind his baroque intellectual interests, lay a desire to reveal the truths of anarchism, and show the explanatory power of his aestheticized reading of the tradition. For Read, this cultural politics offered an avenue into understanding the totality of experience.

Kropotkin, Read, and system building

There is a famous scene in Charlie Chaplin's *Modern Times* (1936), where Chaplin's hapless production line worker, made manic by the frenetic pace of his work, is sucked into the gears of the machine on which he works. Others have appreciated the significance of this as a critique of the dehumanising nature of industrial labour, and Chaplin, like Read, had the dubious distinction of being a self-professed anarchist and a knight of the realm.[114] In a way though, this image of the defenceless individual trapped in the bowels of some great machine mirrors the flight from systematic philosophy that has informed contemporary challenges to Kropotkin's work. Chaplin is propelled through its inner-workings by an unstoppable force; he is pulled in different directions by a power that has no regard for his body; and at the end, he is spat out, dazed and confused, as the machine trundles on unawares. At its worst, opponents accuse, the kind of systematic philosophy preached by thinkers like Kropotkin echoes this cavalier disregard for the individual. Determinist, essentialist, and fatalist, these philosophies lose any sight of individual uniqueness, as it is consumed by this machine of cool logic.

Kropotkin rooted his social thought in a self-consciously scientific epistemology, but for all its potential to reduce the world to the whim of iron laws and immutable quiddities, his thought was subtler. He may have been engaged in a conversation with the key architects of sociology, but this was a frequently critical dialogue, and one that informed a particular ontology. Instead, his approach to positivism focused on its use in making knowledge coherent: recording, cataloguing, and tracing connections. The vision of the cosmos that this informed emphasised tension, agitation, and ephemerality, as he affirmed that modern science had uncovered the increasing elusiveness of any notion of centre. Wordsworth saved Mill, but Kropotkin would have disagreed with the poet. We do not kill to dissect; instead, the rational analysis of the universe uncovers a wondrous and beguiling complexity.

If nineteenth-century sociology was a buttress for Kropotkin, for Read it could be an impediment, even if he praised Kropotkin's bold synthetic efforts. Writing at a time when these systematic ambitions were unfashionable, and brought to mind a particularly uninspiring form of Marxism, a markedly different temperament infused Read's philosophy. It was more Nietzsche than Spencer. Yet, for all his seeming resistance to this tradition of systematic philosophy, Read's anarchism was a dominant presence in his multifarious projects, and formed the basis of an attempt to offer an expansive explanation of social phenomena in which art was primary. It may have been expressed in a new metre, but Read was following more closely in Kropotkin's footsteps than many have appreciated.

3
Statism: The Power of History

In 1897, Kropotkin travelled to Toronto to participate in the annual meeting of the British Association for the Advancement of Science at the invitation of his friend, the Scottish-Canadian economist James Mavor. After delivering two geographical papers, he then embarked on a tour of the east coast, lecturing on the theory of mutual aid, and the history of Russian literature. It was a productive trip. He was invited back to deliver a series of lectures at the Lowell Institute in Boston, thereby laying the foundations for his book *Russian Literature: Ideals and Realities* (1905), but also meeting the editor of *The Atlantic Monthly*, Walter Hines, who commissioned *Memoirs of a Revolutionist.*[1]

While British reporters reacted to Kropotkin's presence with equanimity, American newspapers had more difficulty adapting to his prominence as a revolutionary agitator. The *Boston Daily Advertiser* noted, perhaps with disappointment, that his trip had been uneventful. 'He has not once been arrested', it reported, 'and has not even been followed by government agents'. Aside from betraying the *Advertisers'* lack of faith in the clandestine abilities of American law enforcement, the journalist made a critical mistake in explaining Kropotkin's views. Providing an unexceptional summary of one of his speeches in New York the day before, it appeared under the title, 'Kropotkine Says State Socialism Is Thriving in the U.S.'[2]

As any assessment of anarchism will emphasise, hostility to the state is a defining characteristic of anarchist political thought. Indeed, given the breadth of ideas placed under this rubric, it is common to present antipathy to state power as the sole unitary feature of the various strands comprising anarchism.[3] Useful as the identification of this core belief can be, it can also have the unintended effect of reducing the depth of this critique of the state. During his stay in the United

States, Kropotkin also met the individualist anarchist Benjamin Tucker: a meeting of two men self-identifying as anarchists, but denying the anarchism of the other. That Tucker defined the goal of liberty as a consistent 'Manchesterism' hints that his formulation was at odds with Kropotkin's communism.[4] Despite Tucker offering a searching criticism of the state, for Kropotkin his defence of individual rights ended with him being 'driven into the liberal individualism of the classical economists', with the insidious 'return of the state idea' following in its train.[5] Tucker, defining anarchism as 'absolute liberty, nothing more' similarly argued that Kropotkin's vision of communistic ownership undermined this goal. Coercion remained, since while he proclaimed the importance of freedom, he denied this in 'production and exchange, the most important of all liberties'.[6]

Tucker and Kropotkin clearly drew different inferences from their criticism of the state, but what is important is that this criticism itself was not uniform. Anarchists reject the state, but do so in different ways, and built upon the foundations of this rejection are their utopian visions of a post-statist society.[7] Drawing stark comparisons between individualists and communists makes this clear, but looking at Kropotkin and Read, nominally acting within the same tradition, it is apparent that at times they too defined this rejection differently. Principally, these differences were a product of necessary contextual revision. The death knell of anarchism in Britain would have rung much clearer if ideas formulated in the period between William Gladstone and Herbert Asquith were reiterated, unedited, in the age of Stanley Baldwin and Winston Churchill. So too, Read's role as a political commentator was largely secondary to his interest in modern art, and while his politics ran through his aesthetics, this focus often added fresh gloss to conventional arguments. In turning to Kropotkin's ideas, these values acquired different resonances in a new context, and he teased out aesthetic implications from otherwise narrowly political statements.

To both thinkers, though in different ways, historical research was a particularly penetrating arrow in their analytical quivers. With the nineteenth century witnessing the formation of history on recognisably disciplinary lines, the utility of historical argument was not lost on Kropotkin. Not that the ambitions of this formalised discipline would have appealed to him. As the prefatory note to the first issue of the *English Historical Review* conceded – published the year he arrived in Britain – while it rejected the narrow concentration on 'past politics', 'states and politics will ... be the chief part of its subject'.[8] While mainstream history celebrated the ineluctable rise of the nation-state,

Kropotkin turned to history to challenge this narrative. Casting a glance across European history, a different story seemed obvious. Standing before the inquisitive was an 'absolutely unshakeable argument for anyone who has reflected on history', that the 'essence' of the state has been to 'shackle... local and individual initiative, to crush individual liberties, to prevent their new blossoming... [and]... subject the masses to the will of minorities'.[9] Read would have agreed with this assessment, but in the immediate, history held other attractions. Convinced of the ubiquity of the aesthetic impulse, he turned to history in order to prove also its timelessness. As much as this endeavour, emboldened by a contact with the neo-Kantian ideas of contemporary German art criticism, might seem a decidedly academic pastime, for Read it also possessed a political edge. History then was as much about the present as the past, as indeed it was for Kropotkin, and when Read moved to deduce the political implications of his researches into the history of aesthetic feeling, he reached for Kropotkinian concepts and principles. For both, the power of history lay in constructing a searching critique of the present, and the fetish of the state.

The Place of Anarchism in Socialistic Evolution: Kropotkin's history of ideas

The journalists writing about Kropotkin during his first tour of America struggled to find a suitable appellation for him. One opted for 'scientist and political economist' in an attempt to convey the variety of his interests, while another chose the looser 'sociologist'.[10] A similar struggle ensued across the Atlantic, where British journalists variously plumped for 'scientist of distinction', 'economist', the ambiguous 'traveller... and scientist', 'social economist', and occasionally 'geographer'.[11] Modern appreciations of his thought have tended to follow suit, while reflecting increased disciplinary specialisation by narrowing the exact area of his influence: from, for instance, geography to social geography. Given Kropotkin's synthetic ambitions, this diversity is not surprising, but what is peculiar is the lack of attention devoted to his historical ideas. Those that have commented on his historical writing usually present it as further evidence of his ranging intellect, but in reality, the development of a distinctive historical sociology was one of his fundamental ambitions.[12] Its importance is revealed by the fact that the distinct historical narrative he crafted across a number of works, sought to reflect the ontological principles expounded in his theoretical writing: conflict, transience, and change.

While declaring these principles of plasticity, a common criticism is that Kropotkin erred in developing a conception of the historical process that was, in its static fatalism, the very antithesis of this ethos. By drinking deeply at the fount of evolutionary theory, some commentators trace the inheritance of a narrative of steady progress that both undermines his revolutionism, and sits uneasily with the commitment to flux professed elsewhere.[13] When the otherwise sympathetic Martin Buber opined that Kropotkin was 'no historian', he had this translation in mind, seeing in his perception of history as a process of evolutionary development the obliteration of any appreciation of the real complexity of the past.[14]

From the dawn of his career, however, Kropotkin was clearly thinking historically. The early polemical articles that comprised *Words of a Rebel*, many of which subsequently appeared as pamphlets in Britain and would have introduced Kropotkin's ideas to English readers for the first time, displayed a keen historical sense. In *Law and Authority*, which appeared in several editions in 1886, Kropotkin explored the history of the French Revolution and argued that a 'bonfire of laws' must be the first incendiary act of future revolutions. Failing to light this pyre in 1789 was the revolutionaries' first error, he added, with the defence of law by 'Montesquieu, Rousseau, and Voltaire' against 'royal caprice' transformed into the dominion of 'lawyers' intent on quelling the popular tumult. His following argument, that law was initially 'a compendium of customs useful for the preservation of society' perverted by 'rich idlers' into formalised inequalities, also displayed a clear historical imagination. In this case, looking across the ages to 'primitive people' uncovered a moral dualism at the centre of life: a compulsion to common 'social feelings', and a competing 'desire to dominate'.[15] This idea would become the cornerstone of his moral theory, as he added flesh to these bones in a number of lengthier works.

Historical examples appealed to Kropotkin as a means of armouring his critique of present iniquities, but a sense of history also shaped his self-identification as an anarchist. Several of his key books thus begin by placing anarchism in a broader history of socialist thought, and this too exhibited a particular reading of European history. Revising his utopia *The Conquest of Bread* for reissue in 1907, he appended a preface that deemed the search for communism a perpetual human quest, before jumping to the French Revolution as an attempt to realise it concretely. Spending a paragraph discussing the Revolution, Kropotkin then skipped to the birth of modern socialism as an intellectual tradition, which he saw as a direct product of 1789, mentioning the importance of Charles Fourier, Henri de Saint-Simon, Robert Owen, and, with his own politics in mind, William Godwin. An important consequence of the French Revolution was that Kropotkin saw it inaugurating a rift in socialist thought. On one side was an 'authoritarian' creed growing from the tradition of 'secret societies' like those of '[Philippe] Buonarroti and [Gracchus] Babeuf', and a libertarian socialism represented by thinkers like Fourier and Owen on the other.[16] There is a clear polemical thrust to this reading, and Kropotkin had one eye on contemporary divisions between anarchists and Marxists when he elaborated on this division in *The Great French Revolution*. Here, he depicted *Enragés* like Jacques Roux and Jean Varlet as proponents of 'communalised' commerce and economic equality as a prerequisite for democracy, against the communism via 'conspiracy' preached by Babeuf.[17] Advancing the familiar anarchist argument that the 'means' of securing change must reflect the 'ends' desired, Kropotkin criticised Babeuf for being an 'opportunist', adding that 'his conceptions, as well as the means of action... belittled the idea [of communism]'.[18] Similarly, offering a wilfully anachronistic reading, he praised the discussion of distributive communism by the Convention in 1793. 'What a pity' that this failed to 'prevail among... nineteenth-century socialists', he mused, with 'the "collectivism" of [Constantin] Pecqueur and [François] Vidal, which was preached in 1848' winning out, 'now being dished up again under the name "scientific socialism" '.[19]

The stage was set in Kropotkin's narrative for modern socialism to emerge from the wings, but at this point he saw a period of reaction emerging in the aftermath of the Napoleonic Wars. Yet, the triumph of autocracy was itself only transient, and in the July Revolution of 1830, and the simultaneous emergence of a 'reform movement' in Britain, he sensed an air fit for the revival of socialism. The ascension of Louis Philippe in place of Charles X may seem a peculiar hinge on which to hang the renewal of socialist sentiment, but what Kropotkin really had in mind was the inherent political instability it represented. Indeed, a number of historically significant radicals appeared in this period. Communist thinkers like the ascetic Étienne Cabet, whom Kropotkin disliked, and Louis Auguste Blanqui were active in the Revolution.[20] Socialist ideas grew healthily in this invigorated climate, with figures like Victor Considerant, Ferdinand Lassalle, Vidal, Pecqueur, Lorenz von Stein, and Pierre-Joseph Proudhon all struggling to define a distinctive politics in the ferment and its aftermath. Reaction was again on the horizon though, and whilst socialist principles effervesced in the lead up to the revolutions of 1848, the result of this conflagration was simply 'the middle-class republic' and 'broken hopes'.[21]

It is characteristic of Kropotkin's undulating narrative, however, that while ennui set in as the barricades were cleared from the streets of Europe, he also saw these revolutions as a fillip to further dissent. In a grand sweep he combined 'Garibaldi's rising', the abolition of slavery in the United States, 'liberal reforms in England', the ending of 'serfdom and the knout' in Russia, the overthrow of the 'philosophical authority of Schelling and Hegel', and the rise of Russian Nihilism as the inheritors of this spirit of revolt.[22] Elsewhere, Kropotkin appeared to advance quite the opposite case, seeing in the post-1848 world the furious persecution of radicalism to the point that for the 'next twelve or fifteen years the very traces of socialism disappeared'.[23] His position was that whilst socialism floundered, scientific and liberal innovators of the age drew 'their scientific courage' from earlier socialist ideas, observing that Darwin, Jeremy Bentham, and David Ricardo were early followers of Robert Owen. There was indeed a significant relationship between Bentham, Ricardo, and Owen, but Kropotkin's appreciation is rather misleading. Bentham was an early backer of the New Lanark venture, but Ricardo, despite his friendship with Owen, was a noted critic.[24] Wincing at the suggestion made in a parliamentary debate in 1819 that there was 'plenty of commonable land' in the 'neighbourhood of Mr. Ricardo' fit for an Owenite scheme, Ricardo responded that he was 'completely at war with the system of Mr. Owen'.[25]

Kropotkin's logic is therefore rather slippery. He presents anarchism as something that historically ebbs and flows in wider tides of social progress and reaction, but even at low water exercises a formidable hidden influence. Viewing socialism as an essentially organic product of communities engaged in struggle is one avenue out of this problem, but at the same time, he also attached anarchism to a familiar narrative that saw socialism emerging in the afterglow of the French Revolution.[26] An obvious casualty is historical acuity, witnessed in problematic formulations such as 'we may say... that Jacobins and Anarchists have existed at all times among reformers and Revolutionists'.[27] That Darwin owed much to Owen, or the notion that the abolition of slavery in the United States was a product of 1848, is also highly dubious. The root of these problems is primarily methodological, as Kropotkin sought to realise the scientific approach he venerated. Darwin's brilliance, he once observed, stemmed from an ability to 'embrace an immensely wide range of phenomena in one single generalization'.[28] The price of this was accuracy and analytical verve, but these problems were eased when Kropotkin shifted from adumbrating this historical sociology, to more focused examinations, exemplified in his work on the French Revolution.

Despite these issues, history held an important place in Kropotkin's corpus for two key reasons. First, his own political position rested on an intellectual narrative that traced the emergence of socialism in Europe, based on two broadly conceived strands: libertarian and authoritarian. Second, aside from history adding intellectual authority to his politics, Kropotkin believed that knowledge of history could be of practical benefit to future revolutionaries. Stating, at the close of *The Great French Revolution*, that any new revolution will be 'heir to all our forefathers have done in France' was not prophesy, but a Jeffersonian warning for vigilance.[29] These two themes intersect at the point reached in the discussion of Kropotkin's intellectual history of socialism. For, although 'grapeshot' silenced socialism in 1848, like water eroding the rocks, socialist ideas were bound to sprout forth again.[30] Crucially, however, Kropotkin confidently believed that this new variety of socialism would learn the lessons of both the Jacobins' silencing of Varlet, and the fetish for parliamentarianism that allowed the bourgeoisie to gain the initiative in 1848.

Stressing the interplay of scientific knowledge and social thinking, Kropotkin saw the years between 1856 and 1862 as an era of awakening. William Grove, Rudolf Clausius, Hermann von Helmholtz, James Joule, and Darwin all pushed the boundaries of science, but 1864 also saw the foundation of the International Workingmen's Association in London.[31] Conscious of the status of the International in both anarchist and Marxist mythology, Kropotkin was cautious, noting that the organisation 'oscillated between several different solutions': the proto-Jacobinism of Wilhelm Weitling; Owenite cooperativism; the collectivism of Pecqueur and Vidal; a competing Saint-Simonian tradition; and Louis Blanc and the 'strong body of Lassalleans' that he inspired.[32] For all the promise that this tumult signified, Kropotkin's serpentine vision of the historical process meant that the progressive gains of the International remained vulnerable, and the Franco-Prussian War (1870–1871) spawned another period of statist ascendancy.[33] Yet in the midst of French capitulation, a beacon flared, not only warming socialist hearts in this time of reaction, but for Kropotkin lighting the path for the concrete realisation of socialism. 'A new idea was born' in the Paris Commune, he wrote, and the form 'most propitious for that great economic revolution' that would see the 'communalizing of all the capital accumulated by preceding generations' was discovered.[34] With his histories mourning the failures of 1789 and 1848, and pressing the message that experiments at introducing socialism through the state were doomed to failure, ideas embryonic in the dreams of Fourierists suddenly seemed achievable. In Kropotkin's intellectual history, it was at this point that anarchist-communism emerged as a fully fledged political creed.

Behind the turn to history in the nineteenth century was always a search for purpose, meaning, and the confirmation of 'identities'.[35] As Thomas Babington Macaulay sat down to start work on what would be his five-volume opus *The History of England from the Accession of James the Second* (1848), it was not just the past that exercised his mind. Defining his purpose, Macaulay wrote that his history would examine how, 'from a state of ignominious vassalage' England rose to achieve the 'authority of law and the security of property', combined with a 'liberty of discussion and... individual action never before known'.[36] For a Whig committed to constitutional reform, notably the 1832 Reform Act, his *History* stressed the value of reconciliation, moderateness, and the foundational nature of the settlement reached in 1688.[37] How lucky we all were, Macaulay would have thought, to be born in an England that was the 'umpire' among nations, rather than that dominated by James II, his heart hardened by 'religious bigotry' and possessed of a 'narrow and stubborn mind'.[38] Just as Macaulay's history was a grand exercise in defining British exceptionalism, and rooting current political action in an understanding of the past, Kropotkin's history hoped to define a uniquely anarchist intellectual position, and ransack the past for clues on avoiding the pitfalls that befell history's dissenting voices.

The obvious issue with this backward gaze, however, is the tendency for an unnervingly coherent story to emerge from the chaos of past events. Marx, architect of his own great plan of history, was not the only one troubled by that persistent 'falsifier' Macaulay.[39] Charting the growth of socialism over swathes of European history, Kropotkin's intellectual history is open to the attendant criticism that it presents simplicity where complexity reigned. His essentially Manichean view of the historical process, with the forces of centralism persistently vying with an anti-authoritarian spirit, casts little light on the movements that he wishes to discuss. There is also an essentially ahistorical thrust to this reading, for while Zeno of Elea, the Anabaptists, and Fourier may well have resisted authority, the historical constitution of these forces of authority was obviously radically different.[40] To see the struggles of Anabaptists against the council of Zürich in the sixteenth century, and the efforts of Fourierists to establish an intentional community in New Jersey in the nineteenth century, as expressions of a shared ethos, is patently problematic. For those seeking enlightenment on history's actors, Kropotkin's pages offered little, but then they ultimately had a different object: to embolden, encourage, and enflame.

Kropotkin's intellectual history of socialism may not be wholly satisfactory, but the broader perception of European history it implied is highly significant. For Macaulay, British constitutionalism was the apotheosis of the historical process, achieving a finely tuned balance between individual liberty and the requirements of political order that other nations ought to emulate. His reading of history, to quote that influential anatomist of the Whig mentality Herbert Butterfield, offered 'a story which is the ratification if not the glorification of the present' emphasising 'certain principles of progress in the past'.[41] Kropotkin obviously did not venerate the state, but it is common to view his history in parallel terms, espying the triumph of anarchy in place of Macaulay's constitutional settlement.[42] Yet, the narrative he presented clearly did not offer a story of steady progress. Seeing in history the continual oscillation between authority and liberty, produced a narrative akin to the ontology outlined in *Anarchism: Its Philosophy and Ideal*. The gains and advances of socialism were constantly vulnerable and often swept away in a tide of reaction following the failure of historical actors to seize the opportunity for expansive change, only to eventually sprout again in the rubble. This antagonism was the logic of history, and an unresolvable tension.

The State: Its Historic Role – Revolutionaries and their historic role

Present concerns dominated Kropotkin's explorations of the intellectual history of socialism. As much as he sought to illuminate the past, he looked to history to help articulate a distinctively anarchist position growing from the panoply of radical ideas that had motivated history's rebels. Fundamental to this project was reading contemporary conflicts with Marxists back into this complex history, seeing Jacobins 'at all times' in an obvious broadside at the 'abominable tactics' of those pursuing socialism through the state.[43] His intervention may have been an important act of self-definition, but Kropotkin's understanding of history was not isolated to the realm of ideas. Indeed, the most significant feature of his historical writing was its exploration of the concrete systems of social organisation that had flowered throughout history. The latter sections of *Mutual Aid* offer an analysis of the varying social forms that have defined human life: the tribe, the village community, and the medieval city-state. In pointing to these social institutions, Kropotkin was challenging the idea that the birth of the modern state was axiomatically progressive, and presenting instead the multiple social forms that had made the struggle-for-life winnable. Just as his dalliances with the history of ideas offered a narrative of European history that was fluid, his history of these entities, while highlighting their great achievements, also emphasised the areas in which they fell short of securing expansive freedom. Importantly, he also insisted that while the growth of solidarity was an essentially organic reaction to pressing needs, the birth of authoritarianism was a similarly organic product. This was a foreboding lesson of history, of which anarchists had to be aware.

The tribe and the village community feature prominently in *Mutual Aid* and *The State: Its Historic Role*, but the most revealing passages are devoted to the medieval commune. Principally this was a consequence of Kropotkin's emphasis on communalism as the basis of a future anarchist society, albeit shorn of the deficiencies that had undermined previous experiments. While straining to avoid romanticising life in the medieval city-state – a common thread in the writings of contemporary left-leaning thinkers like Morris and Ruskin – Kropotkin did suggest that the liberties secured by the communal movement were profound, and were responsible for some of humanity's greatest intellectual achievements.

In his reading, the medieval commune emerged at the point that the early state form appeared on the cusp of total victory. Within the 'barbarian' village community that preceded it, certain groups had started to solidify around vested interests, and these began to unite with baleful consequences.[44] Kropotkin saw this rudimentary state that emerged after the demise of the village community as a tripartite entity, the product of an unholy alliance of lawmakers, warriors, and religious leaders. Rome reoccurred in his writings as the exemplar of authoritarian political control, with every 'province' having 'its capital in miniature, its small portion of Roman sovereignty'.[45] Indeed, 'Roman law' would be one of the factors that later corrupted the medieval commune in his analysis, a catchall term that Kropotkin used for codified laws in general, which he thought weighted in favour of property holders.[46] This stood in distinction, he added, to the inherently flexible decision-making of the village community, where resolutions were enforceable solely through the 'moral authority' of the folkmote; a system lost once law became an 'art' of specialised knowledge jealously guarded by certain families. Soon fused to this juridical arm were those pursuing 'the specialization of the warrior's trade', taking advantage of 'populations anxious to be left in peace'.[47] Whilst these 'brotherhoods' wandered the countryside offering their services to those intent on cultivating the soil they were relatively benign, but once fortification of villages became standard, the peripatetic warriors were employed full-time.[48] Those plagued by 'murrains, pests, fires, or raids' flocked to these fortified villages, and, hypnotised by the promise of stability, unwittingly delivered themselves into servitude.[49] Alongside the legal and military castes, a third element grafted its authority to this conspiracy, in the guise of offering spiritual salvation. What began as witchcraft and shamanism at an earlier period was formalised as religion, and the 'learned man' and 'sorcerer' assisted in duping the dispossessed and desperate.[50]

Gloomy as this portrait is of the considerable qualities of the village community usurped by an egotistical cabal, Kropotkin perceived a glimmer of light on the horizon. With statism poised for domination as the 'last vestiges of barbarian freedom seemed to disappear', with 'a unanimity which seems almost incomprehensible... the urban agglomerations... began to shake off the yoke of their worldly and clerical lords'.[51] The 'fortified village rose against the lord's castle' in a grand repudiation of autocracy, Kropotkin informs us, and medieval communalism was born, defined by a 'virile affirmation of the individual'. In turn, the communes actualised various social measures that prepared the ground for an energetic cultural expression. Their first act was the composition of 'charters' which, while varying considerably and some bearing the seal of royal authority, sought to secure the commune's independence.[52] In their internal organisation too, Kropotkin saw a federal diffusion of power that foreshadowed a potential anarchist society, with 'all households united into small territorial unions' and 'individuals united by oath into guilds according to their professions'.[53] Enshrining and protecting this independence, each of the streets comprising this union had its own tribunal, priest, and militia, and the guild system that structured labour was formative to the 'intellectual movement... described as the 12th century Renaissance'.[54] Stressing the 'oath' that united these guilds, they offered Kropotkin a competing, flexible, institution to the unities that had previously sullied the freedom of the village community. Multifarious, ephemeral, and only cohering to complete a particular project such as the building of a cathedral, they stood in contrast to the leagues of lawyers, warriors, and priests striving to establish and ratify their power.[55] Moreover, he continued, they exercised an important regulatory role, agreeing prices by 'mutual agreement' in order to ensure that key goods were universally available. 'Never... has mankind known a period of relative well-being for all as in the cities of the Middle Ages', Kropotkin concluded boldly, 'the poverty, insecurity and physical exploitation of labour that exists in our own time were then unknown'.[56]

In his panegyric on the medieval commune, it is clear that Kropotkin partially bought into the contemporary veneration of the Middle Ages that was an entrenched trope in nineteenth-century socialism. Morris and Hyndman both mined this vein, and Kropotkin drew on the work of Oxford historian and economist Thorold Rogers, who saw in the guilds' efforts to overcome 'pauperism' a precursor of trade unionism.[57] Implicit in this was a comparative rather than analytical urge, and a desire to highlight the inadequacies of the present rather than appreciate the nuances of the past.[58] As Bertrand Russell once warned, 'if we wish to see a period truly, we must not see it contrasted with our own'.[59] Kropotkin was therefore prone to simplifying a complex history. In presenting communalism as a grand challenge to princely authority, he was insensitive to geographical location and cultural difference. In Italy, 'communard' may have carried with it the status of 'urban rebel', but the movement in England 'never got off the ground', facts that jar with his suggestion that communalism spread rampantly.[60]

Kropotkin's analysis poses other problems too. While he presented the commune as a protest against petty despotism, he overlooked the extent to which it was a desire for economic liberty that lay at its foundation. Although not ignorant of their mercantile basis, he chose instead to stress the idea that medieval communalism enshrined a particular, positive, kind of freedom. On a practical level, the claim that the commune essentially abolished poverty within its walls is dubious. Additionally, while he expended much ink on both the cultural achievements of communalism and the nefariousness of organised religion, Kropotkin neglected the extent to which the cultural expression he praised, drew its *raison d'être*, symbols, and patronage from the Church. So too, when descending to the decision-making units that he believed gave the commune its vibrancy, he tended to offer a questionably rosy picture. New ways of arbitrating disputes were created, he wrote, that 'without imposing' the unrealistic 'obligation of never quarrelling' did mean agreeing that no 'quarrel should degenerate into a feud'.[61] He did not deny conflict, but suggested that it was minimal, and argued that customs developed to ease its consequences, an echo of his idea that codified laws were unnecessary. The sceptic might respond, however, that even fair Verona had its Montagues and Capulets, and point out that the 'vendetta' was a prominent feature of communal life.[62]

For all its simplicity, the real purpose of Kropotkin's histories was to emphasise that anarchists must learn from previous struggles. This is apparent when he shifted to the decline of the communal movement, as despite its promise it too was destined to decay. In pondering its multiple failings, he was not only hoping to show that his reading of medieval communalism was more searching than contemporary hagiography, but also pointed to the sorts of problems that might confront future revolutionaries. Recognisable by the walls that enclosed and protected their freedoms, Kropotkin's first objection was that these ramparts themselves were a fundamental weakness. With liberty confined to the districts and guilds sheltered by these walls, those outside were left isolated as the cities' denizens regarded them 'haughtily from its battlements'.[63] Behind this argument was a warning that the antagonisms between town and country could jeopardise the pursuit of freedom. Marx might have observed that the rise of the bourgeoisie 'rescued a considerable part of the population from the idiocy of rural life', but Kropotkin, as a son of the soil, preached the necessity of conciliation.[64] The mercantile basis of communal wealth led to a neglect of agriculture, leaving the commune in a precarious position. Casting an eye at their prehistory, Kropotkin suggested that this 'estrangement' of the urban and rural populations stemmed from the bitter battles waged by the communes to carve out their freedom in the face of royal encroachments. Distracted, they left the peasantry to fend for themselves, with the 'French Jacqueries, the Hussite wars, and the Peasant War in Germany' that punctuated this period betraying the degree of division. Beyond the neglect of agriculture, the commercial fetish also led to colonial misadventure, as independent city-states pursued territory and revenue.[65] Soon, standing armies and mercenaries replaced the volunteer militias that had united temporarily under the banner of their district.[66]

Conflict was an inherent feature of this period, and the existence of 'oases amidst the feudal forest' presupposed the marooning of vast swathes of the population.[67] Shunned by the cities, Kropotkin argued that the peasants turned to the feudal lords, creating 'royal fortified cities' that were quickly populated with familiar protagonists: lawyers versed 'in Roman law', and the Christian church, 'once a rebel against Roman law and now its ally'.[68] Aside from this formidable league, graver problems confronted the commune. Shifting from the material to the intellectual, Kropotkin insisted that a 'deep modification of leading ideas' exploded the base of the communalist movement.[69] During the halcyon days of the eleventh century, federalism, 'self-reliance', and the organisation of bodies from the 'simple to the composite' had held sway, but 'students of Roman law and the prelates of the Church' had vitiated these principles. 'For two or three hundred years', Kropotkin thundered, 'they taught from the pulpit, the University chair, and the judges' bench' that 'salvation must be sought for in a strongly-centralized State, placed under semi-divine authority'.[70] The mutual aid institutions that had germinated in these cities buckled under this pressure. Due to the fact the guilds worked so successfully they were 'spoliated of their possessions and liberties', and what had been an 'organic whole' was divided and appropriated by the state.[71] Statism had vanquished communalism.

Kropotkin's rejection of the state was a squarely historical endeavour, resting on a definite narrative of European history, and looking to history as a vital rhetorical device in challenging the ambitions of those pursuing redemption under the aegis of state action. The idiosyncratic vision of history that Kropotkin offered also bore the imprint of his overarching ontology. As his discussion of medieval communalism revealed, Kropotkin saw history as a fluid process, in which hard-fought victories were always on the brink of being lost. The 'organic' commune spontaneously flowered to meet various social needs, but equally, his presentation of the state as a parasitic incubus suggested that this too was an organic growth. His histories therefore sound a clarion call for action and alertness: the achievements of today are always vulnerable when confronted by negligence tomorrow. Historical rumination also offered Kropotkin the opportunity to reflect on the kind of society he desired. Discussing the village community and the commune, he juxtaposed an image of the state with local self-sufficiency. The state embodied control, centralisation, exploitation, and the ideological manipulation of the people by a small group, while the city-state pursued the diffusion of power in a melange of temporary guilds, local decision-making units, and autonomous institutions. The real triumph of this organisation though was its power in spurring creativity, and universalising enthusiasm in the cultural and scientific feats of the Renaissance. Crucially, Kropotkin did not see this virtuous engagement as something isolated to the paved streets of the commune. Unintentionally paraphrasing Rousseau, who had seen a bucolic democracy in 'troops of peasants regulating the affairs of the state under an oak tree', Kropotkin saw in the French peasantry of the eighteenth century a tradition of meeting 'under the elm tree' to apportion land and negotiate tax demands.[72] The species of tree had changed, just as the rocky roads of the village gave way to the cobblestones of the commune, but the lesson was obvious. A return to the forms of the past was impossible, but knowledge of their history was imperative.

Icon & Idea: Read's approach to history

In seeing a constant battle between authority and liberty as the threads forming the fabric of history, Kropotkin frequently risked ahistoricism. At first glance, Read seems to replicate this weakness. After all, his idea of the perennial artistic impulse, does not necessarily lend itself to nuanced historical analysis. 'There is no phase of art', he declared in 1951, 'from... Palaeolithic cave-paintings to the latest developments of constructivism' that is not an illustration of 'the biological and teleological significance of... aesthetic activity'.[73] While the breadth of the brush he used to paint this picture of the past may pose problems in appreciating cultural specificity, at the same time, his perception of art as an instinctual practice of supreme existential importance clearly invited historical justification. Read thus turned to the history of art with the ambition of providing his intellectual edifice with this base, but at the same time he was, of course, fully conscious of the inherent mutability of art throughout history.

Approaching the history of art, Read was willing to travel some distance with the Marxist art historians with whom he enjoyed an occasionally fractious relationship. It would be remiss, however, to overstate this animus.[74] He wrote a warm introduction to Francis Klingender's 'classic of art criticism' *Goya in the Democratic Tradition* (1968), and played an important role in publishing Arnold Hauser's epic *The Social History of Art* in 1951, initially in two volumes – a work whose very title betrays Hauser's Marxist credentials.[75] Similarly, when John Berger wrote to Read to apologise for mauling his *The Grass Roots of Art* in *The Tribune*, he lamented the fact that they were often 'forced into the position of opponents'.[76] This rift was evidently healed, as both men continued to exchange friendly letters and offer supportive criticism. In his last surviving epistle to Read at the very end of 1961, Berger observed that 'I think I have reminded you before that the first letter that you wrote to me – in which you were equally generous with your thoughts – was when I was fifteen.' While Berger accused him of misrepresenting 'the Marxist point of view' in his piece in *The Tribune*, Read made clear in an early intervention on art history, that he was content to accept many essentially Marxist propositions.[77] If the 'characteristics of a period' are 'determined in the main by material forces – racial, climactic, economic and social', he noted, it is a truism that they shape its art: 'a country in which wood is plentiful will develop a wooden architecture'. But, he qualified, this alone was not enough, adding that 'material causes can never wholly explain the rise and development of a period in art: material is always the vehicle of a spiritual expression'.[78] Finding Marxism a bloodless guide to the history art, Read developed a complex historical narrative of his own, accepting the utility of materialist explanations, but aiming to probe further. This was a project very different from Kropotkin's investigation into the origins of the state, but at the same time anarchism provided Read with an interpretative framework for when he stepped back to examine the political implications of this narrative. Just as it is necessary to see Kropotkin as a thinker defined by an approach to history, it is also fruitful to consider Read in these terms.

In the final decades of his life, Read began to argue that art was not simply an important source of human expression perverted by capitalist social relations, but was, in a sense, the basis of life itself. Delivering a series of lectures at Harvard in 1953, he expanded ideas presented in the Conway Memorial Lecture two years earlier, published as *Art and the Evolution of Man* (1951). The resulting work, *Icon & Idea*, pushed the aesthetic faculty to the centre of human evolution.[79] Summarising his book in a letter to Stephen Spender, Read wrote that 'society owes everything to the artist... the philosophy and science of any age is but a commentary on its art'.[80] Early references to R.G. Collingwood and Coleridge betray the idealistic origins of this difficult work, in which Read's main contention is that 'far... from a playful activity... art, at the dawn of human culture, was a key to survival – a sharpening of faculties essential to the struggle for existence'.[81] The ability to retain the 'perceptual image', and simply 'imagination', were basic weapons in the fight for life, and led to the development of 'an intelligence specifically human'. Due to their importance, certain images imposed themselves, for instance those related to 'food-getting and sex', and 'throughout millennia' left 'physical imprints' on the brain. These, he concluded, were Jungian archetypes: 'a term in psychology indicat[ing] an inherited structure of the brain predisposing the human race... to the invention of particular kinds of symbol'.[82]

Hitherto Read had used the claim that art was 'in its inmost nature... biological' to imply a certain organicism – that it was the natural impulse of a rounded human being.[83] *Icon & Idea* advanced a stronger interpretation of this thesis, intimating that art is the source of human life itself: the consciousness that begets life as we understand it. 'Art has been, and still is the essential instrument in the development of human consciousness', he argued, before turning to more complex forms of knowledge on the basis that 'the image always precedes the idea'.[84] To illustrate this theory he invoked the ancient Greeks, arguing that their intellectual achievements were a product of their fecund artistic activity. 'What has not been first created by the artist, is unthinkable by the philosopher', he wrote, concluding that:

> The irreducible element in Greek culture is the aesthetic element. It is at the root of Greek mathematics and Greek geometry, and Greek philosophy in general begins as a meditation on universal qualities like geometry and harmony.

Read's intricate historical narrative describes the triumph of classical sculpture in its 'synthesis' of two 'sensuous' concepts: 'vital form' and 'formal beauty'.[85] Looking further back in time, he identified the 'vitalistic' as characteristic of Palaeolithic cave painting, where images were translated into plastic form in a 'desire to "realize" the object on which magical powers were to be exercised', a vision he described elsewhere as 'eidetic'.[86] In Read's schema, the transition from the Palaeolithic to Neolithic periods that preceded Greek culture witnessed the emergence of new aesthetic principles. Noting that the student of art tends to see in the Neolithic era a corruption of aesthetic standards, as the 'deadly monotony of abstraction' superseded the 'accurate depiction of animals', he countered that this period actually marked a 'development of aesthetic sensibility'. Sidestepping the issue of social origins, he presented the budding of new modes of social organisation and new cultural principles as intertwined processes; a position he clarified when returning to the abandonment of the 'vital image'. Just as the *sturm und drang* of the Palaeolithic age was caused by the 'hunting stress' occasioned by precarious food sources, in turn explaining the 'eidetic accuracy' of their art, a similar 'cosmic anxiety, a fear of existence or being' lay behind Neolithic abstraction.[87] 'Fear breeds secrecy', Read argued, and in consequence a 'whole magic lore of geometric signs' emerged, along with a new 'consciousness... *of form itself*'.[88] These 'new elements' reflected a 'new way of life', where agriculture had replaced nomadism, and in which 'inventive and comparative' conceptual skills were now the key to survival.[89]

Before tracing Read's argument through to Greek and Gothic art, periods he deemed especially important, it is worth pausing to compare his historical approach to that of Kropotkin. There appears to be little commonality. Kropotkin's desire to demonstrate that early humans sought social solutions to their problems, rather than descending into a Hobbesian bloodbath, is not Read's primary object. Nevertheless, an ancillary argument for Kropotkin was that it was necessary to take early human history seriously, and despite persistent stereotypes, the period was characterised by relatively complex social arrangements. It is no distortion to see *Icon & Idea* echoing this thesis, for the pages devoted to Palaeolithic and Neolithic art abound in admiration for the neglected sophistication of these cultures. Although never losing the poet's tendency to effusion, it is telling, for instance, that Read titled the chapter on Neolithic art 'the discovery of beauty'. He was also following a familiar modernist trope in turning to historic cultures for inspiration. Confronting the contemporary may have animated modernist art, and modernism itself might have germinated as a critical comment on the forces unleashed by modernity, but the appeal of 'primitivism' lay in its supposed unencumbered purity: a tantalising prospect for post-Freudians.[90] A short essay Read contributed to the BBC's magazine *The Listener*, bristled at the lack of an alternative to that 'ambiguous word "primitive"'. 'Such work', he insisted, 'is only primitive in the historical sense; from an aesthetic point of view it often... surpasses the art of later and more civilized communities'.[91] No doubt Read should also have pondered, just as Kropotkin did in *Mutual Aid*, the appropriateness of the word 'civilized', but he fully accepted the importance of renewed contact with the distant past to the radicalism of modernism. Provocatively dating the birth of modern art to the *Exposition Universelle* held in Paris in 1889, he wrote that the interest shown by both Paul Gauguin and Vincent Van Gogh in 'primitive art' was a reaction to the 'hideous reality' of industrial society. Inducing a feeling of 'anguish or uneasiness' akin to the driving force behind Palaeolithic vitalism, their attachment to the 'artefacts of primitive races' was not an 'amusement', but a highly significant connection. 'The more' the modern artist rejects the 'traditional shams and worn counters of expression', the more 'unconsciously' they express themselves in a manner 'which bears a real... resemblance to so-called "primitive" art'.[92] Like Kropotkin, Read thought that ignorance of other social arrangements prevented appreciation of their variety, vitality, and most importantly, their vibrant cultures.

Read's discussion of Greek art is central to his historical narrative largely because it culminates in a notion of decline, in which formerly vivifying principles become fetters to further innovation. Before turning to this, *Icon & Idea* examined the evolution of the Neolithic age into the classical Greek. Reiterating his thesis that the 'discourse' associated with new forms of knowledge emerged from symbols initially developed in art, he discerned a 'transition from magic to religion' between these epochs. Previous accounts of this change had failed to explain why magic did not endure, Read alleged, writing that 'thunder, or... disaster, or... death' were equally explicable in the context of magical knowledge as they were in terms of the religious. Unsurprisingly, he viewed aesthetics as holding the answer. In contrast to the Palaeolithic mimicking of nature, in the Neolithic age the symbols of nature were 'abstracted', and in so doing, art works were 'given a form and a being that is arbitrary – that is arbitrary because it is a human creation'. For Read, the important change was the introduction of a sense of the numinous, 'the dematerialization of the god' and the rise of a notion of 'transcendence' not found in naturalistic art.[93] Coupled with this change was a renewed awareness of space that overcame earlier, 'sensorimotor', understandings, and newly appreciated it on an 'intellectual level' in the form of 'abstract space'. Geometric ideas spread, and 'plastic sensibility' showed increasing refinement until the dawn of Greek culture. Here, the 'first philosophers – Thales of Miletus... and Pythagoras' came forth, endowed with a geometrical perception 'the artists had made... possible'. Greece made its own vital contribution to art too: an extension of Neolithic art in the 'application of abstract principles of symmetry and harmonic proportion to the human figure', a testament to the profundity of this advance being the rediscovery of Greek principles in the Renaissance, when artists like Donatello gave 'a new representation of it'.[94]

Read's appreciation of the history of aesthetics was not for the faint-hearted, and the callow reader following him this far may have finally put the book to one side upon reaching the warning that 'as we approach the Modern Epoch' the task becomes 'increasingly difficult'.[95] Significantly, he felt that untangling the threads of art since the end of the Middles Ages was particularly onerous because of an increasing 'intellection'. As Edgar Wind recognised in a spectacularly hostile review of his book, at the core of Read's argument, and his broader aesthetic philosophy, was the 'denigration of the intellect in art'.[96] This much is clear in his discussion of Palaeolithic, Neolithic, and Greek art in its vital stages in *Icon & Idea*, but it also pervaded his polemical work. In his powerful essay *To Hell With Culture* (1941), Read hurled invective at those who sought to possess 'culture', asking what these 'students and professors, Bolsheviks and Nazis' understood by the term.[97] Turning to the classical world, he argued that the 'cultured Greeks... hadn't a word for it', hinting at an integrated culture where artistic creativity was woven into the tapestry of daily life. Following Eric Gill, from whom Read gleaned the title of his essay, he looked to a democratisation of art that would nevertheless recognise its unique epistemological status, collapsing the barrier between 'the artist and the ordinary man'.[98]

Disregarding the philosophical baggage that made *Icon & Idea* a cumbersome read, the essential thrust of the text was just this idea: that the culture of a vibrant society grew organically from the soil, rather than existing as a sediment of learning, or collection of musty artefacts, possessed by the few. For Read, the image preceded the intellectual elaboration of ideas; art comes before philosophy; and even mathematics was beholden to the 'geometricization' of Greek sculpture. Yet this intellectualisation – the birth of geometric 'perception' – was a deathblow to the vigour of Greek art, as codification began:

> Hellenistic art, the art which is so ... decadent by comparison with the art of the fifth and earlier centuries, is either an art which has lost all vitality, and mechanically reproduces standardized types according to academic rules ... or it is an art of caricature, a manneristic art that seeks to produce an effect of vitality by exaggeration.[99]

Academicism was the ultimate cultural crime, betraying a poverty of imagination in which artists 'for want of an original style' resurrect the manner of a previous time.[100] This recourse to rules that undermined Greek culture was a sure sign of 'decadence' for Read, but it was a pathology not isolated to the past. Viewing the historical record, he wrote, in a Kropotkinian inflection, that it is clear that 'growth and form, birth, maturation and decadence, are dynamic processes' and an epoch must not be judged on its 'stability', but on its 'display of energy'.[101] Capitalism, for Read, embodied this tendency towards atrophying decadence, and modern art pointed to a way out.

The Reconciling Image: The social basis of art

At this stage, Read's history met his social criticism. In his essay 'The Reconciling Image', he insisted that a new culture was imperative, but that this could not be willed, and must 'appear spontaneously in our midst' rising 'from the collective unconscious through the fiery hands of our lame Vulcans'.[102] The decadence that Read diagnosed in later-Greek art appeared again as the values of the Renaissance became routine – exemplified in Leonardo da Vinci's precepts for good art – and he felt they were evident today, in a bankrupt mass culture that nourished a 'decay of sensibility'.[103] Decline set in once initially fresh principles became commonplace, and the parallel between Read's historical thesis and Kropotkin's discussion of the implosion of the communalist movement is stark. The idea that mercantile torpidity and the jealous protection of liberties undermined the vigour of communalism, is mirrored in Read's vision of the corruption of art, as it is immured in treasure troves and artists resort to sterile formulae.

What motivated Read's plunge into the history of art was a desire to move beyond what he deemed the inadequacy of materialistic explanations of art. This was a position he often reiterated. *Icon & Idea* declared that it was pointless to look for explanations of shapes or geometric patterns in 'materialistic or technical' theories, just as he rejected the idea in *Art Now* that art is a 'mere reflex of social and economic conditions'. Even in one of his final works, he scorned the assertion of unnamed 'Marxist critics' that art is an 'epiphenomenon' of economic forces.[104] For all his protestations, however, Read frequently ventured materialistic explanations of artistic change, captured in his insistence that he had 'no intention' of denying the 'fact that new developments in aesthetic consciousness are set in motion by new economic conditions'.[105] As much then as Read pursued an idealistic hypothesis that art is foundational to the perception of reality, it did not mean that the external world had no impact. 'The vital function of the imagination', he insisted elsewhere, 'is not to escape from reality, but to make it viable'.[106] Material factors therefore obviously shaped art, and in elucidating his theory in opposition to materialistic explanations, he was aiming to carve a space for the autonomy of art, and a position for the revolutionary artist to transcend the confines of the present that he thought missing in Marxism.

In Read's dualistic comprehension of art history, social form thus retained central importance, and in thinking about the kinds of society that prepared the ground for significant art, he clung to Kropotkin as a guide. What impressed itself on Read's mind was Kropotkin's robust defence of mutual aid as a feature of human history, findings that Read thought showed mutual aid's importance as the sole basis of 'any rational hope of human progress and happiness'.[107] It is worth noting that Read's book of selections from Kropotkin drew heavily on his historical work, with *The Great French Revolution*, one of his more overlooked contributions, second only to *Memoirs of a Revolutionist* as the source of plundered aphorisms. The neo-Kantianism of Wilhelm Worringer and Ernst Cassirer may have motivated the thrust of *Icon & Idea*, emphasising the primacy of art in forming a sense of reality, but when Read moved to think about the rebirth of culture, his anarchist inclinations were central.[108] Indeed, there is a clear overlap between Read's perception of the initial vibrancy of certain historical cultures, and Kropotkin's reading of past social forms that had achieved meaningful liberty. Greek art was the product of the Greek 'way of life', Read wrote, and rested on a 'civic virtue' that placed great demands on 'physical fitness'. Similarly, he argued that the art of the Middle Ages was supported, at least initially, by the patronage of the 'social organism', rather than mercantile families.[109] At their height, before intellection took its toll and the Gothic cathedral ceased to be a rumination on the numinous and became instead a way of 'illustrating dogma', these were integrated cultures.[110] Such societies, unaware of a culture that was simply an efflux of daily life, inspired the vision of *To Hell With Culture*.

Kropotkin advanced exactly the same argument in *Mutual Aid*. The 'grandeur' of 'medieval architecture', he remarked, was not simply a product of technical sophistication, but because 'each monument was a result of collective experience'. Just 'like Greek art', Kropotkin continued, 'it sprang out of a conception of brotherhood and unity fostered by the city'.[111] For Read, a real revival of art depended on the achievement of an 'integrated culture' akin to 'those of the past – Athens, Etruria, the Christian communities of the Middle Ages, Venice', societies that had also secured 'political liberation', or at least the vibrancy of political 'confusion'.[112] Read demurred from the 'sentimental' interpretation of the Gothic cathedral as an expression of social oneness, noting that in terms of design they were always the product of a singular will, but he did maintain that the loosened bonds of authority in these societies granted the artist precious room.[113] With the retreat of authority, he saw mutual aid occupying the vacuum, warming a 'temperate... social climate' pervaded by a 'common purpose'.[114]

Like Kropotkin, Read's historical narrative buttressed a critique of the present. A central pillar of Read's appreciation of past experiments in mutual aid was that they were small, assuming a purely 'functional' organisation the value of which he believed Kropotkin had proven in the pages of *Mutual Aid*.[115] Rather than simply a point about decision-making, however, what animated Read's stress on the value of localism were contemporary concerns about the insidiousness of mass culture. Even an abstruse text like *Icon & Idea* forced this point, as he elegiacally concluded with the observation that a 'spiritual' lassitude saturated 'our mechanical and materialistic civilization'.[116] Around the same time, Theodor Adorno similarly despaired at mass culture. Poetically bemoaning the 'neon signs' cluttering our cities and outshining 'the natural light of the night', he warned that this presaged a 'frozen death'.[117]

Read echoed the premise of this critique, but his anarchism hinted at a brighter future. Summoning Alexis de Tocqueville, he excoriated American society for its 'thin, streamlined and synthetic' superficiality, a product, he thought of the triumph of the 'democratic principle'.[118] Venturing back across the Atlantic, he turned to Manchester, diagnosing a prevailing banality:

> These cities fill their Odeons and Majestics... their citizens flock to mass spectacles like football finals and greyhound races... But they have no indigenous art, no creative spontaneity... Art languishes, like a prisoner, in well-guarded art galleries.

'The position is not so very different in the United States', he added, 'except that the guards sometimes carry guns.'[119]

That Read's elitist rejection of contemporary culture had a decidedly anti-state edge is apparent when he turned to the question of patronage. After all, a legitimate criticism of socialists captivated by Greek or medieval art is that its production often depended on aristocratic, plutocratic, or theocratic support. Art would thus seem less an expression of communal solidarity, and more an exercise in power, like the neo-Gothic town halls erected in Britain's industrial cities, as merchants and politicians sought to turn their metropolises' economic might into political influence. Read looked to anarchism in an attempt to negotiate new types of patronage, but in this there was an obvious tension. As a propagandist for modern art moving from the fringes to the centre of the British cultural establishment, he maintained relationships with institutions that it might be expected for an anarchist to resist. As an inveterate joiner of committees – 'eight or nine, chairman of four' he wearily confided to Victor Gollancz – Edward Dahlberg was probably not alone when he erupted that consorting with the 'adversaries of human love' in this manner was unanarchist.[120] Read was not ignorant of this problem and debated the issue with Berger, noting that he was 'fully aware of the shortcomings' of these 'corrupt institutions', but did not see an immediate alternative:

> Take... the British Council, to which I have given so much of my time. It was founded by an imperialist (Lord Lloyd) and its aims are undoubtedly... chauvinistic. But I have not the slightest doubt that through its agency the position... of our artists throughout the world has been immensely advanced.[121]

Proposing instead 'limited cooperation with the belief that one is strong enough to remain incorruptible' in the immediate, Read endeavoured to theorise a way in which such Robespierrean virtue would be unnecessary.

As other high-minded commentators like J.B. Priestley counselled the recently demobbed in 1945 to bravely refuse the 'anaesthetic' of 'Glamour, Sport, Sensational News, and ... De-luxe nonsense', and the BBC introduced the 'dustily academic' Third Programme to improve the nation's cultural diet, Read looked for a solution to cultural impoverishment through a form of patronage that abjured the state.[122] Once again, he turned to the idea of a 'vital community', and in turn to the 'collective patron'.[123] With the appeals to planning that had characterised radical politics in the inter-war years becoming a political orthodoxy post-1945, as those rebuilding Europe strained to create systems that would avoid the instabilities of classical liberal economics that imperilled the peace, Read would seem to have struck a lonely path in rejecting the omnipotent state. But if even those at the apex of political power in the post-war period were afflicted by a characteristically British 'queasy ambivalence' regarding state intervention, Read's resistance was much stronger, and challenged the language of technocratic expertise that was then accruing political capital.[124] Pursuing the questionable line that the triumph of democratic socialism in the West had led to an equalisation of wealth that made earlier forms of patronage impossible, Read drew on his anarchist vocabulary to oppose the idea that the state should cultivate culture. 'The State is ... rightly described as a machine', he said, 'its total effect is inhuman', and its involvement in art would blunt vitality as the anodyne decision-making of 'committees' prevailed. Rebuffing universities, colleges, and museums as 'slaughterhouses' for artistic integrity, he called on the historian, psychologist, and educationalist to examine the social conditions behind history's great art, and to forge an education that fostered creativity.[125] But, of course, Read thought he had already uncovered the answer. 'A lesson of history' is that if we seek a 'natural and spontaneous culture ... we should aim at the division of the world in relatively small and almost wholly self-sufficient units'.[126] In this spirit, he closed his selection of Kropotkin's writings, published in the heat of the Second World War, with a lengthy quotation from *The Conquest of Bread*, arranged under a fresh title 'Art and Society'. Art was decadent, Kropotkin wrote, and it would remain so without radical social change. Revitalisation would only come when 'cities, territories, nations' renewed 'their harmonious life', and art could 'draw inspiration from *ideals held in common*'.[127] This was an answer Read would echo.

Kropotkin, Read, and history

Hanging on a wall in the Museum of Fine Arts in Boston is an early painting by Francisco Goya y Lucientes entitled 'Time, Truth and History'. Completed sometime at the end of the eighteenth century, the canvas details three figures bathed in an aqueous light. One is the winged figure of Time clutching an hourglass in his hand, the other hand clasped around the wrist of the naked figure of Truth. Bats and owls circle ominously over their heads. Time exposes Truth to the observer, but also to a figure in the foreground, perched on a rock. This is History. Intently recording events in a book resting in her lap her focus strays, looking away from her work, out of the canvas at the viewer.

For both Kropotkin and Read, the writing of history had a similarly dual gaze. They both looked to the past pursuing the faithful recording of its events and the recovery of its neglected actors. But at the same time, like the figure of History in Goya's painting, one eye was fixed firmly on the reader of their words, and their actions. Their histories were not just a simple act of scholarly rescue, but a call to action and a demand that the lessons of history must guide activity in the present.

A sense of history defined Kropotkin's thought. His conception of what anarchism meant rested on a rich appreciation of the intellectual history of socialism, and he offered an historical narrative that emphasised the pervasiveness of struggle, and the vulnerability of victories won. Evolution was a central pillar of this interpretation, but, like his explicitly ontological reflections, it stressed contention and change, not teleological predestination. While Kropotkin self-consciously looked to history to enflame the hearts of timid revolutionaries, Read's project appears very different. His densely academic discussion built on a German tradition of art theory to highlight the existential centrality of artistic activity. More than distraction, decoration, or declaration of feeling, art lay at the very origins of consciousness. Diagnosing psychological disruption and cultural facileness in the present, Read believed that re-acquaintance with the practice of art was a pressing need. Here, his history met his social criticism. Drawing on Kropotkin's work on mutual aid, he identified those past societies that had approximated this integrated culture, and in their solidarity, produced an art remembered down the ages. For both Kropotkin and Read, this vitality was a feature of societies that had restricted in some way the incursions of the state and its mechanisms of control. Considering the past showed, for both, the essential vulnerability of the state form, and, even in the imperfect experiments of a distant time, the rich possibility of organising life away from its tutelage. This was the power of history.

4
Revolution: The Journey to Communism

In a 1922 edition of the satirical magazine *Punch*, a cartoon appeared set in a doctor's surgery. The rotund doctor, peering over his glasses from behind his desk, advises his patient that he should take complete rest. 'By the way', he enquires, 'what is your occupation?' Grumpily slouched in his chair, the patient responds 'I'm an anarchist', to which the doctor retorts, 'Well, don't throw any more bombs for a month at least.'[1] Clearly this sketch did not tax the writers of *Punch* too greatly, but the curious thing about the cartoon is that the connection between anarchism and bomb-throwing had much resonance at all in the 1920s. Kropotkin's decision to support the Allies in the First World War, a stance he formalised by signing the *Manifesto of the Sixteen* (1916) along with a number of other prominent European anarchists, including Jean Grave and Christiaan Cornelissen, split the anarchist movement. As embarrassing as this was for many anarchists, who saw endorsement of either side in the conflict as a renunciation of a supposedly deeply held internationalism, the bigger problem was the apparent acquiescence of the working classes. Fenner Brockway, pacifist editor of the ILP's *Labour Leader*, may have written in 1916 that to 'us Socialists' the 'workers of Germany and Austria, no less than the workers of France and Russia, are comrades and brothers', but his was a lonely voice.[2] Anarchism had already faced an uphill struggle making its presence felt in the collectivising temper of the pre-war years, but now it was confronted by even steeper challenges as the state extended its purview. It was an inopportune time for division.

In reality, of course, the invocation of anarchist terrorism by *Punch* owed little to any deep engagement with anarchism, but more to the popular conception of anarchist politics as a creed of deranged villainy. Mined in this instance for its modest comedic value, the era of the

First World War – despite anarchist acts of violence having significantly decreased in the years leading up to it – continued to see the use of anarchism as a label for indiscriminate violence. Indeed, the *Washington Post* was not alone in seeing the spark that lit the conflagration as the product of anarchist activities. 'Young Anarchists Hurl Infernal Machine at Pair in Streets of Sarayevo', a subheading screamed in June 1914, recounting how the heir to the Austrian throne and his wife were 'slain' by the young assassin 'Gavrio Prinzip [sic]'.[3] Once the war was underway, the image of the anarchist retained its utility. Edward Grey, acting as British Foreign Secretary, took time out of a 'luncheon at the Hotel Cecil' in October 1916 to call for 'some agreement' in the future on the 'methods of conducting war'. This was pressing, he observed, as 'Germany has been the great anarchist who had thrown down all barriers which civilization previously built up to keep the horrors of war within bounds'.[4]

The war proves an interesting point of comparison for Kropotkin and Read, not only because as the older man was defending its necessity, the younger was packing his bag for the Front. For Read the war, seen through the lens of his subsequent politicisation, was a pivotal point in his intellectual development, transforming an instinctive hostility to violence to full-blooded pacifism. He was also symptomatic of the broader difficulty that confronted internationalists in 1914, for while he already saw himself as a socialist the 'adventurous romance' of war was too tempting for a boy reared on Haggard.[5] The reality of fighting stripped away some of this allure, and looking back from the perspective of another war in 1939, Read recognised in verse the frustrated potential of the generation that came home in 1918 with the vote, but little else:

> We think we gave in vain. The world was not renewed.
> There was hope in the homestead and anger in the streets
> But the old world was restored and we returned
> To the dreary field and workshop.[6]

Perhaps next time, the field and the workshop could be the site of profounder achievements.

Both Kropotkin and Read cleaved to the idea that the revolutionary transformation of society was imperative, but they conceived of this change in radically different ways. While Kropotkin saw a battle with the agencies of state-power as, in all likelihood, an inevitability, Read saw such violence as undercutting the very values of anarchism. Having experienced war, and having seen from afar the path of revolutions in

Russia, Germany, and Spain, he looked for a different route to redemption. For those anarchists wedded to more traditional conceptions of revolution this was an anathema, a feeling amplified by perceptions of Sir Herbert Read's political dilettantism. Yet, surprisingly, a similar issue confronted Kropotkin. Pessimistic about Britain's lethargic labour movement, commentators often charge that he drifted to a form of gradualism, with revolution superseded by the steady triumph of mutual aid institutions. This is a view apparently reflected in his evolutionary reading of the flow of human history, with the inevitable victory of anarchy making revolution redundant. But despite their differences, both Kropotkin and Read continued to believe in the necessity of a decisive break with current methods of social organisation. In turn, they both expended great energy hypothesising what techniques of change would echo that anarchist shibboleth that the means of transformation must sit comfortably with the goals desired. Envisioning this revolution was therefore vital.

The Inevitability of Revolution: State power, fatalism, and evolution

Soliciting reminiscences of Kropotkin from actors in the early days of British socialism, George Woodcock received a postcard from George Bernard Shaw. Reflecting convention in describing Kropotkin as 'amiable to the point of saintliness', Shaw added that 'his only weakness was a habit of prophesying war within the next fortnight. And it came true in the end.'[7] Shaw's comment was only a minor exaggeration. Kropotkin saw war as a product of the international anarchy nourished by capitalism, and believed that, thirsty for profits, the bourgeoisie impelled their governments to military action to augment their profit margins. Once the product of royal whim, today 'armies are pitted against each other that the revenues of Messrs. Almighty Rothschild, of Schneider, of the Most Worshipful Company of Anzin ... may remain unimpaired'.[8] This joint venture of capital and the state had, for Kropotkin, the ambition of assailing the 'popular institutions' that made life viable for the vast majority. Jacques Turgot had done this in pre-Revolutionary France, he wrote, usurping the 'communal ownership of land', a policy continued by the Jacobins and resurrected by the 'English bourgeois ... in India'.[9] But while 'it may suit Russian and British manufacturers to make a partition of Armenia, or to fight upon the corpses of Armenians', Kropotkin reminded his readership that 'the workers have nothing to win at wars'.[10]

Repeating a premonition until it comes true certainly detracts from the profundity of the vision, but Kropotkin's doomsaying was not a unique reflection on the delicate balance of European politics before 1914. What Shaw did not convey in his postcard, however, is that Kropotkin's thesis was that war was inevitable given that conflict between rival states was a feature of capitalism, and the ranks of the industrialised were constantly being reinforced. Commenting on the 1894 Sino-Japanese War, for instance, Kropotkin saw its roots in the emergence of capitalism in both countries, with the established capitalist powers arming and cheering on the combatants.[11] And the leading economies did not confine themselves to promoting conflict, but actively pursued it themselves. Reflecting on twenty-one years of *Freedom* in 1907, Kropotkin singled out the 'ten years we had a Conservative government' as a particularly odious period, marked by the belligerence of both Lord Salisbury and Arthur Balfour. They 'twice brought the country to the verge of ruinous wars – first with the United States, next with France', he wrote, but perhaps most disgraceful was the 'barbarous, unprovoked war against the Transvaal and Orange Free State'.[12]

All of these narrowly avoided conflicts, and the unsuccessfully eluded – Britain's dispute with the United States over Venezuela and British Guiana, the imbroglio with France over primacy in Sudan, and the Second Boer War – were the product of imperial misadventure. For Kropotkin this fact revealed the synchronicity of capitalism, imperialism, and war, but what was particularly appalling was the apparent complicity of the British working class, with one of the few voices of opposition coming from Herbert Spencer, who 'always protested against the unprincipled policy of the Conservatives' and condemned the 'English aggression' that caused the Boer War.[13] Behind this general collusion, Kropotkin discerned an ideological manipulation, one akin to the illusory promises of parliamentary democracy then making headway in British politics. Come election time, 'agents and electoral committees' make 'promises on all sides' and trick their way into the home of the ' "voter" ', flattering 'the mother, the child, and if necessary caressing the asthmatic dog or cat'.[14] Noting the contemporary popularity of stories reporting 'imaginary wars', ending in the 'capture of Rotterdam by the English, and the triumph of England over the world', he discerned an attempt to place the population on a war footing. 'Ceasing to be an expression of what may be called public opinion', he wrote, 'the Press... applies itself to manufacturing warlike opinion'.[15]

Kropotkin's description of the state in its lead up to war revealed just how powerful an institution it was, and why revolution remained necessary. Aside from marshalling technological, financial, and military power, it exercised an ideological hegemony that endeavoured to 'awaken the lust of war' and promote 'Jingo opinion'.[16] History confirmed this idea too. Kropotkin's discussion of the medieval commune, for example, highlighted a 'swing' in the 'pendulum' of ideas as one of the causes of its downfall, as 'students of Roman law and the prelates of the Church' compromised communalist values.[17] To Kropotkin's eyes, the British working class seemed especially prone to this somnambulism, but the London Dock Strike of 1889 hinted at their slumbering power. He soon incorporated the Strike into his familiar narrative that included the Paris Commune, detailing the tenacity of the revolutionised populace. 'Boldness of thought, an energy of action, an eagerness for work' was apparent in both 1871 and 1889 'of which people have given no proof in previous revolutions'.[18] As much as this was an exemplar of creative potential, it was also another lesson in the danger of timidity. The Commune was never able to cast off its inclinations to secure change through government, and Kropotkin resignedly noted that in the Dock Strike, John Burns and Ben Tillett 'were brought... into prominence', their 'moderation' appealing to the 'Liberal middle classes'.[19] Burns pursued a parliamentary career, and Tillett would later follow him to Westminster.

For Woodcock, Kropotkin's dashed hopes for the Dock Strike induced a pessimism that pushed him from revolution to gradualism, an interpretation that has bolstered the diagnosis of a conceptual confusion over the role of revolution in his thought. Indeed, an influential view is that he began a journey mirroring a broader movement in British libertarianism towards an 'Ethical Anarchism' that eschewed revolutionary change in favour of the power of personal example and 'moral persuasion'.[20] Coupled with his apparent *volte-face* in 1914, a narrative emerges where the aging Kropotkin drifts to the centre ground, capped by his return to Russia in 1917, and his death in relative obscurity in the remote village of Dmitrov.[21] Explaining his retreat from activism, Woodcock offered a host of personal factors, including Kropotkin's precarious health, the birth of his daughter in 1887, and the struggle to support his family through writing. Upon arriving in Britain, he pursued an arduous lecture tour, taking in cities from Aberdeen to Leeds, Dundee to Bradford, and Newcastle to Manchester, but these activities decreased in the period after the 1889 Strike, as he apparently turned to the idea of securing anarchism through a 'ripening of public opinion'.[22] Kropotkin's tone certainly changed. Dropping the 'fire and iron' exhortations that littered his contributions to *Le Révolté* and *La Révolte*, he invested his energies in developing the philosophical sophistication of anarchism, a shift in attention that was, perhaps partly, a product of weariness at the forced nomadism of the rebel-rouser. Yet, to interpret this as meaning that Kropotkin now rejected revolution does not bear scrutiny.[23]

The problem is epitomised in a text like *Fields, Factories and Workshops*, which appeared in book form in 1898. Even contemporary readers tended to interpret this work as a rumination on agricultural and industrial efficiency, with one reviewer noting that those interested in the book should not be 'deterred... on the ground that its author is a Socialist'. In fact, it continued, there is 'very little Socialism... in it', adding that the work could have come from the hand of 'any sound Liberal or Conservative'.[24] While the reviewer may have thought otherwise, *Fields, Factories and Workshops* was not a book that Salisbury could have written, for at its heart was an attempt to provide a more robust theory of revolution than the one he had sketched in *The Conquest of Bread*. Its focus on the decentralisation of industry and the synthesis of 'brain' and 'manual' work were disquisitions on the kind of society desired by anarchists, but it also offered a warning that in the chaos of revolution, it was vital to prioritise the issue of subsistence before hunger killed the spark of ingenuity.[25]

Echoing his seesawing reading of European history, in his reflection on twenty-one years of *Freedom*, Kropotkin hinted at why the patient elaboration of a work like *Fields, Factories and Workshops* remained important. His indictment of Tory ascendency implied a bleak period of reaction, made worse by the fact that the fetish of parliamentarianism even captivated the minds of socialists. In such an inhospitable environment, one where the 'triumph of middle-class ideals and policy' jarred with the lost vibrancy of the period between 1884 and 1886, the duty of anarchists was to 'keep high the banner of Anarchism', and spread 'as widely as possible the ideas of... no-government organisation of Communism'. *Freedom* had 'accomplished a task which will live', he added, prising the stranglehold of centralising 'Social Democracy' from the throats of the working class, and keeping alive the ideas of 'Free Communism'. Glancing at the horizon, Kropotkin concluded that 'we may be certain' that when socialist agitation erupts once more, 'it will bear the seeds of Communism... and of Anarchism'.[26]

A counterpart of Kropotkin's perceived retreat to a kind of Fabian gradualism is the notion that he increasingly saw the triumph of socialism as inevitable. Translating concepts looted from evolutionary theory to the historical process apparently opened the door to this kind of fatalism, leaving an 'ambivalent' legacy for his revolutionary theory.[27]

Purveying a 'facile optimism' inherited from positivism, Kropotkin's sense of inevitably was not Plekhanovian in seeing predestination as a spur to practical action, but rather encouraged withdrawal, a process exacerbated by the waning revolutionary momentum in the aftermath of 1889.[28] Even a notionally sympathetic commentator like Nicolas Walter maintained that Kropotkin erred by following a nineteenth-century tradition of deterministic social thinking. His crime, Walter impugned, was to buy into the 'fallacy that historical methodology can not only trace the pattern of the past but also predict the pattern of the future'.[29]

While Kropotkin's ontology stressed 'ceaseless transformation', and while his historical theory approximated this thesis in delineating a tidal conflict between the forces of liberty and reaction, it is true that he did often speak in terms of inevitability.[30] In the seemingly unequivocal article 'The Inevitability of Revolution', Kropotkin pondered the idea that there 'are periods of human existence when the inevitability of a great upheaval' was obvious. 'One feels the inevitability of a revolution, vast, implacable' thrumming through the social fabric, whipping up a 'wind of noble passions' that will overturn the deadening stasis of the present.[31] Similarly, he often spoke of the immanence of change. Referring to the emancipation of women, a manumission that must apply 'at the gates of the university' as at the 'kitchen and washhouse', he laconically stated: 'It will come.'[32] Perhaps unsurprisingly though, such confident declarations tend to appear in articles composed at the dawn of Kropotkin's career. Indeed, this impetuosity would fade in the fresh context of what he saw as Britain's embryonic socialist movement, but it also rested on a tactical assessment that drew on the philosophy of history he was busily expounding in the lead up to the start of the twentieth century. As he noted in his memoirs, published in 1899, 'Europe' is 'traversing ... a very bad phase of the development of the military spirit', but the time was still propitious for 'a revolution far more important and as widely spread as 1848'. Just as medieval communalism, and 1848 itself, burst forth during the nadir of reaction, the present was rich for possibilities too. The key was to spread this message.

As Kropotkin was fully aware though, the problem was that anarchism was just one of several traditions available to those freshly dejected with capitalism. In this sense, the language of inevitability offered a weight of authority, aiming to convince the diffident activist that history was on the side of anarchism. The fact, however, that Kropotkin abhorred what he perceived as the determinism of Marxism, and tried to sculpt his politics accordingly, suggests that this was principally a rhetorical strategy. In *Modern Science and Anarchism,* he chided blundering Marxists for turning 'certain "correlations" into "laws"', but conceded that as the future was a blank canvas, 'it is possible that we are wrong, and they are right'. When discussing scientific knowledge, Kropotkin was also sensitive to the notion of provisionality. Commenting on the tentative first steps of the synthetic philosophers, he deployed knowing speech marks when writing that their desire was to 'discover new connections between things (new so called "natural-laws")... inspiring us with confidence in the correctness of their conclusions'. He was thus cautious in avoiding an overt determinism that might prove embarrassing in the light of further intellectual advance. This, Kropotkin noted, was Darwin's methodological genius, writing that he had looked upon his theory as:

> Suppositions affording a temporary explanation ('working hypotheses')... facilitating the grouping of facts... but these suppositions were not accepted before they were confirmed by applying them to a multitude of facts... and they were not considered as natural 'laws' – that is, *proved* generalisations – so long as they had not been carefully verified.[33]

Despite his praise, Kropotkin did not consistently apply this benchmark of rigorous verification. Opting for the word 'tendencies' when discussing social phenomena – 'ethical tendencies', 'mutual aid tendency', 'tendencies' to communal work – gave him the theoretical space to appreciate the complexity of the social world, and the room to stress the tentative nature of knowledge.[34] But such a mode of argumentation frequently veered close to being unverifiable, and in turn sits awkwardly with the fact that he also saw mutual aid and its ethical derivatives as in some sense proven by modern science.[35] Intellectually committed to the impermanency of our hypotheses, a desire to bolster the claims of anarchism pulled him in a different direction.

Occasional inconsistency is hardly surprising in a prolific writer like Kropotkin, and it is highly significant that his slides into the language of inevitability occurred primarily in his polemical, journalistic writing. Overwhelmingly, he embraced a metaphysic of malleability, one that, contrary to prevailing interpretations, informed his historical writing as he viewed history through the lens of evolutionary theory.[36] That he sought to understand history in evolutionary terms is clear. Aiming to fit the French Revolution into a 'law of human progress', he wrote that, like a 'line drawn on paper... we shall see this line gradually though slowly rising' in a period of evolution. Revolutionary upheaval amplified this development, but he added, at 'this height progress cannot be maintained' as 'all hostile forces league... against it'. Although Kropotkin noted that subsequent ink strokes would detail a line of development taking 'place on a very much higher level', the notion of inevitable reaction is vital.[37] Indeed, elsewhere, he again explicitly took issue with determinist visions of history. 'Men often speak of stages to be travelled through', he sighed, but 'this seems... to misunderstand the character of human progress and... make use of a badly chosen military comparison':

> Humanity is not a rolling ball, nor... a marching column. It is a whole that evolves simultaneously in the multitude of millions of which it is composed... If you wish for a comparison you must... take it in the laws of organic evolution.[38]

Against an analogy that signified regimented inertia, Kropotkin juxtaposed what he saw as the real meaning of evolution. 'Everything is incessantly modified', he clarified, 'systems, wages, planets, climates, varieties of plants and animals, the human species'.[39]

The root cause of the problematic reading of Kropotkin's fatalism is the historically insensitive appreciation of his concept of evolution. Writing to William Skilbeck in 1909, the incoming editor of the newly renamed *The Nineteenth Century and After*, he revealed the extent to which his evolutionary theory rested on Lamarckian precepts. Stating that he was planning to offer a 'critical analysis of Natural Selection' to the journal, Kropotkin added that this was especially significant given that 'Lamarckianism is coming so prominently to the fore' in recent essays on the subject. Later, he wrote to admit that the task was proving more onerous than he had expected, there being 'such a mass of evidence in favour of the direct action of environment [sic]'.[40] Turning to Darwin's work itself, Kropotkin showed that he too had conceded later in life that natural selection might not be the sole motor of evolutionary change, with environment also spurring direct adaptation.[41] To this end, he offered a revised definition of evolution, stating that variations were 'a combined result of the inherited *possibilities of variation* (determined by all previous evolution of that branch...) *and the modifying influences of a changing environment*'.[42] While astutely observing that Darwin did indeed modify his belief in the omnipresence of natural selection, Kropotkin's deep debt to Spencer's work on adaptability nevertheless shows that he was behind the times – especially in his derisive critique of the German biologist August Weismann.[43] In the light of subsequent scientific research, especially modern genetics, Kropotkin's investigations into the mechanics of evolutionary theory appear arcane, but what it does show is that, again, fluidity is at the heart of his perception of evolution; a concept that he attempted to translate to his vision of history.

An illuminating comparison here is with the work of legal scholar Henry Maine. Kropotkin drew heavily on Maine, suggesting that his studies into the 'embryology of human institutions' had opened a new area of scientific research.[44] This praise notwithstanding, Maine made an odd bedfellow for Kropotkin, not simply because he was politically conservative, but also because Kropotkin looked so negatively on formalised law.[45] Curiously, it was Maine's legal ideas that he drew on, pointing to the lack of codified laws in early societies as a foundation for his attack on the iniquities of modern jurisprudence. As this implies, Maine, looking favourably on contemporary law, hinged his attitudes on a broad notion of progress. Unabashedly Eurocentric, he also presented progress as a discernible feature of the West, but was sceptical that the East could replicate such advances.[46] Despite their shared context and terminology, and despite Kropotkin's admiration for Maine, the difference between their interpretations of evolutionary development is stark. Maine discerned a guiding hand in history, arguing that the 'unquestionable excellences of English law' were lambent when seen against 'the early forms of jural conceptions'. Offering an analogy that alluded to the importance of Charles Lyell to the genesis of evolutionary theory, he observed that 'these rudimentary ideas are to the jurist what primary crusts of the earth are to the geologist'.[47] Looking back over the centuries, Kropotkin offered a different reading of the historical record that did not bear witness to the steady accretion of progressive knowledge. Strife was the dynamic of history, and oases of respite were frequently ephemeral, vulnerable to the forces of reaction clustering in the shadows.

Reaction, for Kropotkin, was both organic and immensely powerful. Regardless of his keen optimism and unerring faith in the possibilities of anarchism, the idea that selfish instincts and self-serving individuals might crystallise into a force that confronted this creative ingenuity was never far from his thought. Revolution remained necessary for this reason. Faced in Britain by a rising tide of popular conservatism and imperial zeal, he turned to the manipulative powers of the state for an explanation. Mirroring Marx's proposition that the state was a committee for the furtherance of bourgeois interests, he espied an insidious coalition of industrialists, politicians, and the media aiming to marshal public opinion behind belligerent adventure. This was not a sophisticated analysis of the popular temper in the late-nineteenth century, but it showed his continued attachment to revolution. The Dock Strike in 1889 affirmed its necessity, with parliamentarianism once again obstructing meaningful change. Kropotkin may have been dismayed at this lost opportunity, but he did not resign himself to a form of gradualism, nor capitulate to a teleological logic at the centre of his system. The power of the state demanded action, and, far from translating a theory of steady progress from evolutionary theory to social philosophy, his vision of evolution was one of constant change. Only the concerted action of mass upheaval could sweep away the embedded power of the state and avoid the errors of the Paris Commune. More important than this though, Kropotkin thought, was the fact that the white heat of this revolutionary fervour would forge an anarchist society.

The Conquest of Bread: Creating the future and revolutionary violence

In 1892, Britain experienced its own modest kind of anarchist outrage, when 'John Borlas, 31, described as an Oxford graduate' fired a pistol near the House of Commons. Accosted by a policeman, Borlas declared that he 'was an anarchist' and that his action was designed to convey his 'contempt for the House of Parliament'. The headlines generated by this event betrayed a difficulty in coming to terms with this singular act. One opted for 'Strange Conduct of an Oxford Graduate', another 'Extraordinary Freak of An Anarchist', a third simply pondered 'Anarchist or Lunatic?', while a fourth answered the question: 'The Lunatic and the House of Commons'.[48] Although plenty were puzzled by Kropotkin's politics, rarely were these principles deemed the product of an aberrant mind. Instead, contrary to the image presented in the popular press, and the cartoon of the sickly anarchist warned to lay off throwing bombs in *Punch*, Kropotkin occupied a peculiar position in being feted for the very values anarchists were accused of lacking.

As some perceptive critics have observed, however, the tendency towards hagiographic appreciations of Kropotkin leaves this idea of his essential benignity in place.[49] He was a revolutionary, and as much as he recognised the practical advantages of limiting discussion of the sanguinary aspects of the transition to communism, he firmly rejected the notion that it would be some kind of Benbowian 'holiday'.[50] There is much more to anarchist conceptions of revolution than reflections on how much blood will flow, and fixation on the question of violence tends to overshadow the attempts anarchists have made to develop a theory of revolution congruent with their broader principles. Kropotkin turned with alacrity to this task, attempting to outline a picture of a future revolution that not only sat comfortably with anarchist organisational premises, but actualised anarchism in the course of the struggle.

While he expended great effort thinking through how an anarchist revolution might develop, a legitimate objection to this task is that it delimits a freedom he saw emerging spontaneously. Given Kropotkin's caustic dismissal of British socialists in thrall to the 'debilitating theorists of the German Social Democrats', who 'fold their hands in expectation of a "historical process"' that will destroy capitalism, it appears contradictory for him then to try to define the nature of the coming revolt.[51] Kropotkin was aware of this tension, and introducing Émile Pataud and Émile Pouget's syndicalist utopia *How We Shall Bring About the Revolution* (1913), he moved to defend the utility of utopian texts, while qualifying their purpose. 'A concrete idea precedes its realization', he reflected, exhibiting his technical frame of mind by pointing out that the idea of humans achieving flight was until recently a fantasy. Desirable as this clarity of vision was, Kropotkin also insisted that flexibility was crucial. 'A book is not a gospel to be taken in its entirety or to be left alone', he added, 'it is a suggestion, a proposal – nothing more'. Repeating a favoured theme of a Germanic proclivity to centralisation and control, he also wrote that it was important to remember that authors of utopias never 'offer us anything unchangeable, anything decreed in advance, like those plans of campaign drawn up by the German general staffs during the during the wars of 1793–1809'. This peculiar example aside, Kropotkin insisted that *à la* Proudhon, a 'general idea of the Revolution' was what was needed, not 'revolutionary recipes'.[52]

Visualising revolution therefore served an important role, not only in thinking through the changes desired, but also in distinguishing an anarchist theory of revolutionary change. In *The Conquest of Bread* – Kropotkin's sustained examination of an imaginary upheaval – he stressed the importance of purging the pathologies of capitalism in the course of the struggle itself. While other forms of socialism remained fixated on capturing the apparatus of power, this overlooked the necessary, local, preparatory work. 'Socialist politicians, radicals, neglected geniuses of journalism [and] stump orators' would quickly fill the 'vacant seats' of the town hall, availing themselves of titles like '"Provisional Government"', but the beating heart of the revolution 'is in the streets'.[53] As the revolution's intellectuals traded verbiage from the benches, Kropotkin urged the risen people to state a simple mantra, that 'everyone, whatever his grade in the old society . . . has, before everything, *the right to live*, and that society is bound to share amongst all . . . the means of existence'.[54] Abiding by this principle, he hoped, would make those debating in the town hall redundant, preventing the revolution from falling under their sway. But, he insisted, the question 'how will you organise the future on Anarchist principles' was contradictory, for 'we cannot organise you. It will depend on *you* what sort of organisation you will choose.'[55] What was key, and had been proven by the vanquished hopes of past revolutions, was that the revolutionary momentum must not be harnessed by any group, 'dictatorship, monarchy or parliament', and that expropriation should be expansive.[56] To 'oust the landowner' and not 'interfere . . . with the swarm of middlemen' would be to 'prepare the way for the triumph of reaction', as given the complexity of modern society, it is 'impossible to reform any one thing without altering the whole'.[57]

Amidst the orgy of collectivisation, Kropotkin recognised that there was one burning issue: 'Bread, it is bread that the revolution needs!'[58] Optimistically, he asserted that in a revolution compassion and the dozing creativity of the population would rise to meet this challenge, with the 'insurgent districts' seizing and distributing food, while also negotiating reciprocal agreements with the 'factory workers'. Rather overlooking the realities of the life cycle of crops, he also suggested that the populace would attack 'unproductive land' with the full force of modern scientific and agricultural knowledge to meet their immediate needs. That this solution would not conquer bread led Kropotkin to rethink the course of revolution in *Fields, Factories and Workshops*. Central also to this revision was a tactical reassessment that rather than pan-European anarchism, different countries would hack different paths through the revolutionary thicket, without 'conforming to any particular rule'.[59] Having already pondered the possibilities of rationalised agriculture, Kropotkin's awareness that revolution would be a process rather than an instantaneous change, encouraged him to clarify this image. Framing his discussion as an attack on Adam Smith's obsession with the division of labour, he identified the tendency for political economy to insist that nations must also specialise: Russia to grow corn, and Britain to produce textiles and industrial goods. What confounded such attempts to reduce countries to points on a production line was their sheer complexity, 'variety is the distinctive feature', Kropotkin wrote, adding that dominant industries tended to call companion-industries into existence.[60] Conceding the efficacy of specialisation, he insisted that only 'temporary' division of labour could avoid the dehumanising impact of the production line, a fact that Smith himself acknowledged, but Kropotkin did not notice.[61]

That strengthening his theory of revolutionary transformation was central to these discussions in *Fields, Factories and Workshops*, rather than the dissection of political economy that was his starting point, is suggested by the fact that as an intervention in economics Kropotkin was about a hundred years late. While the most significant contributions to contemporary liberal economic theory dripped from the pens of W.S. Jevons, Léon Walras, and Carl Menger, these names are wholly absent from his text.[62] Marx receives a mention in passing, and the opportunity to lambast his epigones for their 'abstract formulae' and lack of 'concrete' analysis is firmly seized.[63] But Kropotkin's real object was to show that even Britain, where agriculture had been left fallow for so long, could achieve self-sufficiency.[64] What he was intimating was that if worldwide upheaval severed international trade links, the shortage of bread that killed the Paris Commune, would not necessarily lead Britain down the path of reaction. Indeed, locking horns with the 'pernicious' theory of Thomas Malthus, as he had before in *Mutual Aid*, he countered that over-population was a 'fallacy', for a dense population was a prerequisite for the intensive cultivation made possible by modern science.[65]

Fields, Factories and Workshops demonstrates the impact of British concerns on the development of Kropotkin's thought, shown in his turn to address the practical problems confronting British revolutionaries – and his modest attempts to locate his argument in debates between Anglophone intellectuals. Sadly, he ruminated, Malthus remained the mainstay of 'political economy, classical or socialist', and smashing this false idol was a necessity.[66] Turning to the idea of a British revolution in *Freedom*, his image mirrored its French cousin examined in *The Conquest of Bread*. Paramount would be an anarchist political economy based on the principle that 'production' was the 'mere servant of consumption', informing a revolution whose internal logic was localism.[67] In this way, the organisational ethos of a future anarchist community – localised decision-making, self-sufficiency, and 'agro-industrial' communalism – would be born in displacing the current order. Pointing again to a spontaneous process of the 'communization of supplies', Kropotkin wrote that this opening of the 'warehouses' and 'cattle-markets' of the revolutionary cities would meet immediate needs, forestalling the reaction that would gather momentum as hunger bit. His assessment was that even though this era would demand austerity, with the vibrant possibilities of social change captivating minds, 'one can dine contentedly enough on a bit of bread and cheese while eagerly discussing events'.[68]

Bread, cheese, and the heady atmosphere of revolutionary virtue were not permanent solutions, and Kropotkin admitted that 'Britain will be compelled to reorganise production ... so as to send into the field all the labour left unoccupied in consequence of the stoppage of manufactures.'[69] Although he did not mean that compulsion would be necessary to force people to take up the sickle, trusting their good sense to recognise the required course of action, it is not difficult to pick holes in his quixotic vision. Suggesting that any delay in producing food could be catastrophic, but also seeing revolution as a lengthy process and one probably preceded by destabilising inter-state war, it is no great leap to imagine the cool heads that he saw guiding the revolution overheating. At the same time, Kropotkin was conscious that ascetic social models rarely lasted long, and that it would be crucial to traverse the treacherous waters of reaction before the agro-industrial communes achieved bountiful produce, luxuries, and the meaningful labour that made communism an improvement on the production-line economy of capitalism. Placing his hopes in a 'system of natural communism' akin to that practised in peasant communities, but also in cities, where he suggested that water was supplied in abundance until there was a shortage and then 'citizens ... reduce their consumption', he believed this spirit would bind communities in the difficult times. The accuracy of this image is, again, open to contention, and Kropotkin was well aware, as his philosophy of history showed, that selfish actions would not disappear, perhaps even amplified by the terror of crisis.[70] Yet, the burning question remained, how would such obstructions be dealt with, without sullying the democratic objectives of an anarchist society?

This question leads directly to that most thorny issue in anarchist political thought: the role of revolutionary violence. Although their reputation might suggest otherwise, anarchists like Kropotkin were hesitant to vent visions of apocalyptic class war. Partly a product of recognising that it was unwise for a movement hoping to bolster its ranks through the force of reason to preach violence, it also a reflected the fact that anarchist activists were always vulnerable to official restriction. Kropotkin followed suit, but also avoided depictions of the more lurid possibilities of coming conflict because it distracted from the image he presented of anarchism building on the creative genius latent in the populace. Given that revolution would be a period in which passions ran high and in which the indignant cast off long-endured injustices,

Kropotkin was resigned to the inevitability of violence. Contrary to the tendency to bifurcate his thought between revolutionary and gradualist phases, with violence disappearing in the latter period, the fact is that he always assumed a range of positions on the issue. This is apparent even in a text such as the rabble-rousing *Words of a Rebel*, written long before his immersion in Britain's soporific labour movement. He variously presented violence as a product of not heeding the lessons of previous revolutions, as a necessary reaction to the attempts of the state to fetter the revolutionary spirit, or, as with the Paris Commune, a largely irrelevant issue as the threat of resistance made the government evaporate 'like a puddle of stinking water'.[71] Placing responsibility for the *semaine sanglante* squarely at the door of the state, there was nevertheless a warning here too. Writing that the state often disappeared in the face of meaningful opposition, Kropotkin noted that it frequently merely moved out of the reach of the revolutionary tornado in order to regroup. As the French Revolution testified, 'it took five years of continual insurrection...to batter down' feudalism, and even then it fell short.[72]

Kropotkin's final completed work was the exhaustive study *The Great French Revolution*, and as with *Fields, Factories and Workshops*, while an apparently scholarly intervention, its real object was to strengthen anarchist conceptions of revolution. Reaffirming a common theme of his earlier works, he insisted that historic revolutions were lost once representatives assailed the popular momentum. To restore 'order' in such a tumult would produce predictable results: 'The Social Democrats will hang the anarchists; the Fabians will hang the Social Democrats, and will in turn be hanged by the reactionaries.'[73] Habitually imposing contemporary labels on the past, behind his reading of the French Revolution was an ambition to provide revolutionaries with a number of clear lessons. The most important one being that had it not been for the intransigence of Louis XVI, the surging bourgeoisie would have readily 'help[ed] with all their power to keep the people down'.[74] This mistrust of the political channels of the Revolution informed Kropotkin's theory that a dual current defined the uprising. The power behind the Revolution lay in the streets, in the 'popular movement of the masses', whilst the 'political movement' was a 'middle class' affair, fixated on the badinage inside the National Assembly.[75]

At times, he saw these two forces working in tandem to seize the greatest concessions from the *ancien régime*, but he believed that, seeing the Revolution in uncomplicated class terms, the bourgeoisie always remained wary of the popular initiative. Despite the obvious political thrust of this thesis, some contemporaries noted Kropotkin's service in rescuing the 'action of the masses' in the face of undue fixation on the 'political side of the movement'. So wrote the American historian Fred Morrow Fling, who, as a friend of Woodrow Wilson and participant at the Paris Peace Conference in 1919, was unlikely to entertain much time for Kropotkin's politics.[76] Contrarily, another review noted that, in fact, such short shrift was exactly what the book deserved. His 'concern is not to depict things, but to prove things', wrote one empirically minded commentator, and thus Kropotkin 'glorifies the mob' meaning that 'an anarchist might welcome his latest work...but a Conservative, or even a Whig, of the old school might...be tempted to throw it on the fire'.[77] For those granting the book a reprieve from the flames, *The Great French Revolution* offered the argument that localist logic lay behind the Revolution's key achievements, mirroring Kropokin's image of an anarchist revolution. The concerted action of the peasantry led to the abolition of feudalism, he wrote, accusing modern historians of overlooking the fact that the Convention merely gave legal recognition to an accomplished reality in 1793.[78] Further condemning the selective gaze of historians, Kropotkin noted that only the 'theatrical side' of former revolutions drew attention, while the 'immense work accomplished in France...by millions of obscure persons' is lost to history.[79] The apparatus of Louis XVI's state was dismantled by the 'thirty-six thousand' communes in France, organising daily life and maintaining a healthy distrust of representative government, preferring the '"districts", "sections", or "tribes"' of its popular administration. And while people remained captivated by the blood pouring from the block of the guillotine, the real portent of the Terror was missed. 'Under the pretext of saving the revolution', the 'Robespierres and Saint Justs' were endeavouring to contain it.[80]

For all his discussion of the creative aspects of the Revolution, the most revealing feature of Kropotkin's history was its ambiguity over violence. As Woodcock noted, Kropotkin was willing to go to some lengths to excuse the Revolution's mob violence, whilst excoriating the Terror as a product of, ironically, counterrevolutionaries: 'The creative, constructive spirit of popular revolution, which was feeling its way, was now confronted by the spirit of police management, which was soon to crush it.'[81] He justified the execution of Louis XVI by making a contradictory defence of the 'legal point of view', strikingly at odds with his lifelong call for the immolation of all written law, and he discussed the event with glee, observing that his death meant that 'one of the chief obstacles to all social regeneration within the Republic existed no longer'.[82]

It is not difficult to image Kropotkin echoing Robespierre's mantra, that 'mais Louis doit mourir, parce qu'il faut que la patrie vive'.[83]

As the Revolution transmogrified from a war for the future of France to a war with the rest of Europe, Kropotkin vacillated between enthusiasm for the citizen's militias, and a belief that the conflict entrenched bourgeois hegemony. He spoke of the 'Titanic struggle which the sans-culottes had to carry on against the invaders and the traitors', and seemed drunk with the imagery of the Revolution: 'the tocsin sounding all over Paris, the drums beating in the streets, the alarum-gun ... the songs of the volunteers'.[84] Reflecting his subsequent position on the First World War, Kropotkin's argument was that national liberation and anarchism were not necessarily competing goals, as long as the pursuit of freedom did not ossify into an exclusive nationalism. Resting his decision to support the Allies in 1914 on an interpretation of the long arc of European history, he thought that the liberties wrested from autocracy by the revolutionaries were not all futile. With Germany casting avaricious glances across Alsace-Lorraine, he thought the 'growth of Prussian militarism' heralded a dark future: 'the militarization of all Europe, and the arrest of social progress'.[85] The paradox in Kropotkin's interpretation is that while he saw Germany as the biggest threat to the federalist ideals that were the legacy of the Revolution, in his immediate political context, Germany lay closer to a model of regional autonomy than the centralising Republic of the Jacobins. Steeped as he was in French culture, Kropotkin bought readily into the notion common among French Republicans in the post-Commune era, that despite its reverses, France remained the bastion of Enlightenment thinking, and Germany the epitome of reaction.[86] When he pointed out in his history of the Revolution that Royalist counterrevolutionaries in Alsace-Lorraine 'counted on Germany', this was clearly a warning freighted with contemporary significance.[87]

Presumably, however, being attentive was not enough, and people had to be prepared to take concrete action against insurgent reactionaries. Kropotkin's discussion of violence in the context of the Revolution entailed complications, particularly when it veered towards legitimising formal expressions of political violence. Assiduously avoiding this when discussing the Terror, it is no great leap to imagine the rhetoric deployed to justify the execution of Louis XVI widened to all those imperilling a budding anarchy. The problem is that the line he posited between authoritarian expressions of violence, and the revenge meted out by over-enthusiastic sans-culottes is porous: when do the 'armed bands of Marseillais' hunting 'out the counter-revolutionists' become apostles of authority?[88] In this light, his warning that all will be lost if the Social Democrats hang the anarchists, raises the question: what will be lost if the anarchists hang the Social Democrats? The benevolent distribution of food and housing logically reflects anarchist values, but the physical coercion of opponents would seem to jar with the commitment to consensual decision-making and the emphasis on the force of reason underpinning anarchism. One solution is to argue that anarchists do not reject violence in perpetuity, and it would be legitimate for a future anarchist society to meet violence with violence.[89] Equally though, Kropotkin hoped that an anarchist society would create systems of arbitration durable enough to eliminate the issue of violence more-or-less entirely.

Kropotkin offered few clear answers to the question of violence. Sensibly recognising that an anarchist revolution would not effloresce unopposed, he saw violence as an inevitable reflex of those holding power and occasionally, on the part of the revolutionaries, the product of deep-rooted resentment at their historic abuses. To a large extent it would depend on the wisdom of the ruling classes. After all, he would say, how willingly the state relinquished its power would determine how much blood flowed. Yet, as his lengthy treatment of the French Revolution showed, the state rarely voluntarily abandoned its privileges, and Kropotkin largely avoided the problem of how the treatment of counterrevolutionaries might impinge on the anarchist society he was hoping to achieve. As a revisionist historian of the Revolution like François Furet would have no doubt pointed out, Kropotkin's tendency to divide people into two camps – revolutionaries and counterrevolutionaries – presaged an inherent intolerance, opening the door to systematic violence ahead.[90] Indeed, there is a clear affinity between Kropotkin's dualist view and the utterances of a figure such as Emmanuel Joseph Sieyès, whose influential tract *What Is the Third Estate?* (1789) drew similarly stark lines: 'What Is the Third Estate? Everything; but an everything fettered and oppressed.'[91] Against such an image of the activist as a Nechayevian fanatic, Kropotkin defined the duty of the anarchist revolutionary 'minority' as that of compassionate, earnest propagandising, inspiring by example, rather than forcing particular action.[92] His own attempts to pursue this project in Tsarist Russia, ending with his betrayal and incarceration in the Peter and Paul Fortress, might have suggested some of the hazards of this vocation. Nevertheless, Kropotkin preferred to stress the constructive aspects of an anarchist revolution that would see an anarchist spirit grow from its dawning moments. For Read, however, this did not amount to a solution to the problem, as, he argued, if the means adopted to secure anarchism must not undermine the ultimate objective, the question of violence remained pressing. What would be more effective in killing a blossoming anarchist society than drowning it in blood?

The Romantic Revolution: Knightly politics and education as revolution

Kropotkin's critics may have questioned the logic of certain aspects of his system, but they mostly regarded his anarchism as a consistent doctrine. Consistency, in contrast, was rarely an attribute applied to Read. But just as Kropotkin's alleged move away from revolution is seen as stemming from a dual root – a turn to gradualism caused by his waning faith in the labour movement, and an intellectual commitment to an essentially deterministic view of history – Read is charged with a similar twofold weakness. On one level, his knighthood and his fluffed attempts to explain it away hang over his legacy, apparent evidence of flippant political attitudes cheerfully jettisoned in return for official acceptance. At the same time, others, notably George Orwell, criticised Read for not integrating his aesthetics and politics, arguing that he failed to offer a vision of social change echoing his aesthetic values.[93] Yet, Read thought long and hard about how an anarchist society might come into being, and about the ways that a social order could develop that enshrined cultural vibrancy. In so doing, he also offered a robust critique of the older tradition of anarchist revolutionism represented by Kropotkin, and presented an idiosyncratic alternative.

On 1 January 1953, *The Times* contained the declaration: 'Read, HERBERT, for services to literature'.[94] This brief announcement was met with 'apoplexy' by the Glaswegian activist Frank Leech, as, apparently, 'this great fighter dropped dead' of a heart attack upon reading the news.[95] Although no doubt apocryphal, the story does give an idea of the consternation that met Read's decision to accept his knighthood. The *Manchester Guardian* thought that year's honourees rather undistinguished; indeed, 'when one looks through the massive list of Orders one must be pardoned for thinking that before long there will hardly be a public servant in the country... not entitled to wear his ribbon or medal'. Read, it noted, was 'rather off the beaten track'.[96] General indifference may have met Read in the mainstream press, but he rightly predicted that anarchist circles would treat the news differently. While probably not expecting a coronary reaction, he thought fit to publish a justification for his decision in a January edition of *Freedom*. Pointing out, with references to his work for the British Arts Council, that he was 'an anarchist before any of these unsought distinctions came my way', he insisted that:

> I have never renounced the society in which I have lived; and having lived in compromise with that society in big things and little, I cannot see why, logically, the empty question of a title should be made a matter of indignant protest.

Read urged detractors to 'examine their own consciences' given that they too accepted 'integrally bourgeois' privileges that could only be avoided by living on a 'desert island', and pointed out that 'every glass of beer you drink, every cigarette you smoke, helps to sustain the bourgeois society...you so rightly despise'.[97] What his argument singularly failed to appreciate, as Colin Ward noted, was that some concessions were easier to avoid than others.[98] Rare support came from Augustus John, an artist praised by Read and himself occasionally involved in anarchist politics, although given that John had accepted an Order of Merit in 1942, this move was far from altruistic. Read's blithe reflection that an anarchist being awarded a public honour was a 'paradox that could only occur in England' was apparently incorrect.[99]

Unsurprisingly Read's knighthood led to his ostracism from the organised anarchist movement, a connection that had always been somewhat vague. Future Islamic scholar Robert Irwin, who flirted with anarchism while at Oxford, remembers inviting Read down to address the University's Anarchist Society, and reminisced that they 'barracked' him for accepting the honour.[100] Like John, Woodcock publicly supported Read, insisting that 'a libertarian' had the right 'to make his own choices, even in his relations with the State', while privately criticising him for missing the opportunity of joining a distinguished group of dissident intellectuals that had rejected official honours.[101] Writing to Woodcock, Read said that 'Vero [Vernon Richards] seems to have cut me out of his life, on account of the knighthood business' adding that 'it is really too silly to be so indignant about a matter which has no intrinsic importance'.[102] This became a refrain. Responding to a request from the artist Margaret Gardiner in 1965, who would herself receive an honour, to include his name in an anti-Vietnam War appeal to be published in America, he cautioned against mentioning his DSO, MC or D.Litt, saying they were 'not worth a dime...I prefer to be naked'.[103]

Anxious as Read was to downplay the significance of his knighthood it raises the question of why he chose to accept it at all. His biographer uncharitably points to pressure from his wife Ludo, who, still embarrassed by the stigma of their affair which cost Read his job in Edinburgh, was further humiliated by his unconsummated relationship with the young painter Ruth Francken in the summer of 1952.[104] According to the writer Geoffrey Grigson, who tersely deemed him 'not much of a poet, [and] to tell the truth not much of a writer', Read apparently qualified his acceptance saying that '"I didn't feel important enough to refuse."'[105] Perhaps though, the real motivation lay in an admixture of vanity and embarrassment. Read worked hard to make a living in a literary world dominated by the products of elite educational institutions, many of whom were of independent means. E.M. Forster may have declined a knighthood, but he was made a Companion of Honour on the same day as Read, and his journey from the independent Tonbridge School to King's College, Cambridge, all lubricated by a generous bequest, was markedly different from Read's early years in Halifax, stint as a bank clerk, and aborted degree at Leeds.[106] Whatever the reason behind his decision, Read continued to identify as an anarchist and expound his political ideas for his remaining 15 years. Indeed, he perplexingly wrote that, if anything, his honour would add weight to his social criticism, giving 'force and authority to one's faith'. Missing the objection that it was also a gift to those satirising his politics as intellectually feeble, this was nevertheless a view that he had developed prior to his day at Buckingham Palace. In 'our dead-end civilization', a rather un-festive Read wrote to Woodcock on Christmas Day 1952, no doubt aware of the coming imbroglio, the writer is given 'merely a choice between various modes of compromise' and 'it seems one cannot afford to dispense with the personal contacts of metropolitan life'.[107]

Despite Read's sanguine reasoning that such a triviality would not hinder the power of his critical message, the reality was that it did. Stephen Spender recalled a maudlin meeting with Read in the year that he became a knight, writing that he seemed 'depressed by an overwhelming sense of decay', and that the 'loss of faith in the social ideas' that had sustained his enthusiasm pushed him towards a fatalistic pessimism. His retreat from practical involvement with the anarchist movement would support a reading that sees Read's attachment to anarchism waning, but then his connection to this movement was never particularly formal. Regardless of the embarrassment that his rise into the ranks of chivalry caused his comrades, Read's role had always been that of an influential populariser, and as an engaged intellectual, a thinker striving to expand the horizons of anarchist ideas. But for a political tradition privileging praxis, it is unsurprising that questions were asked about the strength of his commitment. For Spender, repeating T.S. Eliot's characterisation, Read was essentially an 'old-fashioned nineteenth-century liberal'.[108] This was a painful assessment for an anarchist, where 'liberal' was an entry in the lexicon of political abuse, appearing between 'anarchist' and 'Tory', as contributions from earlier political satirists.

Assessments such as these tend to stress personal failings that, despite their awkwardness, had little impact on the intellectual content of Read's politics. Yet, other voices were more willing to take him to task on his ideas. In 1959 Read entered a public quarrel with the scientist and novelist C.P. Snow, after Read had given his famous lecture *The Two Cultures and the Scientific Revolution* a poor review in the literary *The London Magazine*. Snow's separation of literary intellectuals and physical scientists, with future progress resting on the shoulders of the latter, and the literati displaying a worrying 'Luddite' propensity, was bound to provoke Read. Contemplating the romantic reaction to industrialism in Britain, Snow ridiculed Ruskin and Morris for their vainglorious 'screams of horror' and supercilious attempt to 'contract out'. For Snow, one fact was clear, to meet the needs of a rampant global population, 'industrialization is the only hope of the poor'.[109]

Read took issue with all of this. The category of 'literary intellectual' was simplistic, he chided, as critics of 'our technological civilization' included 'philosophers, politicians, and even men of science like Einstein... and Bohr', not just whimsical poets pacing the hills and dales. Echoing his own philosophy, Read suggested that modern intellectuals were not ignorant of science or 'anti-scientific', but concerned by the violence meted out on 'certain mental processes' by industrialism, for these define what it is to be human. Responding to the idea that W. B. Yeats, Ezra Pound, and Percy Wyndham Lewis brought 'Auschwitz that much nearer', and countering Snow's admission that he turned his back on modern poetry because of its tradition of 'imbecile... anti-social feeling', Read pondered whether it was actually the case that Snow simply lacked poetic talent.[110] He did not share the political views of Pound or Lewis, he added, but argued that their indictments of the 'money system' were far from vapid. In a Kropotkinian inflection, Read pointed to political economy, a discipline that had patently failed to produce 'any coherent science of the production, distribution and consumption of commodities', to stress why some intellectuals were wary of scientific hubris.[111]

Smarting from the trenchant critique of his lecture, and no doubt nettled by Read's questioning of his literary abilities, Snow bit back. Seizing on the issue of consistency, he dismissed Read as possessing 'no . . . sense of intellectual responsibility at all', surmising that 'in a serious intellectual sense, his left hand does not know what his right is doing'. Emboldening his case, Snow turned to Read's early essay on Surrealism, first issued in 1936, and recently reprinted in his collection *The Philosophy of Modern Art*. Snow noted, correctly, that an unacknowledged textual revision had occurred:

> Surrealism, like Communism, does not call upon artists to surrender their individuality.

Became:

> Surrealism does not, like Communism, call upon artists to surrender their individuality.[112]

Orwell's *1984* 'never invented anything half as neat', Snow spat, suggesting that someone who masked his shifting opinions in such a manner 'is not worth arguing with', before rethinking this conclusion and highlighting six instances where he felt Read had distorted his lecture.[113] This bad-tempered exchange closed with a response from Read, anxious to defend the integrity of his vision. The textual change, he maintained, was not one of opinion, but a lexical shift:

> What changed between 1936 and 1952 was the significance of the word Communism. It was still possible in 1936 to believe that the word Communism (I did not write Stalinism, or . . . Marxist-Leninism) was not too compromised to stand for the principles of libertarian communism (which I defined in an essay first published . . . a year before the essay now in question).

Read insisted on the consistency of his views, stating that his political principles 'were first formulated in 1914', signalling to his pamphlet *Essential Communism* for support.[114] If Snow still had the stomach for a fight, this would not have helped. Published initially as a Social Credit pamphlet, it appeared in the same year under the title 'Art and the Revolutionary Attitude' in the first issue of the American journal *The Southern Review*. Although admitting to 'drastic revision' in his definitive version, the edits signified a change of direction, having rejected anarchism as 'not a practical policy in the present stage of . . . economic development', to later pointing to 'anarcho-syndicalism' as the 'the practical organization of society' and the 'ideal of anarchy'.[115]

Read's justification of his commitment to libertarian communism in his contretemps with Snow is plausible. The International Surrealist Exhibition that initially sparked this intervention, happened, after all, in London in June 1936, against the backdrop of the conclusion of a massive general strike in France, and, most importantly, ratcheting tensions in Spain. Watching Spanish events was central to defining Read's previously fluid political ideas. This was apparent in his efforts to revise *Essential Communism* in light of these principles – ideas appearing suddenly exhumed from a shallow-grave following their apparent death in the First World War. While Snow pinpointed a paucity of intellectual responsibility, the main problem was Read's prolificacy. The stream of ink flowing from his desk as he battled to carve out a career as a writer left a clear trail of his developing ideas, proving a ripe bounty for the unforgiving inquisitor.

The anarchist political tradition became a rich storehouse of ideas for Read in the aftermath of the Spanish Civil War, and it remained so even after he bent his knee before the Queen. Issuing a collection of his political pamphlets in 1954, this edition was not a requiem for his politics, but an insistence on both their continued vitality, and a call for revolutionary change. Drawing on Albert Camus and Leo Tolstoy in a fresh introductory essay, he averred the necessity of a far-reaching 'rebellion' to induce 'chemical changes within the crystal'. Quietism is either 'morally insensitive or criminally selfish', he continued, but added that if revolt results in a mere 'reconstruction of the societal crystal along another axis, our action has been in vain'. Following Camus, Read argued that his understanding of rebellion hinted at a vital truth: that spontaneous revolt might 'change human nature, in the sense of creating a new morality, or new metaphysical values'.[116] Read was an early devotee of Camus, a writer with an obvious appeal, one commentator noted, for anyone hoping to construct 'a credo for radicals of an anti-Soviet persuasion'.[117] Introducing a truncated English translation of his *L'Homme révolté* (1951), Read offered glowing praise, writing that the book showed the redundancy of narrowly political revolution, and was full of ideas 'close to anarchism'. Read also saw Camus tapping into a rich vein of thinking that saw rebellion as inherently creative, a hopeful message after decades of 'anxiety, despair, and nihilism', and an affirmative response to the abyss opened by existentialism. 'If we decide to live', Read concluded, putting his words in Camus' mouth, 'it must be because... our personal existence has some positive value; if we decide to rebel, it must be because... human society has some positive value.'[118]

Read's enthusiasm for Camus rested on a belief, shared by Kropotkin, that anarchist revolution was an inherently creative endeavour. At the same time, while maintaining that there was 'nothing in the anarchist philosophy to justify indifference' and insisting that cleaving to anarchism demanded action 'consistently directed to a revolutionary end', he conceded that anarchism had 'changed its methods'.[119] Reviewing the omnibus *Patterns of Anarchy* in the pages of *Encounter* shortly before his death in 1968, Read used it as an opportunity to 'review my own anarchist convictions'. Under the telling title 'Pragmatic Anarchism', he wrote that education was an area in which anarchist philosophy had particular resonance. Identifying this as his own primary area of concern, he noted that the conclusion of his research was that it was only possible to understand 'the purpose' of education in the context of 'a libertarian conception of democracy'.[120] This emphasis on pragmatism shows Read expressing ideas that were current in contemporary anarchist theory, often associated with a rediscovery of the work of the German activist, and early victim of National Socialism, Gustav Landauer.[121] The thrust of this reorientation was a shift from cathartic revolution to creating 'practical anarchist alternatives to specific issues within the framework of society as it now exists', reflecting Landauer's dictum that the state is a 'set of relationships' rather than a 'mechanical superstructure' that can be smashed.[122] The most successful attempt to translate this concept for a British audience is usually discerned in Colin Ward's *Anarchy in Action* (1974), distilling ideas elucidated in the influential journal *Anarchy*, which he edited between 1961 and 1970.[123]

The reach of this rethinking of revolutionary tactics was deep, and Read was an important pioneer looking to aesthetic education as a new weapon in the arsenal of anarchist rebellion. His sustained engagement with the problem, *Education Through Art*, had an unlikely provenance for a book preaching the values of cooperation, written as it was between 1940 and 1942, as bombs fell on London and Eliot left a suitcase of clothes at Read's Yorkshire home in case he lost everything to the Blitz.[124] Rather than discouraging him, Read thought that the 'vacillating background' to the book, as the war on the Eastern Front ground to a halt and the two sides paused to 'count . . . their dead and wounded', made the call for a 'democratic revolution' all the more pertinent. His book was a challenging intervention, optimistically hoping to 'inspire . . . teachers and administrators', of the necessary pursuit of an education that fostered 'a sense of mutuality'. For those missing the radicalism of this message, Read made it plain, stating that: 'I now proceed to make practical suggestions for the reform of our education system, they... have no other end than the basic ideals of a libertarian society.'[125]

At the core of *Education Through Art* was a familiarly Readian call for the reintegration of the personality, through a renewed, reciprocal relationship between the individual and society. 'Coercive discipline', 'authoritarian mentality', 'social convention', and 'mechanical toil' had all retarded the 'spontaneous creative ability' of the individual, and only revolutionary change would loosen these bonds. Decrying in his final years that many had neglected the anarchist nature of this book, Read was evidently aware at the time that the 300-plus pages choked with lengthy quotations from Plato, Jung, and Trigant Burrow blunted its rebellious edge. The year after its publication, he decanted its arguments into the pamphlet *The Education of Free Men* (1944) for Freedom Press, summarising his argument and stating that there was a 'pattern of moral virtue in nature' and by 'habituating' children to this pattern, it was possible to achieve 'true happiness'. As 'aesthetic laws are inherent in the biological processes of life', nurturing a 'relationship of reciprocity', in contrast to the 'constraint' guiding modern schooling, was central.[126] Spontaneous creativity brings spontaneous discipline, he added, shown in the control, focus, and poise fundamental to artistic creation.[127] An aesthetically guided education could cure social ills by promoting the values of tolerant reciprocity, while simultaneously allowing the individual to flourish in the context of an integrated social unit.

Given that *Education Through Art* appeared in the years of the Beveridge Report and, even more significantly, R.A. Butler's Education Act of 1944, Read's model of libertarian schooling clearly faced an uphill battle.[128] It was however one of his principal lasting achievements, as under the auspices of his post-war involvement with UNESCO, he helped establish the still-existent International Society for Education Through Art.[129] For all the official recognition of his educational ideas, Read remained committed to the idea that they were a pragmatic means of achieving anarchism. After all, he reflected, the notion that 'it is possible to organise a society on the basis of voluntary associations and mutual aid' was a common belief only inhibited by 'our political institutions'.[130] This idealistic message obviously provided Read with intellectual sustenance, for he was lukewarm about his dealings with UNESCO. Following its first meeting in Paris in 1946, during which its constitution was ratified, he expressed concern that UNESCO's attempts to actuate change seemed destined to fail. In a world recovering from the travails of war, and coming to terms with the full extent of its barbarities, its formation reflected a situation 'universally recognized as desperate'.

Despite the urgency of the need for renewal, Read noted that following the sanction of its constitution, it looked wholly inadequate for the task. Its message did not 'reach the common man', he argued, dismissing its 'effect on the cultural situation' as '*nil*'.[131]

Unimpressed by UNESCO's tottering early steps, Read reached for his anarchism to explain this failure, and plot an escape. A propensity towards intellection was one key problem, a habit of 'confusing culture with learning and education with propaganda', and a tendency to lock decision-making behind the uninspiring doors housing 'conferences and committees'.[132] Mirroring his distaste for state patronage of the arts, and his rejection of the language of technocracy purveyed by a thinker like Snow, this view rested on his broader assumption that the position taken on the value of institution-led reform pointed to an important distinction between liberalism and anarchism. While liberals looked to institutions as safeguards of liberty, he argued that in reality this was exactly the 'kind of tyranny' that the post-war state perpetuated. 'Institutions... are megalomanic, self-perpetuating and viviparous', he colourfully wrote, 'they legalize tyranny and spread its invisible tentacles into every cell of life'.[133] UNESCO's ambition of quantifying, classing, and analysing, was also an affront to his organic view of art, failing to acknowledge that 'culture is not a concrete material which can be... bartered like butter or steel... [but] ... a spiritual growth... like the grass in the fields'.[134]

Failing to recognise these Readian truths, the organisation promulgated well-meaning but impotently liberal goals. Questioning its campaign against illiteracy, Read saw here too the pall of its 'intellectual atmosphere', and an assumption that 'knowledge about the structure of the universe, about history, geography and economics' constituted 'human progress'. On the heels of literacy, he concluded, 'objective textbooks of history' would arrive, repeating the Renaissance crime of academicism that he saw killing a once impressive artistic vibrancy.[135] Invoking Plato and Aristotle for support, Read wrote that the synchronous stimulation of the 'minds and emotions of children' was vital, a connection severed since the Middles Ages by the Church's assumption of moral education, and the subsequent secular supervision of 'intellectual' education. The collapse of religion as a force in social life left a vacuum, but its resurrection was not the solution. Instead, Read argued, morality was a form of 'discipline', and the purpose of education was to adjust 'the plastic mind of the child, to predetermined patterns of thought and behaviour'. For a champion of freedom this formulation obviously had sinister implications, but Read moved quickly to draw a distinction between the 'arbitrary and ideological' patterns 'imposed by the Jesuit, the Communist or the Nazi', and patterns that are 'physical' and 'if they are good... we call them beautiful'. Rehashing the argument of *Education Through Art* and *The Education of Free Men,* Read insisted the way to secure moral growth was through aesthetic education, with its contemplation of universal forms and technical discipline. Despite his associations with authoritarianism, Read admitted that this was a lesson he had gleaned from Plato: the defining connection between 'moral virtue and aesthetic training'. Closing this restatement of his principles, he returned to the futility of UNESCO, and the call for a necessary revolution. Preservation of peace may be its *raison d'être,* but its fetish for intellectual values would be less successful than a system of education promoting aesthetic contemplation, underpinned by an ethos of mutual aid, and recognising global 'multiplicity and diversity'. Only here, focusing initially on 'small things', might the seeds of a new culture germinate.[136]

Read placed great emphasis on the curative powers of his educational philosophy, reflected in his discomfort with the path pursued by UNESCO. Both his theory of art education and engagement with the United Nations might appear to exist at some distance from his anarchism, but behind both was a reassessment of existing approaches to revolutionary change. This did not, as Eliot and Spender might have hazarded, amount to a slide towards liberalism, shown in the fact that his rejection of UNESCO rested on a critique of liberal institutionalism that drew directly on his anarchist vocabulary. Nevertheless, as Read looked askance at state-led efforts to rebuild war torn Europe in newly carpeted committee rooms, he was drawing inspiration from a theoretical re-examination of the tactics that had led past activists down so many disastrous dead-ends. As he observed in 1947, the 'romantic conception of anarchism – conspiracy, assassination, citizen armies... barricades', was redundant in the era of the 'atomic bomb', which had rendered struggle 'on the plane of force' hopeless. Rather, the most 'effective action is molecular', and he suggested that the success of any social revolution rested on changing the 'actual disposition of men'.[137]

This vision of creative experimentation in the present that would displace the controlling instincts of the state in the future became a cornerstone of Read's revolutionary theory. He echoed this in his assessment of UNESCO, ruminating that the real potential of radical pedagogy was in the 'new institutions... new methods of education' that will 'spring up piecemeal, in... unexpected places' and 'precede a new civilization'.[138] In private, this pragmatist vision was also at the forefront of his mind, as he defended it a few years later in another testy exchange with Edward Dahlberg. While the American writer commented that Read's establishment connections and ability to get on 'with the well-to-people [sic]' showed the superficiality of his anarchism, Read's riposte offered a different take on his politics:

> I don't believe I shall bring the anarchist ideal one step nearer by joining an artificial commune . . . or wearing a loin-cloth in a sub-arctic climate . . . I believe I can best serve that ideal by cultivating my small-holding . . . by establishing a sense of community in this village, by living at peace with my neighbour, by creating . . . a cell of good living.[139]

Such molecular imagery was a persistent feature of Read's thought at the time, but he insisted that a focus on local and individual action did not amount to quiescence. 'Moral indifference' was not a state of virtue, and recent history had confirmed the truth of Martin Niemöller's famous poem: 'there were millions of good respectable citizens in Germany, and we can now see . . . that their inactivity was perhaps the greatest crime of all'.[140]

The Pre-requisite of Peace: Pacifism, pacificism, and violence

Read was a pioneering figure in British anarchism. Castigated for theoretical feebleness and personal inconsistency, he was nevertheless at the forefront of attempts to fathom processes of radical social change that would sit comfortably with anarchist principles. And in this, he was not simply hitching his ideas to those of Kropotkin, but was engaged in a sympathetic critique of the anarchist tradition. A distinguishing feature of this new politics was the centrality of nonviolence, a prominent theme in the second wave of British anarchism. Vernon Richards betrayed the reach of this view when discussing the Spanish Revolution, writing that 'recourse to violence . . . is an indication of weakness', and concluding that 'the revolution with the greatest possibilities of success' is that in which 'violence is reduced to a minimum'.[141] This was not a pacifist formulation, and Richards took issue with the Dutch anarchist Bart de Ligt, author of *The Conquest of Violence*, a book that exercised an important influence on British anarchists after its translation into English in 1937. While Richards looked to the reduction of violence as a positive goal in the transitory stages of radical social change, Ligt opposed it entirely, declaring that in the face of 'total war... we must oppose total peace'.[142] Read kept abreast of these debates over the role of violence, and followed the permutations of the commitment to nonviolence with a partisan interest. Ligt's book graced the shelves of his personal library, along with the *satyagraha* textbook *Training for Peace: A Programme for Peace Workers*, by American radical Richard Gregg, who had travelled to Mohandas Gandhi's ashram in the 1920s to seek enlightenment from the source.[143]

The case for seeing Read as a quintessential pacifist – a hatred of violence forged through first-hand experience of war and reinforced by dissatisfaction with anarchist theories of revolution – initially looks compelling. Certainly for his critics this is the case, condemning that 'diluted hyphenation pacifist-anarchism' or, like Walter, seeing Read's later tactical purism as evidence of 'never follow[ing]' his politics 'through to its uncomfortable conclusions'.[144] Read's own statement that having ruminated on the problem of war and peace for 'thirty years' he had concluded that 'peace is anarchy' also appears categorical.[145] As the dispute between Richards and Ligt implied though, even those resisting violence were wont to disagree, just as the word 'pacifism' has historically covered a range of positions and rested on shifting etymological sands.[146] While arguing that he emerged from the First World War convinced of the correctness of pacifism, it was not, in fact, until the late-1940s and early 1950s that Read's philosophy of nonviolence found consistent expression. Prior to this, Read steered a meandering path between, to adopt A.J.P. Taylor's useful but inelegant distinction, pacificism and pacifism – a general opposition to war, versus a principled commitment to nonviolence.[147]

Like many of his generation, Read often returned to his experiences in the trenches. Aside from his writing, he played an important and unacknowledged role in the publication of the English translation of Erich Maria Remarque's *All Quiet on the Western Front* (1929), a work that was central to the return to the war as a source of inspiration by British literary memoirists in the late-1920s.[148] Corresponding with Remarque to find English translations for portions of the text's idiomatic German, the former adversaries bonded over the shared scars of conflict. As Remarque commented, he started writing his book 'without ever having considered it earlier', because he felt that 'so many of my comrades, although after all we are still young, nevertheless lead an often joyless, bitter, resigned life without knowing why'. The glowing reception of the book must have been some consolation, and Remarque thanked Read, attributing this success 'not least to your activities'.[149] Other writers looked to imitate this success, but while the main British chroniclers of the 'soldier's story' – Siegfried Sassoon, Edmund Blunden, Richard Aldington, Robert Graves – turned to verse and prose to confront their memories, Read added political polemic to the list.[150] In contrast to their sullen silence, Read discussed the political implications of his experiences often, with his early essay *Poetry and Anarchism* hinting at his complex reactions to a conflict in which he witnessed great horror, but also uncovered depths of personal 'courage and endurance' surpassing 'some of the heroes of the playing-fields of Eton'. This democratising conclusion aside, he concluded by saying that he demobbed a pacifist, 'a pacifist who could speak of the horrors of war with the authority of experience'. Having established his credentials for discussing violence, he then proceeded to offer a perplexing discussion of two schools of pacifism, one based on 'humanitarian' values, the 'pacifists proper', and the other based on reason. His personal perspective remaining unclear, Read soon shifted to an uninspiring psychoanalytic argument that both pacifists and belligerents suffered from a perversion of the 'destructive instinct', turning outwards to produce sadism, or inwards for masochism. The upshot of this was that the origins of war lay in the experience of childhood, a situation for which he concluded there was no 'ready alternative' – before offering a ready alternative. Revolution was the only solution: a change in the social structure that eschewed the centralism exhibited by both capitalism and Soviet Communism. If 'nationalism persists' and 'collectivism masquerades as socialism' unchallenged, conflict will also continue, as will the 'psychosis' caused by the repressive practices of government. War and centralism were symbiotic, he decided, and only the flexibility of anarchism would bring peace.[151]

In spite of the glib psychoanalytic garb of his argument, Read's narrative is significant because it is not a rejection of violence *in toto*, but a repudiation of war. Given that it was published in 1938, at the height of appeasement and as Hitler annexed the Sudetenland, his preoccupation with international sabre rattling had clear contextual origins. Yet also, Read had not developed a concrete conception of nonviolence. His resistance to state violence would develop into a broader distaste for all violence, but at this time he possessed more traditional views. Maintaining in an early article that the 'necessary principles' of anarchism existed in the 'works of Marx, Engels and Lenin', he noted a 'sad deviation' when it came to revolutionary tactics. Here, Bakunin was right, and Marx wrong, for revolution was not the invention of a 'trained and disciplined' proletariat, but a 'spontaneous... explosion of forces'. Similarly rejecting the evolutionary implications of Marx's contention that revolution depended on the ripening of capitalism, he astoundingly stated that while 'Marxian revolution' takes years, 'anarchist revolution is a question of hours'. Quickly recognising the simplicity of this view, in a subsequent article he redefined his position as opposition to the idea of a disciplined revolution necessarily passing through several stages, deeming this a fertile bed for apathy.[152]

Alongside Bakunin, in his early article on revolutionary change Read invoked another formative influence: Georges Sorel. Although Sorelian ideas were no doubt in the air at the Leeds Art Club, Read's real engagement probably came via exposure to the work of T.E. Hulme, who later translated *Reflections on Violence* in 1916. Read was enthused by reading Sorel's major work during the war, writing that it sated his thirst for 'imaginative qualities' absent in Marx, and contributed an unlikely letter to *The Yorkshire Post* in which he argued that Sorel 'perfects' Marxist philosophy.[153] For a future proponent of Gandhian *ahimsa*, devotion to Sorel, the apostle of proletarian violence, entailed an obvious tension. In his 1938 article on revolution, Read's debt to Sorel appeared in an anti-deterministic interpretation of revolution, as he wrote that there was 'nothing inevitable' about it, and that revolt depended on proletarian aloofness, their ability to form 'a new spirit, a new ethics, a new philosophy of life... established with catastrophic violence'.[154]

Dating his conversion is difficult, but it seems that Read grew disenchanted with the idea of violent revolution before Gandhian principles grew to prominence in the British peace movement in the 1950s. Indeed, as much as Read waxed lyrical about his indebtedness to Sorel's privileging of spontaneity and feeling as necessary revolutionary components, this attachment waned. As early as 1929, he expressed misgivings about the tyrannical potential of revolutionary 'enthusiasm', seeing it epitomised in Lenin and Mussolini, and Read's political testament included Gandhi but not Sorel, although he did insist on the sustaining value of the 'myth'.[155] Underpinning his transition from Sorel to Gandhi was the fresh experience of warfare in 1939, and an assessment that Hiroshima had made a direct confrontation with the state suicidal. Going into this new war, Read wrote that he was optimistic that the conflict would lead to the social revolution postponed in 1918; a view that actually echoed his youthful Sorelian thesis that war 'tends to accentuate... class differences', and in consequence provoke a 'heroic and revolutionary class spirit'.[156] Diminishing his call for violence, yet maintaining the idea that the toils of combat had enfeebled the state,

Read saw the war creating new opportunities for anarchism. In 'France, Belgium, Italy, Greece, and now Germany' the leviathan state wobbled, and he suggested that a 'non-governmental society' might rise from their ruined cities.[157]

Quixotic it may be, but Read's statement on the revolutionary situation reveals how complicated his views on revolution and violence were. The idea that 1945 was a ready 'revolutionary situation', with most of Europe still under arms and the state apparatus of the victors possessing unequalled dominance over domestic life, is certainly moot.[158] That aside, while some commentators have traced Read's break with the classical tradition over the issue of violence, this often confuses his opposition to the war with a more general hostility to revolutionary violence.[159] Like Kropotkin in 1914, he ended up begrudgingly seeing the necessity of the Second World War, a view he similarly substantiated by arguing that there were British liberties worth defending. Discussing the particularity of British culture, its elegiac poetry, and romantic landscape painting, he stated that 'we are fighting this war precisely because in these respects we refuse to be changed'.[160] For all that his Baldwinian outlook on Englishness informed this obstinacy, Read continued to locate the war in a narrative of potential radical political change, although he tended to shift the epicentre of this revolt from the 'streets and docks ... slums and factories' of Britain, to the bruised polities of continental Europe.[161] Writing in *The New Statesman*, he lambasted those that saw the future of Europe as one of newly established states of either a capitalist or state socialist persuasion, echoing, in a sense, the speculative conclusion of the Yalta Conference that the 'dismemberment' of Germany might be the most sensible safeguard of world peace.[162] What about a 'third way', he commented, involving 'communities of self-governing industries' practising 'mutual aid'?[163]

Hesitancy about the utility of violence became entrenched once Read began to formulate his emancipatory vision of aesthetic education, and by the cessation of hostilities he had firmly moved away from traditional conceptions of revolution.[164] The immediate post-war context also witnessed his most sustained period of political involvement. In 1945, four editors of the anarchist newspaper *War Commentary* were put on trial for encouraging desertion, which given that the charges were levelled in 1944, when Allied victory seemed assured, provoked protests on the left. Read became heavily involved in their defence when the case went to trial, penning articles and helping to establish the Freedom Defence Committee, of which he was the chairman. While failing to keep Vernon Richards, John Hewetson, and Philip Sansom from prison – Marie-Louise Berneri avoided prison on a technicality – the efforts of the Committee attracted support from a range of prominent intellectuals, and raised awareness of the need for a group that safeguarded civil liberties. Orwell, Victor Gollancz, Henry Moore, and Harold Laski expressed support, and Read roped in both E.M. Forster and Bertrand Russell. Despite his support, Forster was somewhat concerned that the preponderance of anarchists in the Committee might make it less effective, asking Read, 'wouldn't it strengthen the letter if no anarchists signed it?'[165] The Defence Committee endured beyond the trial, and conceded Forster's call for less doctrinaire political objectives. Enshrining this political catholicity, the constitution of the Committee stated that it would 'maintain particular vigilance towards the exercise of any extraordinary powers restricting the freedom of political action or... expression of political opinion', and promised support for all 'individuals or organisations irrespective of their political views'.[166]

Ultimately, though, the Freedom Defence Committee fizzled out. Read confided to Gollancz that both he and Forster thought that there was 'something fundamentally wrong' with the Committee, and that it needed 'more dynamic management'. Given that the vice-chairman was the stricken Orwell, who 'has been almost continuously ill', the burden fell on Read, and he wrote that he had been trying to recruit fresh leadership: 'I tried Clem Davies', recently elected leader of the largely irrelevant Liberal Party, 'but he would not play.'[167] Although the Committee signified the apogee of Read's active political involvement, the death of the Committee, and the knighthood that came shortly thereafter, did not completely curtail his activity. When Harold Macmillan allowed the housing of American Polaris missiles on Scottish soil in early 1960, the resurrected anti-nuclear movement revived Read too, and in the ensuing fiasco the strength of his pacifism came to the fore.[168]

By 1960, Read was expressing a commitment to nonviolence that now possessed deep roots, and had developed from his conclusion at the end of the Second World War that anarchist approaches to revolution needed rethinking. By 1949, he had clearly begun to identify with the pacifist cause, as he made apparent in a review of Gandhi's autobiography published in *The Listener* that year. The book, he noted, was a bold examination of the 'universal truth' of nonviolence, only marred by the turgidity of the prose and Gandhi's 'egotistical' views on sex.[169] By 1956, Read was viewing world affairs through the lens of his pacifism. As Soviet tanks rolled into Hungary, he responded to a request from Arthur Koestler, Stephen Spender, and George Mikes to speak out against the invasion, by offering a restatement of his pacifism. Penning a spirited criticism of the USSR, and tying Hungary to the Suez debacle of the same year, he pointed to these events as evidence of the need for an end to government by 'Edens and Kruhschevs (sic)', and called for an ambitious policy of 'world resistance to government'. But, he cautioned his correspondents, the Hungarian rebels pursued an 'illogical' path in fighting the Soviet war machine on the plane of force: 'I am a pacifist' and the 'only way to end war is to refuse to fight'.[170]

Putting this intellectual commitment into action a few years later, Read participated in the 'non-violent mass sit-down' outside the Ministry of Defence on 18 February 1961, calling for disobedience against Polaris to unleash:

> The imagination of the people so that they become fully conscious of the fate that is threatening them, and we can best reach their imagination by our actions, by our fearlessness, by our willingness to sacrifice our comfort, our liberty and even our lives.[171]

Yet, in spite of the stirring rhetoric, his experiences would be unedifying. A founding signatory of the charter that established the Committee of 100 in 1960, attracted by its policy of nonviolent direct action and its status as a radical alternative to the orthodoxy of the Campaign for Nuclear Disarmament, Read's enthusiasm soon waned.[172] Following violence at a demonstration at the US Airforce base in Wethersfield, Essex, on 9 December 1961, he distanced himself from the movement. In a letter to fellow member John Berger the following day, Read mentioned that he had written an ignored appeal to the Committee of 100 speaking out against such confrontational tactics, and that such violence was 'alienating public sympathy', adding that abiding by a policy that 'may be all right for teenagers ... is neither clever nor effective'. This was further evidence for Walter of Read's half-heartedness, but Berger concurred. And when, in the year before his death, Margaret Gardiner recruited Read to publicly oppose the Vietnam War, she encountered a man still intractable on the issue of violence. He thanked her for sending 'coals of fire' in the form of Frantz Fanon's book, probably his recent incendiary work *The Wretched of the Earth* (1961). Read was clearly struck by Fanon's insistence that Africa must pursue its own path, and the vision of the 'Third Word starting a new history' and setting 'afoot a new man', rather than sending back to 'Europe ... an ideal reflection of their society'.[173] Expressing hope that Africa would 'get rid of the European image ... the bourgeois image, the image of "progress"' and its trappings '(= canned food, refrigerators, television etc.)', he added that he thought this sadly unlikely.[174] Aside from missing the difficult to deny advantages of refrigeration in a hot climate, Read's comment shows that he was struggling to keep pace with the changing realities of life in the 1960s, and people's shifting priorities. Coming two years after Hugh Gaitskell encouraged a fresh direction for the Labour Party at its Blackpool conference, noting that now a 'new way of life based on the telly, the frig. [sic], the car and the glossy magazine' mattered to voters, Read was startlingly out of touch.[175] But while he might have seen Fanon as an ally in this campaign against modern banality, he stubbornly rejected violence as 'not merely evil, but insensate'.[176] The true anarchist is 'compelled' to be a pacifist, he concluded elsewhere, holding that anarchism must be secured 'piecemeal', creatively, and through the power of earnest reflection; in other words, exactly the kind of society he hoped to achieve.[177] Read had travelled a long way from Sorel.

Kropotkin, Read, and revolution

Published the year before Kropotkin's study of the French Revolution, Jack London's genre-blending 1908 novel *The Iron Heel* plotted the course of a fictional revolution. In fact, it examined two. Narrated from the distant future by a scholar, Anthony Meredith, who disinterred the manuscript from the trunk of a Californian tree, Meredith provides contextual footnotes to the story of star-crossed lovers Avis and Ernest Everhard. Committed revolutionaries, they combat the oligarchic 'Iron Heel', then controlling the North American continent, and, living up to its name, intently 'crushing mankind'. Both hurl themselves into the First and Second Revolt against the evil empire and both meet a tragic fate. Their execution is unconfirmed but certain in the bloody reaction that followed the failed uprisings, as the Iron Heel, the epitome of the heartless state, punished the dissenters: 'impassive and deliberate... without mercy and without malice'. Across an ocean of time, in a new age where the 'Brotherhood of Man' stands atop the ruins of the Iron Heel, Meredith reflects on the tragedy of their story. 'Little did... [they]... realize that the tortuous... evolution of the next three centuries would compel a Third Revolt and a Fourth Revolt, and many Revolts, all drowned in seas of blood, ere the world-movement of labour should come into its own'.[178]

Kropotkin and Read ended up sharing this perspective that revolution was a process, rather than a decisive, cathartic event, although there were clear differences in how they imagined its course unfolding. While both have seen their attachment to revolutionary change questioned, it is clear that they expended considerable energy attempting to devise a coherent method of social change that would give birth to the principles of a new society as it progressed. Looking to history, Kropotkin saw that, like London's fictional revolution, combatting the forces of reaction would be a necessity, but that the key for anarchists was to concentrate on the creation of alternative social practices. Retribution would probably be inevitable, but unleashing the thwarted ingenuity of the oppressed masses was worth far more attention than fixating on the lurid possibilities of tomorrow.

As indebted to Kropotkin as he was, Read became dissatisfied with this visualisation of revolution. Having experienced the 'blood and shit' of war first hand, he was less relaxed about the question of violence, even though he took time to reach this position.[179] For him the problem was that Kropotkin had indeed shown the creative vibrancy at the heart of anarchism, but what would sully this objective more than having to traverse a Virgilian river foaming with blood? Instead, Read stressed the utility of cultivating anarchism locally, of contracting relationships that, in a 'cellular' way, would ultimately displace the state. Enacting anarchist principles in the present – and what better way, he thought, than through education – would mean that the eventual confrontation with the state would not mirror the drawn-out battle against the Iron Heel. Anyway, what use was the barricade in the age of the atomic bomb?

5
Utopia: Imagining Post-capitalist Society

In the afterword to the second German edition of *Capital*, Marx offered his response to a review of his book in the Parisian periodical *Revue Positiviste*. Particularly irksome, he thought, was their reproach that he confined himself 'to the mere critical analysis of actual facts', instead of 'writing receipts [recipes] (Comtist ones?) for the cook-shops of the future'.[1] Marx's substantial critique of the 'utopian socialists' rested on this foundation, as he argued that the energies spent by Robert Owen, Henri de Saint-Simon, and Charles Fourier in imagining future societies, distracted from the real duty of the dissident intellectual – developing a robust scientific theory. Theorising before capitalist social relations had ripened, they were unable to see the conditions that would endow the working-class with political consciousness, instead looking for 'historical action... to yield to their personal inventive action'. Consequently, they pursued futile dreams, waiting like Fourier in a café for the benevolent capitalist to bankroll his scheme, and composing 'duodecimo editions of the New Jerusalem'.[2] Fourier dined alone.

From the mid-twentieth century, opposition to utopianism took a different form, and often manoeuvred Marx into the tradition he ridiculed. For liberal critics like Karl Popper, Isaiah Berlin, and Leszek Kołakowski, utopian thinking often contained a distinctly illiberal kernel. Adopting and adapting Kant's dictum that out 'of the crooked timber of humanity no straight thing was ever made', Berlin offered a threefold critique of the utopian impulse.[3] First, like the worlds satirised by Aldous Huxley and George Orwell, he discerned a latent authoritarianism in inflexibly outlining future modes of social organisation. Pushing liberty to the forefront was no solution, for somebody was destined to lose out: 'total liberty for wolves', he observed, 'is death to the lambs'. Second, while most of these utopias promised some kind of equality, Berlin denied that securing it would necessarily be a moment of triumph. Citing Goethe's take on the Baron d'Holbach's *Système de la nature*, he pointed to the tendency for utopian societies to be 'grey, Cimmerian, corpse-like ... devoid of colour, life, art, humanity'. Finally, he charged, utopian dreamers tended to forget the inevitable plurality of human values. All 'Utopias ... are based upon the discoverability and harmony of objectively true ends, true for all men, at all times and places', he wrote, a fault repeated across the spectrum of utopian ideas, from the work of Plato, Zeno, Thomas More, and Tommaso Campanella, to Saint-Simon, Fourier, Owen, Étienne Cabet, William Morris, and Edward Bellamy.[4]

Such trenchant critiques of the utopian tradition pose legitimate questions for anarchists, who have traditionally been more willing than most political traditions to ponder the shape of things to come. Indeed, Berlin's post-mortem suggested that anarchist utopias might inadvertently kill the very attributes they held most dear: seeking cohesion, monotony supersedes vibrancy; desiring order, authority trumps freedom; and in imagining a golden age of consensus, they ignore the complexity of life. Yet, confirmed utopians as they were, Kropotkin and Read were not ignorant of such objections. Many of the protests raised by the mid-century anti-utopians were pre-empted by Kropotkin, who confronted contemporary efforts to build utopia in the present in a parallel fashion. This was important, Kropotkin thought, because such attempts had done so much to sully the utopian method, with their histories tending to abide by the opening witticism of Marx's *The Eighteenth Brumaire of Louis Bonaparte* (1852), and appearing 'once as tragedy, and again as farce'.[5] Read's engagement with these issues was partly a product of historical location; with Popper and Berlin notable contemporaries in the world of British letters, he engaged directly with them. At the same time, Read was consciously building on a tradition of utopian social critique that pre-dated their interventions, and was impressed by Kropotkin's prescient attempts to elucidate a utopian vision conscious of these very criticisms. Impeccable Kropotkinian credentials aside, Read made his own important contribution to anarchist utopianism. Filtering Kropotkin's vision of communalism through his cultural theory, Read developed an image of a potential anarchist society adorned by a rich aesthetic sensibility, and in which association became a fertile bed for the growth of individual uniqueness. The administrators of Yevgeny Zamyatin's dystopia *We* (1924) may have aimed to 'unbend the wild curve' to create the 'great, divine, exact, wise straight line', but Kropotkin and Read dreamt of a world of crooked timber.[6]

What Must We Do?: The utility of utopianism

Berlin's critique of the utopian mentality rested on a characteristically deep, if also perturbingly sweeping, reading of European intellectual history. He argued that a quest for 'rational organisation' was a thread through time, connecting the 'benevolent sages of [the] modern' age with Campanella, Cabet, and the 'bureaucratic fantasies' of Auguste Comte. They imagined 'fantastically tidy worlds' peopled by individuals 'joyfully engaged in fulfilling their functions' within a grand, 'rationally ordered' hierarchy of the perfect society.[7] For Kołakowski, the conviction and dogmatism nurtured by this conception of perfection could lead to 'less innocent political values' than a panorama of liberation. If, as was often the case, only a minority held this unimpeachably true vision, it could warrant supreme inhumanity. 'Believing in a higher-order reality', he wrote, that is there in the present but might not be recognised, 'justifies utter contempt for actually existing people' and 'gives legitimacy to all kinds of cultural vandalism'.[8] As many of the key anatomists of the utopian mentality suffered themselves at the hands of those hoping to build a brave new world in the present, this hostility had, in part, obvious biographical roots. Modernity, as Zygmunt Bauman observes, another thinker fleeing a grand project of social rebirth, 'is an age of artificial order ... the era of planners, visionaries, and ... "gardeners" who treat society as a virgin plot of land'.[9] Such gardening frequently led to more sinister locales than the artisan's workshop of Morris' imaginings.

Underpinning these interpretations of the utopian mentality is an implicit contrast with the openness and plurality of liberal democracy.[10] Kropotkin's politics appears vulnerable to challenges such as these, and though they rarely indicted him directly, references to anarchistic thinkers were clearly a synecdoche for anarchist thought in general.[11] That he often gave vent to images of future societies, and spoke admiringly of thinkers shuffled into the utopian tradition (Fourier, Comte, Morris) strengthens this association, as does the accusation shadowing Kropotkin that he spent his time outlining ineluctable historical laws. For all this, and despite the weight of intellectual authority ranged on the anti-utopian side, Kropotkin was himself, in a sense, an anti-utopian utopian. Built into his utopianism was a critique of the utopian mentality that would find echo in the later writings of Berlin, Kołakowski, and Popper. Not only did this amount to a contribution to anarchist theory that would remain central to subsequent thinkers like Read, but Kropotkin endeavoured to present a form of utopianism that avoided the errors committed by other utopians.

In the anarchist tradition, Bakunin has notably drawn criticism for confirming Berlin's fear that utopianism often supports a dangerous fanaticism.[12] His habit of composing detailed catechisms outlining the rules governing future societies left him open to this accusation. Although he wrote infrequently about his compatriot, Kropotkin was keen to challenge this vision of Bakunin, no doubt antagonised by contemporary attempts to limit his historical importance in comparison to Marx. H.M. Hyndman, for instance, had written a scathing appreciation in 1883, declaring Marx 'much superior' in 'original capacity and acquired knowledge', and deeming Bakunin's theory 'hasty', his methods 'semi-Asiatic', his influence 'distinctly reactionary', and his anarchism based on 'wholesale devastation'.[13] Kropotkin moved to dispel such an unforgiving reading, noting that, in contrast, Bakunin was an open-ended thinker. His writings 'contain no ready-made recipes for political cooking', he commented, echoing Marx, 'those who expect to find in a book the solution to all their doubts, without having to pass through the process of thinking, will not find that in Bakunin's works'.[14] Whatever the accuracy of Kropotkin's judgement, it is clear that the purpose of this tactical reading was to marshal Bakunin into an anarchist tradition conscious of the problems of blueprint-based thinking.

Kropotkin's remarks on the continued utility of Bakunin's work therefore mirrored his qualified endorsement of Pataud and Pouget's syndicalist utopia, where he stressed that while clarifying images were useful, they remained contingent on the vicissitudes of tomorrow. This was an important proviso, as his attempts to envision an anarchist utopia appeared during a general surge in utopian fiction, and many of these works explored decidedly illiberal societies. Discussing Edward Bellamy's influential *Looking Backward* (1887) in *La Révolte* two years after its publication, Kropotkin noted its appeal, observing that it led 'le grand précurser de Darwin', A.R. Wallace to 'déclaré dans la presse que ce livre lui avait démontré la possibilitié du Socialisme'. The book's emphasis on the 'prodigiously multiplied efficiency which perfect organization can give to labor', and Bellamy's militarised system of ranks in his 'industrial army' clearly did not appeal to Kropotkin, who complained of the 'beaucoup de préjudés autoritaires' it contained, and stated that it resembled 'une armée de Bismarck'.[15] Bellamy's utopian speculation was far from being a voice in the wilderness, and his work echoed numerous contemporary efforts by political commentators, and envoys of the emerging genre of science fiction, to imagine different tomorrows. Richard Jeffries' *After London* (1885) pictured a post-apocalypse

England falling 'quickly into barbarism' and a return to nature, while one-time Republican Congressman Ignatius Donnelly offered *Caesar's Column* (1890), where a wide-eyed visitor witnesses the wonder of a future New York, before seeing its 'vast, streaming, endless swarms' of 'the condemned' poor, 'marching noiselessly as shades to unavoidable and everlasting misery'.[16]

Kropotkin did not mention these works. Nor did he cite books like William Dean Howells' indictment of modern American capitalism *A Traveler from Altruria* (1894), feminist utopias such as Mary E. Bradley Lane's *Mizora* (1890) and Elizabeth Burgoyne Corbett's *New Amazonia* (1889), or W.H. Hudson's pastoral utopia *A Crystal Age* (1887). Nevertheless, the glut of utopian speculations at the end of the nineteenth century formed a clear context for his intervention. Abjuring the fantastical conceits of these books, Kropotkin sought to root his own utopian speculations in what he felt was the practically possible, yet he was cautious in avoiding the overt determinism that this stance could entail. Pondering the idea of 'the permanence of society after the revolution', he argued that while anarchism would provide a firm foundation, 'we cannot by ordinance regulate the condition of posterity; our descendants must see to that... themselves'. Similarly, his assessment that anarchism was just one social form in a cornucopia of possibilities, led him to suggest that geographical factors would influence revolutionary action. 'We do not believe that these Communes will make full application of our Anarchist principles', he concluded, 'but we do believe that while the revolution will be the result of all revolutionary parties, our ideas... will have their effect.'[17]

Yet, as much as Kropotkin eschewed the writing of detailed plans for future social systems, it is apparent that he did possess a relatively clear picture of the kind of society he desired. He stated as much, writing that *The Conquest of Bread* was an attempt to 'sketch a Communal Utopia', and this work itself echoed Kropotkin's earlier attempts to think about the future. Indeed, his earliest surviving political statement bore the unequivocal, if uninspiring, title *Must We Occupy Ourselves with an Examination of the Ideal of a Future System?* (1873), a question he answered at the outset with a laconic 'I believe we must.' This was not an anarchist proclamation, but just as he did thirty-seven years later in his revised version of *The Conquest of Bread*, he defended utopianism as an exercise in expressing 'our hopes, aspirations and goals', and timidity on paper boded ill for achieving far-reaching change when the opportunity arose. Despite the continuity over the usefulness of utopian thinking, there is much in the earlier statement that would have embarrassed the older Kropotkin, notably his idea that recalcitrant individuals might be 'compelled' to earn their livelihood.[18]

One enduring aspect of his argument in *Must We Occupy Ourselves* was the importance of local organisation in providing a life preferable to that under the state. But as Kropotkin himself shifted geographical contexts, the vocabulary he used, and the examples he upheld, changed. Writing in Russia, the *obshchina, mir*, and *artel* were pinpointed as models of living in which a degree of direct democracy and communistic distribution pervaded. In advancing this argument, Kropotkin was operating within a defined seam of Russian radicalism. Alexander Herzen, for one, had returned to the peasant commune as an example of socialism in action after growing frustrated with the docility of Western European workers.[19] Bakunin held a less magnanimous view of the 'parfaitement ignorants' peasantry and the patriarchalism of the *mir*, but nevertheless the commune remained the mainstay of his politics.[20]

Moving West, Kropotkin recognised that this agricultural example would hold less appeal for Europe's industrial workers, and he searched for alternatives. In France, the historical gaze at the forefront of his polemical writing presented two obvious examples. As was clear in his reading of the French Revolution, rather than *philosophes* or budding politicians, the urban workers and peasants provided the dynamic element of the revolt. Recent history offered a better example though, and in the Paris Commune Kropotkin saw his belief confirmed that communalism was not a social form confined to bucolic isolation, but practical in the context of a teeming metropolis.[21] The example of Paris in 1871 informed Kropotkin's attempts to translate anarchism for the British, but his new environs, and the channels open to him to present his views, entailed a shift in audience that in turn demanded recalibration. Alongside journalistic pieces for *Freedom*, his main avenue was James Knowles' periodical *The Nineteenth Century*, a self-consciously intellectual vehicle with a middle-class readership. Here Kropotkin continued to propound his anarchism, but the motifs of British urbanism superseded illustrations plucked from rural Russia and revolutionary Paris: museums, free libraries, parks, pleasure grounds, and tramways.[22] His point, somewhat tendentious in these examples, was that as forms of social organisation already existed that rejected compulsion in favour of mutuality, the common objection that anarchism held an unrealistic appreciation of human nature was unfounded. While not models to implement, these institutions allegedly showed the practicality of anarchism's organisational ethos.

Patient librarians were one thing – and Kropotkin noted that one of Herbert Spencer's quirks was that he 'grumbles at having to give a copy of his writings to the free library of the British Museum' – but he was also confronted by the political assumption that state-led reform was the key to solving Britain's social problems.[23] With Sidney Webb's defence of 'municipal socialism' clearly in view, a project that Webb thought was capturing the political scene and marked a rejection of Spencer's 'anarchist principles', Kropotkin offered a different reading of events in Britain's provinces at the end of the nineteenth century.[24] Rather than seeing municipalism as a triumph of local state infrastructure over free enterprise, Kropotkin saw it as a valiant 'experiment' that 'confirm[ed] the Anarchist conception of how the Social Revolution will probably proceed'. Looking to the municipal ownership of docks in Liverpool, and more curiously a rabbit farm in Torquay, he suggested they reflected a truth enshrined in the Paris Commune: that 'every revolted city' will 'organise the supply . . . of all the first necessaries of life' before anything else. This he read as a bold reversal of the fixation on production in conventional political economy, but it was also an example of local action, independent of Westminster. An obvious objection to this is that rather than a groundswell of working-class action, municipal projects were frequently exercises in opportunism by ambitious politicians. Birmingham was an example at the forefront of Kropotkin's mind, and while he saw the origins of reform in the creative energy of the city's people, others might emphasise the flamboyant Joseph Chamberlain's role. But whatever the success of these municipal projects, Kropotkin pointedly insisted that revolution remained the only course. After all, just as nascent authoritarians usurped the institutions of the medieval commune because they worked so well, a 'home-made Pierpont Morgan' lay ready to pounce.[25]

A central demand of Kropotkin's revolutionary theory was that the tactics employed must sit comfortably with the social goals pursued, and that, therefore, the new society would germinate in the rubble of the old regime. This had an ethical and practical component, implying that the relations of reciprocity and benevolence that were crucial in coping with the stresses of revolution would endure, as would the new methods of meeting pressing needs. Municipalism showed this latent potential, and Kropotkin felt that the distributive ethic it implied must be enshrined at the foundation of a new society. There is an echo of his overarching ontology in this, in that equilibrium is the spontaneous product of multiple individual and communal actions. Placing great store on rationality, Kropotkin suggested that the ability of revolutionary actors to recognise urgent needs, would mean a practical inclination to communism – a form apparently so just, that it would survive in the post-revolutionary world.[26]

Alongside the communism that grows to meet immediate needs, he also argued that the cooperation demanded by revolutionary change would fuse fresh networks of decision-making. As the reach of written laws retreated with the state (or perhaps were burnt along with their enforcers), Kropotkin saw 'mutual agreement' filling the vacuum. Pointing to the European railways, whose interlacing networks traversed the borders of nation-states, he argued that their cooperation was not the product of a 'Napoleon', but rather a 'hundred divers companies' slowly coming to a satisfactory arrangement. Given the financial dividends involved, this was an awkward example, and Kropotkin was aware of the tension. Accepting the tendency for large companies to oppress small ones, the 'scandalous fraudulency' of the railways in the United States, the lengths they would go to in order to drive wages down, and the importance of state-sponsored monopoly in ensuring their dominance, Kropotkin stuck to his guns nonetheless. While in France, the 'land of centralization', he wrote, the number of companies dwindled, in Britain where there are a 'hundred and ten' they 'agree remarkably well'. The central lesson, he held, was that when these companies negotiated amongst themselves it did not involve the state, but 'congresses composed of delegates... [who] submit proposals, not laws, to their constituents'.[27]

The importance of this example for Kropotkin lay not only in the fact that this model of negotiation had great social potential, but also in the fact that it was already in operation elsewhere. 'The Russian *mir* spends sometimes three or four days before a hundred householders come to a *unanimous* agreement' he wrote, 'but they come nevertheless'.[28] Central to his argument was the diminutive scale of this unit. Its size allowed Kropotkin to suggest that unanimity was possible, and thereby sidestep the problem of majoritarianism, while also seeing in the body a 'plasticity of organisation' that enabled it to quickly adapt to new challenges.[29] While anti-utopians discerned an inherent inflexibility in utopia, Kropotkin wanted to enshrine this flexibility in the very institutions that defined the society. Echoing his reading of evolutionary theory, he depicted these forms securing:

> The most complete development of individuality combined with the highest development of voluntary association... in all possible degrees, for all imaginable aims; ever changing, ever modified... constantly assum[ing] new forms.[30]

Such malleability, he hoped, would kerb the spread of authoritarian principles that undercut previous experiments in communalism, with these new institutions flexible enough to adapt to meet unexpected challenges.

His emphasis on the commune as a site of individuality shows that Kropotkin was sensitive to a common objection that the pressure of agreement underpinning communal living enforced a tyrannical conformity. This was a protest not isolated to the anti-utopians, but also expressed by liberal theorists like Tocqueville and John Stuart Mill, who saw the 'social tyranny' of the majority as a potentially more odious tool of coercion than formal methods of punishment.[31] While proposing a number of ways to limit this potential, for Kropotkin the very structure of the commune aimed to avoid it. His insistence that association would be free, temporary, and convoked to address a specific need, intended to prevent the sedimentation of particular interests. Even though he championed small decision-making units, Kropotkin nonetheless rejected local experiments in utopian living of the kind that had flourished in the United States in the nineteenth century. Paradoxically, he argued that while keeping '50 or 100 persons' in 'full agreement' was difficult, it would not matter in a community of '2000 or 10,000' as 'they only need to agree as to some advantageous methods of common work'.[32] Bigger communes would also reduce the inevitable tensions of close living. 'Even for two real brothers to live together in the same house' is not always conducive to 'harmonious' family life, he noted, something echoed in the experience of steamboat passengers who soon begin to 'hate each other for small defects of individual character'.[33] Kropotkin's image was not therefore a commune in bucolic isolation, and he went as far as to argue that in fact 'commune' no longer referred to a 'territorial agglomeration' but was a 'synonym for a grouping of equals'.[34] Here, a cosmopolitan attitude would reign, with the burdens of labour reduced, and individuals free to move between groups filling their time building a grand piano, enjoying astronomy, or whatever the 'thousands of associations chose' to do.[35]

Behind Kropotkin's quaint image of the commune populated by virtuous individuals intently working to fill the common-pot before retiring to pursue wholesome intellectual activities, was a desire to show that anarchism met both collective and individual needs. For those anarchists inclined to preach the economic value of communism, carving out a space for the personality was a pressing concern, particularly when trying to disentangle the communalist tradition from associations with a history of 'Communist-beehives', like those pursued by followers of Cabet and Fourier.[36] Max Nettlau offered an answer to the problem in the title of his essay 'Anarchism: Communist or Individualist? – Both', insisting that in economic affairs neither tradition 'will ever disappear'.[37] Beyond offering a rounded picture of communalism, Kropotkin was also aiming to undercut the appeal of competing brands of anarchist thought. As his comments on individualist thinkers like Max Stirner and Benjamin Tucker show, while he praised these figures as brave custodians of individuality in a time of crushing conformity, he saw this defence unwittingly developing into a fetter on individual growth. Stirner's 'rehabilitation of the "I"' stressed the supremacy of the individual, but also allegedly warranted a callous 'right to oppress all mankind' in the assertion of individual uniqueness. For Kropotkin, the economic dimension of this argument was a familiar one, pushing them towards the 'liberal individualism of the classical economists' that had also undermined the social radicalism of Tucker, and indeed Spencer. This rhetorical move allowed Kropotkin to position his anarchism, in the face of objections from both individualists and Marxists, as the sole doctrine securing individual and social freedom. Communalism would allow the individual to fully develop, he wrote, and 'reach full *individualization*, which is not possible either under… *individualism*, or under any system of state socialism in the so-called *Volkstaat*'.[38]

Spending so much time painting pictures of future worlds was a perilous pastime for a political activist, leaving Kropotkin open to objections of an out-of-touch whimsicality. More sinisterly, as Berlin and the anti-utopians impugned, the utopian tradition frequently withheld the freedom it promised by offering a blueprint of the perfect society; this ordained crystal city offering such a wonderful existence, that any act that brought it closer was legitimate. The practicality of Kropotkin's utopian vision is certainly open to dispute, especially as he attempted to vault certain pitfalls by seeing anarchism as offering everything: solidarity, cooperation, and economic sustenance, but also individual freedom, room for dissension, and meaningful labour. His idea that communalism preserved localised decision-making, but was also outward looking, encouraging cosmopolitan encounter rather than parochial seclusion might also be seen as wishful thinking. Similarly, the image of communal individuality might be one of anarchism's original contributions to the history of political thought, but it is not an obviously achievable goal.[39] Yet, while these questions remain unresolved, Kropotkin would no doubt have pointed to this very lack of resolution as evidence of the vitality of the image. His utopianism did not rest on 'models' but suggestions for how a different life could be lived; a life in which these inevitable tensions could be played out without tearing the social fabric, or demanding the deadening arbitration of the state.[40] This, for Kropotkin, was a preferable kind of social arrangement, and one that burned the blueprint on the same fire as written law.

Brain Work and Manual Work: Labour, creativity, and communism

For all its rooting in agricultural statistics, *Fields, Factories and Workshops* was also a utopian text, offering a vision of an economy in which human needs were central. Kropotkin's call for political economy to shift from fixating on production to study whether 'bread... is wanting in the peasant's... cottage' became his mantra, but his definition of needs stretched far beyond simple necessities.[41] A bit of bread might tide over an effervescent populace during a revolution, but time would increase their hunger, and luxuries were essential. Built into Kropotkin's emphasis on luxury was a critique of the tradition of utopian experimentation, led by people who had fled to anonymous 'American deserts' with the ambition of creating a new world. There, locked in a battle with an unforgiving soil, rather than a New Jerusalem they won an arduous existence, perhaps only relieved in the 'music-room in which the 'brothers' could strum a piece of music'.[42]

As the United States continued its unstoppable journey west, followers of Owen, Cabet, and Fourier were drawn to the vast expanses pregnant with limitless potential. These were different kinds of pioneers from those caravanning towards the Pacific, and most chose Illinois and Ohio as the sites of their new beginnings.[43] While the exact composition of these communities tended to vary, as did the forbear they identified with, most were committed to a clear set of principles: socialised property; an idea of the dignity of labour; commitment to equality; the primacy of the community; and a stress on the value of modesty and austerity.[44] For a pluralist like Berlin, this was an anathema. Clashing values was the crucible for the 'richest development of human potentialities' he wrote, and for individuals to prostrate themselves before 'a single ideology' induced atrophy, or as Kołakowski judged, 'stagnation' was 'an inescapable condition of... utopian happiness'.[45] Nathaniel Hawthorne's image, in his novel *Blithedale Romance* (1825), based on his own experiences in the intentional community of Brook Farm, Massachusetts, of communalists spending a wearying and cold night debating the name of their community – 'Sunny Glimpse', 'Utopia', 'The Oasis' – suggested a depressing reality of these schemes.[46] When utopians were not busy killing each other in pursuit of their projects, life would be a dull affair.

Cleaving to the trope of the renewed dignity of labour, Kropotkin nevertheless developed this idea into a vision of an economy that might avoid the pitfalls of utopian banality. Central to *Fields, Factories and Workshops* was a concern over size, and he looked forward to the overcoming of agricultural and industrial zoning for two key reasons: first the localisation of consumption and production would tide a community over during revolution; but also such an integration would impact positively on quality of life. To Kropotkin's mind, this was a view sanctioned by studying European economic development. Britain might like to think itself the workshop of the world, but the idea that an equilibrium would emerge where others met the country's needs in raw materials was a myth, as the logic of innovation meant competing economies benefited from accumulated technical knowledge.[47] With 'Russia' starting 'where Manchester and Saxony' now reached, competition, which political economists saw as the motor of efficiency, only induced further impoverishment, and the spectre haunting Europe was the emerging productive capacity of the United States. As instability brought 'pitiless oppression ... pauperism, and insecurity', Kropotkin thought that there was just one solution: a 'return to a state of affairs where corn is grown, and manufactured goods fabricated, *for the use of those very people who grow and produce them*'.[48]

Framed as a 'return' it might be, but unerring faith in the possibilities of science tempered Kropotkin's romanticism, leading him some distance from the medievalism of Morris or Thorold Rogers. Indeed, he chastised Morris, unfairly given the complexity of his views, for failing to recognise the 'gracefulness' of the machine, concordantly rejecting the notion that 'industry ought to return to its hand-work stage'.[49] This appeal to the exponential power of machinery also allowed Kropotkin to address a fundamental weakness of the ancient city-states and medieval communalism: that their political liberty came at the expense of slaves, and the *de facto* slavery of the agricultural population.[50] Rich living on the back of the exertions of helots and serfs was not a solution Kropotkin's faith in direct democracy allowed, but technology supposedly offered an answer. Crucially, in contrast to Theodor Adorno's purported statement that Marx 'wanted to turn the whole world into a giant workhouse', Kropotkin argued that rationalisation would lead to localism, not the 'mammoth farms' of Iowa or 'leviathan factories'.[51] Pointing to a plethora of schemes that might boost agricultural productivity, from 'thermosiphons' heating the soil to cheap 'glasshouses', he argued that all of these had the added boon of reducing necessary labour time. This, he added elsewhere, should be the real object of agricultural researches: '*an increase of the quantity of produce, together with a reduction of labour and of the area required for growing that amount of produce*'.[52] With global economic uncertainty ahead, and world-trade destined to falter, Kropotkin wrote that industrial nations would have to 'revert to agriculture' to meet their needs. This was not, however, a retrograde vision, but premised on a novel synthesis: the 'agro-industrial commune'.[53]

Opposition to centralisation was a patent feature of Kropotkin's political theory, and he translated this into his economic attitudes. As the logic of capitalism clustered workers in ever-larger factories, turning them into the 'flesh and bone' appendage 'of some immense machinery', he pointed in a different direction, to a localised consumption and production, realised in the 'factory amidst the fields'.[54] Blending these romantic and rational ideas – with the productivity of modern industry softened by its rooting in the soil of the country – Kropotkin's spatial understanding of this system became opaque. While deeming communalism an ethos of inter-personal relationships rather than an entity, his image of the fusion of industrial and agricultural land nevertheless implied a definite space. At the same time, while stressing localism, Kropotkin was conscious of the objection that institutions like the *mir* were, in Engels' unrestrained words, symbols of an almost 'oriental despotism'.[55] Addressing the problem of parochialism, Kropotkin wrote that 'each group in the Commune will... be drawn towards similar groups in other communes', building a dense patchwork of exchange that nurtured an essential cosmopolitanism.[56] This answer demanded a considerable leap of faith, and rested on a conversation with the tradition of communal experiments in the United States that had done so much in recent history to tarnish the communalist cause. As much as the vast horizon of the American landscape promised endless possibility, in the end, it also augured an unyielding isolation.

The loneliness of the American utopian pointed to a far deeper problem with these experiments, and one that the medieval communal movement, for all its faults, had dealt with more satisfactorily. 'Man is not a being whose exclusive purpose in life is eating, drinking and providing shelter for himself', he wrote, and an anarchist society must look beyond simply securing the necessities of life. Kropotkin's first suggestion was that a revised work process might overcome this tendency, with the division of labour replaced by 'temporary division' and a 'variety of pursuits'.[57] Following the integration of industrial and agricultural workspaces, labour would gain the flexibility to move between roles. Heightened application of machinery would also free time for individuals to pursue their goals, as mundane chores were mechanised. 'Hairdressers already' had machines for 'brushing glossy or woolly heads of hair', Kropotkin wrote, selflessly pointing to an innovation that would have been little use to him. While machinery took up the slack in the manufacture of 'plain goods', he denied the argument that intellectual advance depended on freeing engineers and scientists from toil.[58] Mentioning Galileo, Newton, and Linnaeus, he argued that the gulf between manual work and natural philosophy never used to be substantial, and that these scientists all honed their skills crafting objects that also fuelled their scientific imaginations. Aside from confirming his belief that varied labour would not induce decline, Kropotkin's comment led to an educational conclusion. Like Read, although looking to physical rather than artistic techniques, he rejected the usefulness of 'parrot-like repetition' in favour of encouraging children to 'discover...proofs by themselves' and building their own instruments.[59]

Read may have been the thinker obsessed with creating the right conditions for the artistic temperament to grow, but Kropotkin also looked to this potential society as a birthplace of cultural vibrancy. Enlivened by its diverse labour, renewed education, and spirit of solidarity, he was keen to show that intellectual life would not stagnate. Pointing to all the thinkers that had grappled with the problem of evolution before Darwin, he wrote that an anarchist society would have shortened the gestation period for a book like *On the Origin of Species*. An anarchist Darwin would simply have 'made an appeal to volunteers for facts and partial exploration', and then been inundated with assistance, he concluded, missing the fact that this was both exactly how Darwin worked, and why his book took so long to write in the first place.[60] Besides science, liberated leisure would also rekindle art. Invoking the Greek sculptor chiselling 'his marble...endeavour[ing] to express the spirit and heart of the city', and the 'grandeur' of Raphael and Murillo drawing inspiration from the 'life itself of the city', Kropotkin stated that the 'decadence' of contemporary art could be overcome. Again, in terms that Read would echo, he referred to academicism as the cause of the pitiful state of modern art, noting that recourse to books would not lead to renaissance. The cure was to correct the atomism of the 'town', to 'renew...their harmonious life' creating a sense of community that gave a 'vital' energy to emerging artists.[61]

While these reflections could have come from the pages of *To Hell With Culture*, Kropotkin and Read parted ways on the types of art they predicted would embody these luminescent values. 'The best canvases of modern artists', Kropotkin proposed, 'represent nature, villages, valleys and the sea with its dangers, the mountain with its splendours.' Yet they all ultimately failed the test of truth, lacking the 'strength' that only came through acquaintance with nature. Only the artist who had clung to the creaking boards of a fishing vessel, the artist who had spent time in a factory and 'forged metals by the vivid light of a blast furnace', and only the artist 'permeated with popular feelings' could truthfully convey them. Summoning Ruskin and Morris, he concluded that it was necessary to infuse society too with these artistic values. 'Everything that surrounds man, in the street, in the interior and the exterior of public monuments, must be of a pure artistic form', he wrote, but added that this could only come with a 'breaking' of the 'present bonds' of humanity, and a 'new start in the higher principles of solidarity'.[62]

Kropotkin's depiction of the moribund culture of the late nineteenth century reflected current fears over cultural decadence, although his philosophy diverged from the implicit elitism behind many of these critiques. The organic analogy beloved by contemporary social thinkers – in Kropotkin's rendering an image of the self-righting, self-ruling nature of complex societies eternally plagued by the vampiric state – carried with it an organicist conceptual vocabulary. In cultural terms, decadence possessed connotations of a sense of the 'exhaustion' of bourgeois culture and, in turn, the 'youth' of burgeoning cultural alternatives.[63] As much as this mentality was a manifestation of *fin-de-siècle* paranoia, the questioning of the narrative of progress had deeper roots in the cyclical histories of the Enlightenment. After all, for Edward Gibbon, the hugely influential chronicler of decline and fall, decadence played its part in the 'corruption' of Roman virtue.[64]

While less fatalistic, Kropotkin, particularly in his early years, dwelt on the proximity of cataclysm, detecting the putrefactive stench of bourgeois cultural decadence. Addressing the youthful artist in his celebrated pamphlet *Appeal to the Young* (1880), he contrasted the 'sacred fire' burning in the great artists of the past, with the insipidness of modern art, where 'mediocrity reigns'.[65] The pinnacle of art had become 'realism', the meticulous representation of the 'suffocating mud of a sewer or the boudoir of a lady of love'. Kropotkin was thus unimpressed with Émile Zola, a writer whose realism he thought tinged 'with a tremendous amount of ... romanticism'. Bereft of an 'idealistic aim' Zola's writing was impoverished, a backward step from the realism of Honoré de Balzac, or better Nikolai Gogol, whose words not only mused on the basest features of real life, but the 'highest ones as well'.[66] Zola's selective vision failed the test of realism, but was also enervating. Just as art should not simply 'decorate the parlours of shop-keepers', so writing should strive for more, and the attentive artist, 'the true poet' listening 'to life' and 'confronting the sea of suffering', cannot stay aloof. If they do, art 'can only degenerate'.[67]

Degeneration was a common conceptual sibling of decadence, but a term even more laden with biological overtones.[68] Frequently uttered in the context of concerns over declining racial standards, interest in nascent eugenic theories was not a minority interest in turn-of-the-century Britain. Here too, as social thinkers fell into the arms of science, anatomists of utopianism discern a worrying trend. As Bauman commented on the Holocaust, for instance, it 'arrived in a factory-produced vehicle, wielding weapons only the most advanced science could supply, and following an itinerary designed by scientifically managed organization'.[69] Yet, at first, eugenics did not only appeal to the political right.[70] Karl Pearson, first incumbent of the quickly renamed Galton Chair of Eugenics at University College, London, was of the left, and a friend of Charlotte Wilson, who helped found *Freedom*. Pearson's reading of eugenic theory revealed that the 'path of progress' tarmacked over the 'hecatombs of inferior races', adding that denying this natural law would lead the 'superior race' to 'degenerate itself'.[71] Such notions underpinned the revived imperialism of the late-Victorian age, seeing the destined triumph of the West in racial terms but also, paradoxically, inducing a sense of pessimism, particularly as the flower of the British manhood was revealed to be so decrepit during recruitment for the Second Boer War.[72]

Given this pedigree, it is perhaps surprising to find Kropotkin praising the scientific work of both Pearson and Francis Galton, while also attending the First International Eugenics Conference held in London in the summer of 1912.[73] Delivering the plenary, Arthur Balfour sounded a cautious note, the *British Medical Journal* reported, reminding the delegates that 'every faddist seized hold of the eugenic problem as the machinery for furthering his own' method of 'bringing the millennium upon earth'.[74] As the conference proceedings show, faddist opinion was well represented, notably by Charles Davenport, who would later be an important influence on Nazi eugenic thinking. Kropotkin's critique of Zola's realism makes it apparent that while he refused to see degeneration as a dominant feature of contemporary society, it remained an empirical reality. In his own speech to the Conference, entitled 'The Sterilisation of the Unfit', Kropotkin adopted eugenic terminology while demurring from the conclusions of scientists like Davenport. Praising the Italian economist Achille Loria, who in a previous discussion had challenged the elitism of the sterilisation debate, Kropotkin turned to evolutionary theory, noting that proponents of aggressive measures failed to appreciate 'the influence of surroundings upon the soundness of what is transmitted by heredity'.[75] This echoed an idea that he had developed much earlier, notably in his exposé *In Russian and French Prisons* (1887). Applauding Cesare Lombroso for uncovering that many criminals had 'some defect in the organization of their brains', he conceded that 'we cannot endorse in full' his conclusions. What Lombroso missed was that rather than 'exterminat[ing] all people having defective structure of brain [sic]', we must examine the social conditions that turned these pathologies into propensities to criminality, and through 'fraternal help' encourage 'higher instincts'.[76] Anything else, Kropotkin concluded, attacks the 'race solidarity – the best arm ... in the struggle for life'.[77]

A fundamental challenge to utopian thinking is the objection that the kinds of life sketched in these utopias are a bare improvement on the present. Valuing austerity – both moral and economic – the denizens of these imaginary cities pursue lives devoid of colour, variety, and art. From Kropotkin's perspective, surveying the abandoned farmhouses of utopian experiments littering the prairies of the United States, this history of failure had economic and social origins. Locked in a struggle with an unforgiving environment, and pervaded by a spirit of unforgiving fanaticism, such communities were destined to fail. Kropotkin therefore mounted an attack on communalist endeavours that Berlin and Kołakowski would echo, and offered a counter-vision of communities harnessing their productive capacities to create purposeful labour, a fusion of agricultural and industrial space, and luxury. Familiar *fin-de-siècle* anxieties animated Kropotkin's interventions and provided his intellectual vocabulary. But the journey he plotted out of the current malaise was one defined by the extension of solidarity and the triumph of an ethic of cooperation, rather than the efforts to condemn, control, and coerce preached by some of his distinguished competitors. Popularising these values of mutual aid, he believed, would be far more effective in liberating the poor and oppressed from Britain's dank and miasmic cities.

'Uniformity is death': The incommensurability of values in utopia

The problem with Kropotkin's faith in science, confidence in the power of rational persuasion, and commitment to social rebirth, is that it suggests an inherent inflexibility. This has become a familiar refrain in recent critiques of his politics, but it rests on a more intellectually rich appraisal of the history of European ideas propounded most vividly by Berlin. To his mind, the essential dogmatism at the heart of the utopian project grew from a particular reading of Enlightenment rationality, and was manifest in 'three principles'. First, that all 'genuine questions can be answered', second, that 'all these answers are knowable', and third, that 'all the answers must be compatible with one another'. Such a yearning for a 'unitary pattern' fitting 'the whole of experience, past, present, and future, actual, possible, and unfulfilled' informed a search for the 'one and only' plan of human history.[78]

Beyond countenancing barbarism in pursuit of this essential truth, Berlin argued that hypothesising about a golden age of consensus overlooked the importance of value conflict to healthy societies.[79] As Ruth Kinna notes, given the associations with determinism, scientism, and teleology that dog Kropotkin, it is not difficult to move him into this tradition.[80] The very foundation of his utopia, a Berlinian inquisitor would argue, looks to moral unity, apparent in his belief that the distributive ethic tiding a community over in its revolutionary stages would endure. Those turning to understand Kropotkin's position on 'human nature' have certainly thought so, espying a Panglossian habit of seeing individuals as 'naturally good' that supported his rejection of the state, or, conversely, seeing him recognise the existence of anti-social feelings but thereby undermining this very rejection.[81] The reality is though that Kropotkin, like the liberal opponents of utopianism, recognised the vivifying nature of value conflict. Acknowledging the importance of egotistical impulses, at the heart of his utopian project was a desire to formulate new methods of dealing with such conflicts: fresh approaches to arbitration that would not splinter an anarchist society, stultify dissenting voices, nor allow authoritarianism to re-emerge. Imperfect as they were, this concern demonstrates the importance of value plurality to his utopian society.

Although in awe of Spencer's synthetic achievement, Kropotkin believed that he had erred in letting his political values encroach when turning from exploring cooperation in animal societies to human. Accusing Spencer of possessing 'ready-made ideas, the ideas of middle-class radicalism', Kropotkin has drawn similar complaints, and been faulted for looking at the natural world through the spectacles of his anarchism.[82] As Kołakowski claimed, in *Mutual Aid* Kropotkin argued contra the 'Darwinists' to see 'aid and co-operation' at the centre of life, from which he 'drew the comforting conclusion that… natural inclinations… would ensure the harmony of society'.[83] In fact, Kropotkin's thesis in *Mutual Aid* was subtler than this, a point he made in the introductory note appended to the articles when compiling them as a book. Thinkers 'like... Spencer', he observed, maintained that the 'war of each against all was *the* law of life' a view 'too willingly repeated' since the time of Thomas Hobbes. Proleptically observing that he might be accused of representing nature under 'too favourable an aspect', Kropotkin conceded that this was 'unavoidable' given the crust of misinterpretation that had settled over Darwin's work. He therefore clarified his objective: 'It is a book on the law of Mutual Aid – not on *all* factors of evolution.'[84]

Defining his polemical purpose in this manner, he proceeded to offer a refutation of a series of ideologues that he saw elevating individual struggle to the status of a law.[85] While subtle in his observations of animal societies, he was less so in his reading of the figures indicted. An article by T.H. Huxley, 'The Struggle for Existence and Its Bearing Upon Man', published in *The Nineteenth Century* in 1888 sparked particular ire, with Kropotkin deeming it 'atrocious'.[86] While he took issue with Huxley's vision of nature as a 'gladiators' show', the true thrust of Huxley's argument had been that nature was not a laboratory for theories about human ethics.[87] Aside from Spencer and Huxley, Kropotkin littered his text with the adjectives Hobbesian and Malthusian, seeing such readings of the state of nature as overly 'pessimistic' and presenting only a 'narrow' vision of struggle.[88] Rejecting the omnipresence of conflict, he also thought that the obverse formulation was incorrect. Writing before the birth of modern science Rousseau, like Hobbes, offered an errant picture of nature, this time seeing it 'as nothing... but love, peace and harmony'. Rather missing the point that both Hobbes and Rousseau looked to the state of nature as a means of envisioning a humanity unencumbered by social norms, instead of as an empirical reality, he observed that the briefest perambulation in the forest exposed their crudely 'impartial' interpretations.[89] Kropotkin might have been guilty of some tactical misinterpretation of his own, but his argument was that the reduction of the Darwinian notion of competition to skirmishes between individuals was itself a misreading. Struggle was indeed the locomotive of evolution, he suggested, but this was a war against 'all natural conditions unfavourable to the species', and in this fight those societies that reduced individual competition, ensured their 'higher' development.[90]

As much as Kropotkin's book was a paean for the importance of sociability, behind this argument was a vision of conflict as generative. Shifting his focus from marmots to medieval communalists, he reiterated that the tension between the principle of solidarity and that of individual assertion formed 'the substance of history', but that the latter had been 'analyzed, described, and glorified from time immemorial'. The concentration on mutuality was, he therefore concluded, a legitimate one. At the same time, the periods that Kropotkin deemed 'the greatest . . . in history – the ancient Greek city and medieval city' were not defined by the kind of consensus that Berlin thought so banal, but productively managed internal conflict. Their strength lay in the delicate interplay of communal and individualistic values pulsating within their walls:

> The study of the inner life of the medieval city and . . . Greek cities reveals . . . the combination of mutual aid, as it was practised within the guild and the Greek clan, with a large initiative . . . left to the individual and the group by means of the federative principle.[91]

The complex political structure of the commune nurtured this vitality, combining households organised in small territorial groupings, with multiple professional guilds uniting individual workers. Unified by temporary bonds, and convoked to meet a certain need, he saw these guilds achieving an admirable flexibility that offset the chance of their bureaucratic ossification. This fluidity also granted great latitude for individual 'initiative', he added, with the city giving 'full liberty of expression to the creative genius of each', a fact immortalised in its art. 'The progress realized in all arts', he enthused, 'is the best proof that the system was no hindrance to individual initiative.'[92]

Kropotkin remained confident that rather than anarchist communalism witnessing the dissolution of the individual in the collective, like the medieval city-state, it might allow a communal individuality to flourish. But he also did not imagine that this would be a golden age of Zamyatin's straight lines, in which dispute, contention, and conflict disappeared. Rather, just as the medieval guilds had, Kropotkin believed that the key was to develop non-hierarchical systems of arbitration, while also forestalling antagonisms that might split an anarchist society, in the very fabric of that society's organisation. Chief amongst these was the ephemeral nature of the groups that comprised it, meaning that an individual could disentangle themselves from an association with relative ease, and without damaging their interests. In other words, the lifestyle of the pariah did not await those unwilling to join a group whose functional remit they found unappealing, although there was an obvious practical difficulty with this solution that other anarchists had tried to grapple with before. Bakunin's solution was making 'work . . . the basis of all political rights', and Kropotkin initially followed suit, insisting that the 'parasite' that 'shirks work' must not 'receive money' or a portion of the finished labour.[93] His journey from populism to communism meant that Kropotkin left his belief in money behind, and similarly led him to abandon this coercive language.

In *The Conquest of Bread,* he pondered the issue of recalcitrance in more depth. Responding to the rhetorical objection that without 'a bait of lucre' people would be unwilling to work, he pointed to the recent promulgation of this argument: once by American 'anti-abolitionists', and a second time by the Russian nobility before the liberation of the serfs. The 'eagerness' with which the freshly liberated went about their work, 'proportionate to the completeness' of their liberation, revealed that the whip and knout were not perquisites to toil. Looking to an anarchist society marked by the beautification of labour and the reduction of its burdens through machinery, Kropotkin foresaw an even more vigorous enthusiasm for work. Laziness was also essentially a myth, he proposed, frequently a product of misplaced energies; like the idle schoolchild subjected to 'Greek or Latin' who 'would work admirably were he taught science'. But what if there remained individuals reluctant to participate? Modifying the tone of his earlier argument, Kropotkin placed the refractory individual in a denser patchwork of 'producing groups'. He imagined a commune, defined by a number of productive enterprises, allowing this individual free use of their products on the proviso 'you consecrate four or five hours a day to some work recognized as necessary'. If they still refused, the community had a number of options, which Kropotkin deliberated in an imaginary conversation. One, deeply idealistic solution, was that if the community had sufficient resources, 'we shall be delighted to give' the 'necessaries of life' freely; another was that the individual was at liberty to 'go look' for preferable conditions 'elsewhere'; a third that they were welcome to 'seek adherents and organize with them on novel principles'.[94] Such reasoning may give rise to the objection that Kropotkin paints a troublingly benign picture of a future community responding to antisocial acts. Yet, despite his sense that the iron bonds of shared conviction would unite such a society, it is apparent that he did not see friction and dissent disappearing.

The fluid boundaries of the guilds of the city-states served as an historical example which anarchists could develop, but Kropotkin pointed to other ways in which they managed conflict. He noted, for instance, that upon entry into a guild, each 'brother' swore an oath that any future quarrels must not 'degenerate into a feud', without agreeing to the impractical 'obligation of never quarrelling again'. Moreover, any member involved in an external feud, was guaranteed the support of his fellows, with the intention of 'bringing things to a peaceful end'. If called before a court, Kropotkin maintained that support would continue, and even if the individual were found guilty, they would 'not let him go to ruin'. The only exceptions to this being if that individual was guilty of 'secret aggression', or if 'a brother' had broken 'the faith towards guild-brethren'.[95] His reading is no doubt naïve, something Dante would attest. Encountering a relative in Hell, in his epic poem *Divine Comedy,* the man scuttles away from Dante, angry at the failure to avenge his death – '(Which is disgraceful to our Family)' – suggesting that this is a dubious model to approximate.[96] For Kropotkin though, its power was not as a system to copy, but as an example to illustrate the possibilities of difference. Its key difference, he added, was that it bypassed the codified laws he saw as characteristic of Roman inflexibility. Instead, the city-states adopted an especially 'just' principle, where 'the whole community took responsibility for the misdeeds committed by its members'.[97]

Judging that this notion of communal responsibility had valuable anti-authoritarian implications, Kropotkin returned to it in an explicitly normative context. Ruminating on the question 'are prisons necessary?' in *In Russian and French Prisons,* he responded negatively, suggesting that 'fraternal treatment' was the best answer to antisocial behaviour. 'If we have our share in the achievements of the geniuses of our century', he admitted, 'we have our part of shame in the deeds of our assassins.' Revolution and rebirth would not be a panacea, even though it would address the economic inequality behind most crime. Rather than prisons, he invoked the treatment of 'lunatics' as an example for wider emulation. The physiologist Philippe Pinel found a novel treatment for those regarded as 'possessed by the devil' in the late eighteenth century, breaking the chains binding them to asylum walls. His solution, Kropotkin concluded, was simple: 'liberty'.[98] Beyond helping the afflicted, he thought that Pinel's humanistic approach pointed to a fresh, social, treatment of criminal and antisocial actions, a method that could be enhanced by the broad inculcation of fraternal values 'from the earliest childhood'. Imbibing such principles in their salad days, Kropotkin wrote that the individual brought up 'to feel himself *one* with... humanity' would instinctually act in a socially conscious way. When, for instance, confronted by a drowning child, such an individual would not dither on the riverbank as they contemplate Bentham's felicific calculus, but jump in 'by instinct'.[99] Similarly, a society purged of the 'unbridled individualism' of capitalism would discover a newfound neighbourliness, with every communalist gaining the 'courage to say aloud in anyone's presence what we think of such [antisocial] acts'. Often, vocalising criticism would be unnecessary, for 'the look' was fortified with the power to condemn 'cowardice, deceit, intrigue'.[100]

Kropotkin pointed to a number of ways in which a communal society might address disruptive actions without, theoretically, mirroring the coercive practices adopted by the state, ranging from the fluidity of temporary association, to the powers of fraternity gleaned from Pinel's example. As much as this shows that Kropotkin was conscious of the criticism, later popularised by liberal anti-utopians, that utopists lacked an accurate conception of human diversity, and indeed the importance of value conflict, serious objections remain. The appeal to Pinel and the tradition of medical thought suggests that Kropotkin essentially conceived of antisocial behaviour as pathological, and that this pathology would be more-or-less cured as a renewed society attacked the foundations of inequality and injustice. While he did more than most to unflinchingly examine these potential issues, Kropotkin's optimistic deferment of the problem until after the moment of social catharsis leaves the issue under-theorised. In turn, suggesting that moral censure and social treatment were preferable solutions to the existing legal structures is also questionable. Tocqueville and Mill both foresaw this problem, but Michel Foucault, revelling in the paradox, argued that Pinel and his English counterpart Samuel Tuke, were disingenuous when urging the curative power of 'air and liberty':

> In fact Tuke created an asylum where he substituted for the free terror of madness the stifling anguish of responsibility... In one and the same movement, the asylum becomes, in Pinel's hands, an instrument of moral uniformity and of social denunciation.[101]

The shackles restraining the prisoners may have been broken, but in recasting the metal into the bonds of social conformity, an arguably greater tyranny was unleashed. Yet, to censure Kropotkin for failing to appreciate the incommensurability of certain values is patently incorrect. He may have elided some of the complexities that this commitment entailed, but in writing that '*variety, conflict even, is life, and... uniformity is death*', he was clearly tapping into a notion of plurality that some anti-utopian thinkers deemed the sole attribute of liberal societies.[102] Read, at any rate, thought so. Reflecting on the ideal society several generations later, as the Battle of Britain played out in the skies above him, making the possibility of an anarchist community seem at best a distant dream, he concluded that, 'I have nothing to add to what has been said by Kropotkin.'[103]

The Republic of Roncador: Read's early utopianism

Yet, Read did have something to add, and in an unexpected place. Escaping Edinburgh in early 1933 after the scandal of his affair, Read found solace, indeed, 'the happiest period of my life' he noted later, in a 'nest of gentle artists' perched on the edge of Hampstead. In penurious circumstances, the diaspora of Yorkshire artists nesting in this area of London came to his aid. Henry Moore lent Read his studio for a brief period, and with Ben Nicholson and his wife Barbara Hepworth in close proximity, as well as the artist Cecil Stephenson, the feeling that Leeds' artistic avant-grade had decamped to leafy Hampstead made this an especially attractive environ. Soon Read acquired his own studio near the others, and there, ensconced in a wooden hut that he built himself, he sat down to write.[104]

The product of his labours that summer was a peculiar novella, entitled *The Green Child* (1935), marking Read's sole published excursion into literary fiction. Appearing the year before the Spanish Civil War decided his political attachments, the book nevertheless examined a number of utopian themes, and juggled a range of political ideas that Read found wanting. Despite enthusiasm for the imaginative power of the work, initial interpretations were generally bewildered. 'There are odd novels, and then there are very odd novels', wrote one reviewer, rediscovering the work in that symbolic year 1984, 'Sir Herbert Read's *The Green Child* is one of the very odd ones.'[105] A contemporary observed that while his 'ideal... is an agreeable and well-sustained invention', it lacked a 'moral' that would have made it complete.[106] Subsequent history has not been kind to his book, and those spotting a moral missed by this reviewer, have seen a contradiction between the world explored in *The Green Child* and Read's developing politics. A.L. Morton, for instance, who was perhaps instinctually sceptical of Read's politics given his Marxist attachments, discerned a longing 'for order and beauty' in the text and a fundamental pessimism that held 'little hope for the future'.[107] Following suit, David Goodway sees *The Green Child* offering a vision akin to the 'bloodless, cerebral' politics of George Bernard Shaw, while others discern ambiguity over which of the 'book's societies is utopian, [and] which is dystopian'.[108] With the work apparently casting weak light on Read's politics, exegeses have tended to concentrate on the book's status and worth as a literary creation, limiting its relevance to his political thinking.[109] In spite of the confusion and scepticism, the origins of *The Green Child* in a period in which Read's political inchoateness gave way to firm conviction, makes the novel all the more significant. Indeed, the central feature of the book, missed by so many commentators, was its ironic skewering of the kind of 'blueprint' utopianism condemned by Berlin and Popper, a position inspired by his reading of anarchism, and ideas that seemed to have a brighter future the year after the book's publication.

The triptych structure of *The Green Child* begins by following Oliver, or 'Olivero', a South American dictator, as he fakes his own assassination in order to return to the English village of his birth. This idea of homecoming, as his friend Graham Greene pointed out in a complimentary introduction to the book, was a prominent autobiographical theme in Read's life. Not, admittedly, flight from the life of an autocrat, but a desire to escape the frenetic pace of London's literary scene that eventually drove him north to the scenes of his childhood.[110] Oliver similarly returns home to the village that nurtured him, but here events take a phantasmagorical turn. Encountering a stream running backwards, he follows the course of the water to a mill, through the window of which he spies the miller, Kneeshaw, forcing a green child (Sally), who is bound to chair, to drink lambs' blood. For all its peculiarity, Read based this aspect of his tale on, nominally at least, recorded history. The twelfth-century historian William of Newburgh, a fellow Yorkshireman, presented in his post-Anarchy *History of English Affairs* (1196) the story of the Green Children of Woolpit, East Anglia. The tale told of 'a boy and a girl, completely green in their persons, and clad in garments of a strange colour, and unknown materials' emerging from a freshly harvested field. In Newburgh's version, the two children gradually assimilated. Having 'learnt our language', they changed colour, eventually receiving the 'sacrament of baptism' after which the boy dies prematurely, while the girl survives and marries into the community.[111] Read was evidently taken by this evocative story of cultural assimilation, having mentioned in *English Prose Style* that it was the 'norm to which all types of Fantasy should conform'.[112] In his rendering though, the green child experiences a different fate.

Helping Sally to escape, they both trace the course of the mysterious river into the heart of the moor above the village. Realising that the waterway does not flow into the sea, but reaches its terminus inland, they paddle in the limpid pool at their journey's end, and the green child begins to slip through the silt in its depths. Oliver rushes to her aid and they both sink 'below the surface of the pool'. Thus ends the first section of the book, with the second recounting the comparatively parochial journey Olivero took to South America, and his promotion to the head of a military junta. In contrast to the fantastical events of the first portion of the novella, Read emphasises a stark change of tone by spending several pages outlining the constitution of the fictional Republic of Roncador. The document, written by an Olivero fortified by 'yerba tea' and with 'frequent recourse to Rousseau and Volney' drew on Plato too, and caps a regime that is essentially a Josephinian-enlightened despotism, in which modest social reform guided from the centre countervails military strength.[113] Cultivating a 'Golden Age' devoid of 'conflict, of contending interests', he fears that 'moral flaccidity, a fatness of living' burdens the Roncadorians. Convinced that 'escape' is the only means of redemption, he plots his fake assassination.[114]

The final section begins where the first ended, in detail and style. Encased in an air bubble, it transports Oliver and Sally to the depths of the pool, and eventually to the green child's home. Passing through a series of caves, they return to the community she left thirty years before. Here they stay, in a world structured around a series of 'ledges': the first characterised by the 'pleasures of youth'; the second, 'the pleasures of manual work'; the third, 'the pleasures of opinion and argument'; and finally, 'the highest pleasure' that of 'solitary thought'. Oliver transcends these steps quickly, moving from bodily gratification to intellectual sophistication, accepting the maxim:

> The only sensual perception which is true is that which shows us in everything an unchanging Order; other perceptions ... of the manifold variety of things ... tends to create a sense of Disorder, and are the cause of error.

Questions of absolute beauty begin to crowd his mind, and he yearns for solitude. Surmounting the final ledge, he calmly prepares for death, surmising that the 'harmony of the universe' is like the 'harmony of the crystal' – 'obeying ... immutable laws and proportions'.[115]

That *The Green Child* would not be a source of edification for anarchists is obvious. While Kropotkin's utopia portrayed a vibrant society in which an integrated agro-industrial economy and localised political forms encouraged cooperation, but also managed a generative conflict, Read's imagined worlds explored the obverse of this openness. The Republic of Roncador, aside from the fact that its power emanated from military force, achieved political stability but through a desiccated constitutionalism that sapped the vitality of its inhabitants. And neither is the world beneath the water an anarchist utopia. In contrast to the witless and listless Roncadorians, its inhabitants enjoy the fruits of intellectual speculation, yet it is also a hierarchical world, and the path to liberation is secured through a turning away, and turning inward. What Read's critics tend to overlook, however, is the extent to which his book was a comment on the utopian tradition, rather than an image of the kind of society desired. Later, this was precisely how he framed his book, placing *The Green Child* in the context of Popper's anti-utopian *The Open Society and Its Enemies*, which 'set the terms of the debate' after it appeared in 1945, by yoking together utopianism and totalitarianism.[116] Rooting his book in this argument, Read wrote that the purpose of his intervention had been to demonstrate 'symbolically' that 'the realization of a rational blue-print leads to the death of society'. He nevertheless diverged from Popper, insisting that the 'utopian mentality' remained vital and was, in Anatole France's words, 'the principle of all progress'. The egregious obstacle to this 'progress', however, was the co-option of the utopian method by those beholden to the 'rational framework'. With Kropotkin's utopia of flexibility in mind, Read noted that the 'most terrible utopias are the scientific utopias of the marxian socialist and ... monopoly capitalist', who with 'their rational instruments ... advance on the spontaneous sources of life itself'.[117]

Read's rejection of the scientific utopia echoed his scepticism regarding the purity of scientific knowledge, but it also reflected his distaste for the kind of technocratic utopianism championed by a figure like H.G. Wells. Wells rejected the scientific aspirations of sociology, especially that of those 'pseudo-scientific interlopers' Comte and Spencer, but his suggestion that the 'proper and distinctive method of sociology' was the 'creation of Utopias' would have had a sinister ring in Read's ears, particularly in an age where the power of the state came in the form of technical experts armed with clipboards and propelling pencils.[118] Indeed, this desire to couch his work in the language of science he thought was Wells' main error. Coming close to 'the sense of pure Fantasy' in his best writing, Read diagnosed a tendency to err, 'imparting to his fantasies a pseudo-scientific logicality'.[119] Mainly though, Read was unimpressed with his oeuvre. *The New Machiavelli* (1911) was 'the best novel Wells has written', he declared privately, before sarcastically qualifying that 'that isn't saying much', and concluding that 'the man is damned artistically ... his style ... is positively rotten'.[120]

Although Read was temperamentally predisposed to be uninspired by the scientific aura pervading Wells' works, his political nomadism and tendency to vent decidedly authoritarian visions would also not have appealed. While damning *The New Machiavelli* with faint praise, Read noted that Sidney and Beatrice Webb were obvious subjects of the book's satirical needling. Having joined the Fabian Society in 1903, Wells' relationship with the group was not plain sailing, remaining a member for just four years, with one historian suggesting that 'he and the Society reacted to each other like a ship' with a 'cannon loose upon its deck in a high sea'.[121] The development of Wells' politics in the late 1920s suggests that Wells might indeed be the proverbial loose cannon. Addressing an audience at the Sorbonne in 1928, Wells noted, in a refrain that Read would have accepted, that modern democracy was failing to 'produce inventive and original', 'resolute', or 'far-thinking' governments. With this in mind, he urged his listeners to look to 'the Communist Party and Fascism' – notwithstanding his 'strong dislike for many aspects of Fascism' – as models approximating 'a World State ruled by a self-devoted organisation of volunteers'. Read owned a copy of this address, but four years later Wells brought this message closer to home, calling for the peculiar political synthesis of 'Liberal Fascism' at the Young Liberals Summer School in Oxford.[122]

Placing too great a stress on Wells' incautious attempts to remain politically current in this period would give the wrong impression. He was neither a fascist nor a communist, but as Wells himself noted in his Sorbonne speech, what fascism had apparently shown was the validity of ideas he had examined 'more than twenty years ago'.[123] Wells was thinking of *Anticipations* (1901) and *A Modern Utopia* (1905), works published before fascism became a frame of reference, but both emphasising the value of political elitism. In *Anticipations*, rather than withering away the state, he raised it to omnipotence, also investing it with the eugenic ambition of monitoring 'philoprogenitiveness' and preventing its citizens from 'propagating weakness'.[124] *A Modern Utopia* softened some of these edges, but explored his concept of the 'World State' and 'the samurai' that shaped it, a clique of administrators encompassing 'all our head teachers ... our judges, barristers, employers of labour ... medical men, [and] legislators'.[125] In his autobiography, published in 1934, Wells observed that this book had had a far-reaching impact, and affirmed his belief in the 'basal notion of the Samurai', a group he thought the Fabian Society could become, and a model emboldened by his observation of 'successful organizations [such] as the Communist Party and the Italian Fascists'.[126] Wells was a prominent public figure, and as much as these ideas would have entered Read's orbit, the trenchant critique of them would have encroached too. J.D. Bernal, for instance, observed that appeals to scientific expertise in the management of society had an ancient lineage, but were hampered by the fact that most scientists were 'manifestly . . . unfitted to exercise control'. With Wells' hope for an intellectual elite emerging through democracy checked, Bernal expressed concern that 'Fascist solutions' might begin to appeal.[127] Shortly before this, the Russian intellectual D.S. Mirsky, who pursued the unusual path of White Army officer to London-based Bolshevik convert, to victim of the Gulags, concluded more assuredly that Wells 'is drawing nearer and nearer to fascism'.[128]

Read was unsurprisingly hostile to Wells' emphasis on technocracy and his concept of a world state, and he made this clear when Wells contacted him in 1943. Discussing a series of letters that Wells had contributed to *The Times* regarding the Allies' war aims, which later went through several editions as a pamphlet, Read reacted warmly to the endeavour but suggested a series of Kropotkinian clauses.[129] Wells' efforts were no doubt motivated by the fact that the Nazis were busy attempting to actualise a world state of their own, but Read urged him to remain steadfast in abandoning this principle. 'You have removed my particular bogey', he wrote, 'the suggestion of a world state with all the obsolete machinery of government . . . [but] . . . why perpetuate the idea of money?' He also suggested that 'some sort of guild organization of industry' was important, and in turn proposed the insertion of a new article, '4. Right to Membership of a Community' defined as 'an association of like-minded people for mutual aid'. Closing his letter, he turned to his recently published *Education Through Art* and, promising Wells a copy, stressed a general point dividing the two writers. His chief aim, he wrote, was to show the 'uniqueness and the fluidity of the personality which I want to preserve at all costs, and it can only be done . . . by a process of education which is fundamentally aesthetic rather than logical'.[130]

Viewed against the backdrop of Read's engagement with Popper's anti-utopianism, and his resistance to Wells' scientific utopias, his project in *The Green Child* comes into clearer focus. For a thinker who would later comment that 'all biological, social and individual progress depends on resistance to conformity, fixation and centralization', it is apparent that the Republic of Roncador was not a model to emulate, but a way of satirising coolly logical political thinking.[131] Olivero's intricately designed constitution is hollow when juxtaposed with the regime that he heads, in which he revels in the improvements he makes to his soldiers' uniforms, and parades in public like a supercilious Napoleon atop a 'white horse' receiving 'the full ceremonial salute'.[132] Read's reflection on the torpor that encourages Olivero's escape is a resonant echo of Kropotkin's critique of communal asceticism, and foreshadowed Berlin's influential paean on the value of value conflict. With 'immoral and anti-social tendencies' purged, the Republic loses its dynamism, and the 'mirthful and contented' inhabitants trudge on into a 'spiritual lassitude'.[133] Unlike Wells, who observed that his utopias were less 'expectations for mankind as my desires', Read's book was not, in this sense, a utopia.[134]

The ethereal final section of *The Green Child*, source of the greatest confusion, was also a critical comment on the kinds of utopian thinking that accentuated the fixity both Kropotkin and Read abhorred. His cave-dwelling green people, enjoying their spiritualized lives beneath the water, stand in contrast to Wells' cultureless and cannibalistic Morlocks, as well as the happy but soporific inhabitants of Roncador. Their aesthetically rich existence intoxicates Oliver, who spends his time on the labour of 'the highest type of workman', polishing crystals, encouraging a sensuality, contemplation, and philosophical speculation absent in his previous life as a despot. Indeed, Read's description of this labour mirrored his own burgeoning aesthetic sensibility, especially his notion that art represented a search for truth. Polishing these crystals, Oliver notes, 'might be regarded as a science itself, for on it were based, not only all notions of the structure of the universe, but equally all notions of beauty, truth and destiny'. Oliver then stumbles upon the kind of dialectical relationship that Read saw in the relation between the artist and nature. With 'no law but his own instinct to guide him beyond the limits of natural forms', he experiments, discovering forms 'whose perfection was other than the perfection of nature'.[135]

Mastery of this enterprise allows Oliver's progression to a state of self-consciousness and, with his death, the attainment of a kind of *nirvana* in which he comprehends the laws of harmony. Yet, as much as he gains this knowledge, Read pressed the point that these laws are relative. The cave-dwellers, 'not knowing fire, not being subject to inclement seasons, not afflicted with thunder', lack a perception of 'Disorder', and laugh at Oliver when he initially posits that 'Order and Disorder might be taken as polar opposites that together constituted a single harmonious whole'.[136] This metaphysical dualism is closer to Read's own position – seen, for instance, in his proposition that the aesthetic faculty is innate, but also shaped by context – and is at odds with the fixed conceptions of the green people. Their world of rock, crystals, and perennial twilight gives rise to a philosophy of stasis, offering a partial explanation of the world and its natural laws, but one patently at odds with the logic of organic life.[137] This was not a utopia, but a critique of dogmatic philosophy and an inflexible utopianism that could never encompass the variety of human experience. As the Republic of Roncador failed to create a perfect world in pursuit of a blueprint, so too, on a philosophical level, the intellectually hubristic green people did not offer a coherent vision of life, contemplating a motionless universe with death at its apex. This attack on the static conception of life and the draughts and diagrams of social engineers was the point of *The Green Child*. As Read commented to Edward Dahlberg in 1949, 'there is a certain sense in which form kills life, and my "Green Child" was written to demonstrate that fact'.[138]

A Civilization from Under: Read's aesthetic utopia

Read's initial contribution to utopianism may have taken a self-consciously fantastical form, but beyond the rich suggestiveness of *The Green Child*, his blend of artistic and social criticism produced more detailed speculation on the possible shape of the future. Politely declining the offer in 1946 to join an experimental community in Paraguay, where the members engaged in 'land work, ranching, gardening', Read noted that while he fully supported their efforts 'in heart' and 'mind', 'now I am 55', a new life in the saddle was not realistic.[139] Such projects in building intentional communities may not have appealed, but while Read modestly asserted that he had little to add to Kropotkin's utopian vision, his rich aesthetic sensibility led him to theorise an anarchist society textured by artistic values, raising ideas latent in works like *The Conquest of Bread* to the status of a revolutionary objective. As much as Kropotkin pre-empted many aspects of the anti-utopian temper that grew in tandem with the rise of totalitarianism, Read, who fully devoted his attention to the idea of utopianism in the late 1940s, was writing at the zenith of this reaction. This context is important in understanding Read's defence of the utopian impulse, a project he frequently approached by tackling the work of Popper, in particular, head on. While insisting on the continued utility of the imperilled utopian method, and making his own contribution to the anarchist utopian tradition, Read's interventions bore the imprint of Kropotkin's fusion of industrial and agricultural spaces. This blend of the rational and romantic, as Orwell pointed out, marked a tension in Read's thought between the productive techniques of modern industry, and the image of the thoughtful artisan central to his utopianism. Read was steadfast, insisting *à la* Kropotkin on the appropriateness of local control in the context of a modern society, and adding that this was the key to a sublime existence.

Read agreed with the spirit of Popper's rebuttal of utopian thinking, but rejected what he termed its fundamental 'despair'. The danger, he continued, was that Popperian 'nihilism' could induce acquiescence:

> Dismissing any hope of a perfect society ... he casts his eyes to the ground and contemplates ... the piecemeal methods of the mole. He makes his little burrow, throws up a little hill to show that there is 'work in progress.' But the wide acres that stretch all around ... are in danger of being destroyed by approaching storms of which he is unaware.

Against such pessimism Read urged the value of remaining an 'idealist', even if the 'ideal society is a point on a receding horizon' that can never be reached, a myth that guards against retiring from the struggle.[140] Observing that such dreaming underpinned all the advances in political philosophy, Read still followed Popper in seeing an authoritarian thread running through many utopian visions. 'Totalitarianism is nothing but the imposition of a rational framework on the organic freedom of life', he wrote, echoing the thrust of *The Green Child*, 'and is more characteristic of the scientific ... than poetic mind.'[141]

Read's distinction between the scientific and poetic mind was a broadside at Marxism, and Popper's two-volume opus *The Open Society and Its Enemies* added a weight of intellectual authority to this critique. Nevertheless, these ideas were current both within the historical anarchist tradition, seen in Kropotkin's scepticism at the scientific claims of contemporary Marxisms, and prominent in Read's immediate intellectual context. As Marie-Louise Berneri noted in her posthumously published *Journey through Utopia* (1950), which offered a survey of utopian ideas from Plato to Huxley, there was a dualism at the heart of utopianism. On the one hand, she observed, there was the pursuit of 'happiness ... through material well-being, the sinking of man's individuality into the group, and the greatness of the State'. On the other, a perception of 'happiness' as 'the result of the free expression of man's personality ... [that] ... must not be sacrificed to an arbitrary moral code or to the ... State'.[142] Reviewing Berneri's book in *Freedom*, Read noted that its object paralleled Kropotkin's in *Mutual Aid* and *Ethics*, namely a step towards 'the sociology of knowledge' rather than simple 'anarchist propaganda'. But he too was struck by the paradox of the utopian mentality, noting that while utopianism was in the vanguard of the movement for 'freedom of thought', there was a baneful 'tendency towards authoritarianism' in much utopian speculation. There is 'in the human mind an itch for tidiness', Read judged, that is crucial in laying the foundations of modern science, but problematic when utopists overlook that 'life itself is not tidy'.[143] Drawing on Popper, Read accused Marxism of perpetuating this crime, arguing that Marx had been 'under the spell of Plato'. Popper had demolished 'Marx's method', he continued, suggesting that authors of 'laws' of historical development always resort to the 'sanction' of 'force' and 'the power of the State' to 'enforce their "law" '.[144]

Yet Popper's dissection of the order-obsessed utopian mind only told part of the story, and Read insisted that utopianism remained a fruitful way to 'take possession of new forms of life, new fields of consciousness'.[145] From his perspective, high aesthetic standards must define these new forms of life, but merely improving design was insufficient. Instead, an appetite for art 'must exist as a normal state of health', something wholly absent in 'the chaos of ugliness which the industrial age has created'. Competing ideologies – 'communism, fascism or capitalism' – postured as the map to this cultural rebirth, but Read was unpersuaded, pointing to the 1937 *Exposition Internationale des Arts et Techniques dans la Vie Moderne* in Paris as evidence.[146] Although one American newspaper noted that the extravaganza promised a 'gay Parisian summer', the main objects of attention were the German and Soviet pavilions. Erected facing each other, the rich 'symbolism of their juxtaposition... [and]... the defiance of one to the other' was not lost on spectators. Albert Speer's 'heavy and solid' swastika-bedecked building squared up to the Soviet construction, the *Washington Post* noted, the latter adorned with 'superb sculptured figures of a man and a woman, defying the world together, advancing' their 'raised hands holding the scythe' pointing 'towards the conquest of a distant... future'. 'It is', the enraptured critic noted, 'by far the best piece of sculpture in the Paris Exposition'.[147] Read disagreed. 'The exhibits of Russia and Germany were among the worst to be seen', he observed, but conceded that those of 'the other totalitarian state, Italy, were surprisingly good'.[148]

Despite its striking achievements in paving a road to modernisation, for Read the USSR was a clear example of how not to create a new world. As much as he objected that the 'prevailing industrial system' of the Western world cultivated 'decadent qualities', while simultaneously curtailing the leisure time necessary to develop a discriminating aesthetic sensibility, he nevertheless insisted that he was not a romantic reactionary. Modern industry was, after all, perfectly capable of creating objects 'with aesthetic qualities' like 'aeroplanes and motor-cars'. Writing as the Soviet army began to reverse its catastrophic defeats in the

East, *The Politics of the Unpolitical* (1943) observed that in spite of the regime's 'magnificent efficiency', Read's belief that culture 'must come from under' as the 'spontaneous expression' of 'joy in life, of... joy in work' meant that the USSR was a poor model. With its inhabitants suffering the indignities of war, hunger, and oppression, it was hardly a crucible for artistic rebirth, and its state patronage was similarly self-defeating. Individual artists may prosper under tyranny, as rulers 'weave a cloak of culture to hide their misdeeds', but the 'judgement of history is absolute' and aesthetic standards remain the ultimate test.[149]

Read's vision of the USSR – in later Cold War parlance a 'realized utopia' – drew on his reading of the history of utopianism, and his corresponding perception of Marxist determinism.[150] At the same time, it also presented the opportunity to offer an anarchist counter-vision, and Read stressed two factors that were crucial to the development of a vibrant culture: an economic system guaranteeing 'security to a class, and preferably... the whole people', and 'spiritual liberty' defined as freedom of expression. Neither condition was sufficient in isolation, for economic stability did not ensure 'spiritual energy', and this factor itself grew from 'social integration... from mutual aid and from unity of aspiration'. Making this claim in the same year that he published *Education Through Art*, Read insisted that this change must occur free from state tutelage, and should not mimic the tactics of previous revolutions. Pointing to the family, the school, the workshop, the parish, and the borough, he claimed that these units must lead this revolt, always avoiding the imposition of cultural values, in favour of encouraging 'a public standard of taste (decent design) comparable to the public standard of behaviour (decent conduct)'. There is a 'final correspondence between what is efficient and what is beautiful and what is true', he concluded, a fact that our current industrial society failed to appreciate.[151]

Vague as it was, Read's image of the ideal society drew explicitly on his Kropotkinian conceptual vocabulary. Rejecting the idea that it was possible to impose a vigorous culture from above, he looked to local initiative, and to a multiplicity of organisational bodies as the soil from which a sophisticated aesthetic sensibility might grow. On a deeper level, like Kropotkin, Read's thought was animated by a desire to blend decidedly romantic and modern precepts. He may have been a doyen of modern art and a theorist of industrial design, but Read insisted that he was also 'by birth and tradition a peasant'.[152] While excoriating the banality of mass society, his solution was not a return to agricultural toil, but following Kropotkin, a humanisation of machinery as a precondition for social renewal. Indeed, Read embellished this Kropotkinian theme, suggesting that the beautification of industrial production was logical, and denying that standardisation necessarily mutilated aesthetic appeal: 'machine products are exact replicas... if one is beautiful, the rest are beautiful'.[153]

Stressing the compatibility of anarchism and British modernity was an important, if often weakly theorised, feature of Read's political thought. For while he lambasted the 'deserts of cinders and smoke' and 'rivers of filth' flowing through Britain's cities, he was keen to show that anarchism would not entail a Morrisian 'reversion to handicraft and outdoor sanitation'.[154] Yet Read's parallel assertion, that effectiveness was 'in inverse ratio to... size', and his corresponding commitment to small-scale units, drew the natural objection that this was paradoxical. As Orwell commented when assessing Read's politics, anarchism 'rules out the kind of air-conditioned, chromium-plated, gadget-ridden existence which is now... desirable'. The construction of technologically sophisticated items, he continued, demanded a 'planned, centralized society with all the repressive apparatus that implies'. Moreover, while Read saw the aeroplane as a potential object of aesthetic value, Orwell denied the link between mechanical reproduction and beauty. A 'beautiful' poem 'read aloud five thousand times... would seem the most hideous collection of words that has ever existed'.

Orwell's objection that Read did not offer a convincing argument for anarchism staving off technological stagnation is not without merit. Responding, Read conceded much of his critique, but protested that Orwell had missed a vital feature of mechanical reproduction, in that 'I want to see a million copies of "Animal Farm" diffused by the most efficient... means... but I don't want... to consume a million copies.'[155] He chose not to prolong the dispute, but like Kropotkin, a central pillar of Read's thinking was that the attributes of planning and modern scientific knowledge were not the sole property of Washington or Moscow. Turning to the problem of Britain's agricultural weakness, Read drew on *Fields, Factories and Workshops* to challenge George Bernard Shaw's suggestion in *The Times* in 1940 that Stalinist collectivisation was worth emulating.[156] Raising the point that Shaw showed little regard for the 'cost' of Stalin's project, Read pursued the curious argument that, in fact, collectivisation was the child of Kropotkinian rather than Leninist logic. 'The orthodox Marxist scheme was a tragic failure', he considered, and so 'State farming was abandoned' in favour of 'co-operative or collective farming'. Despite the errant reading of the situation in Russia, Read's argument was that decentralisation of both farming and industry presented the opportunity for the socialisation of technology and science.

Just as the 'dust-bowls' on the American plains suggested that heavy industry was not a model for sustainable agriculture, neither was the abolition of the tractor preached by a 'mystic like' Jean Giono. 'What we want is a common-sense use of the power and products of modern science', Read concluded, 'remembering that these should be used for the benefit of mankind.'[157]

To Read's mind, the principles of quality design and the comforts of modern life were compatible with local control. Even if, however, his interpretation of these comforts was out of step with the changing priorities of Britain's burgeoning consumer culture. Late in life he tended towards a bucolic rejection of the encroachments of modern civilisation, turning against 'weed-killers, motor cars, tractors... urbanization (words as ugly as the things they signify)' and looking to rustic solitude where 'poetry and intelligence... arose as naturally as poppies and cornflowers'.[158] In the 1940s and 1950s, however, Read endeavoured to stay up to date, highlighting the Kropotkinian significance of contemporary developments. Visiting George Woodcock in Cambridge in the late 1940s, for instance, Read spent most of the time discussing the supermarkets that he had seen during a recent trip to the United States. Stripped of their cashiers, he proffered these as a 'model for free anarchist communist distribution', replacing Kropotkin's antiquated storehouses.[159] In the late 1950s, he also seized the opportunity to visit China, then in the midst of its Great Leap Forward. Perhaps strangely, Read found the trip invigorating, seeing in the country's agricultural communes 'my idea of anarchism come into being, in every detail & practice', with these institutions exercising autonomy and showing remarkable productive capacity. These 'new industrial cities' he believed mirrored the 'decentralization of industry advocated... in *Fields, Factories and Workshops*', but reaching the industrial heart of Wuhan he found the scene less appealing. 'There can be no doubt by the end of this century China will be the most powerful nation in the world', he wrote, but at what price? 'The destruction of natural beauty, congested roadways & death on the roads, lethal fumes, lung cancer & juvenile delinquency', he answered. This was the Janus-faced nature of modern China, he felt. While the communes looked to a new way of life, industrial China moved towards repeating 'the mistakes of the capitalist world'.[160]

One anarchist captured his feelings about Read's comments on China in the subtitle of an essay: 'Commentary on an eyewitness who did not see'.[161] Yet, as much as Read appeared oblivious to the fact that the formation of the communes he visited was the product of authoritarian dragooning rather than spontaneous cohesion, his divided feelings over China's future path encapsulated the complexities of his view of the relationship between modernity and meaningful liberty. Following Kropotkin, he looked to an expansive communalism that remained in touch with the soil, but was also rooted in modern science and production. Read did not add much to these broad Kropotkinian contours, but his innovation was seeing this system as the crucible of cultural rebirth. And like Kropotkin's vision of socialised machinery – sensitively imbedded in local communities and with its capacities turned to meeting real social needs – Read saw this as fully compatible with aesthetic value. Such an image of communalised production stood in stark contrast to the youthful observations of Leeds and Halifax that excited his political thinking in the first place, but it also grew from a concern over the disrepute into which the utopian method had fallen in contemporary radical philosophy. As Popper pricked utopian hubris, and the USSR and Nazi Germany discredited the utopian tradition by building their own cathedrals in awe of a coming order, Read remained convinced of the value of an anarchist utopia.

A Community of Individuals: Stirner, Jung, and Kropotkin

Kropotkin stressed that anarchist communalism would not demand the dissolution of individuality in the sea of social conformity, but rather that such a society would provide the base for freethinking actors to emerge. A component of this idea was that those political traditions nominally privileging individuality – principally Spencer's radical liberalism, and the anarchist individualism of Max Stirner and Benjamin Tucker – ultimately undermined this goal in preaching the vitalising qualities of individual competitiveness. If anything, Read's enthusiasm for Stirner, and the trajectory of his art criticism, which tended to eulogise the contributions of gifted individuals, suggests a significant departure from Kropotkinian communism. Indeed, for one art historian, Read's thought demonstrated that he was 'essentially a kind of individualist-anarchist rather than a communist-anarchist'.[162] In fact, as much he roved widely in diverse philosophical fields, Read's appropriation of Stirner, and Carl Jung who would become a major influence on his thought, was always refracted through the lens of Kropotkin's attempt to introduce parity to individualism and communism.[163] Drawing on a richer stock of concepts, and looking to the necessarily fraught relationship between the community and the artist as an example, Read aimed to embroider Kropotkin's communalist tapestry with a more vibrant thread of individuality.

Writing that he had read Stirner in his youth and, 'to use our vivid English metaphor: it stuck in the gizzard', Read's callow appreciation developed into a belief that twentieth-century psychoanalysis had shown the German's perspicacity. Suggesting that 'Jung, [Trigant] Burrow, [Otto] Rank and [Erich] Fromm' would subscribe to Stirner's argument that freedom is 'essentially self-liberation – i.e. that I can only have so much freedom as I procure for myself by my ownness', he qualified that this was not an expression of selfishness, but as Fromm had shown, a meditation on the meaning of 'love'.[164] To self-loathe, he clarified, denoted a constant anxiety and self-obsession supporting selfishness, whereas loving with 'the consciousness of egoism' reveals a real 'fellow-feeling with every feeling being'. Marx's savaging of 'Saint Max' in *The German Ideology* had neglected this 'subtlety', Read added, and the real value of these reflections lay in their elucidation of the personal aspect of real freedom.

This was the contribution that stuck in the gizzard, hinting at a reconciliation of the tension examined in psychology between the concept of 'a Self' and 'the hypothesis of a collective unconscious'. While it offered no ready answer, Read maintained that the 'dialectic of our existence' oscillated between these poles: 'ego-consciousness or self-will', and the 'pre-determined patterns of collective consciousness or social patterns of behaviour'. His educational theory pointed to the idea that aesthetic education was attentive to both strands, cultivating 'uniqueness' but also a mentality of reciprocity. Education should thus aim at 'individuation, but also… integration'.[165] In his political testament 'My Anarchism', he fused Stirner, Jung, and Kropotkin to illuminate this truth. Jung, he argued, had shown that the 'emancipated individual' could not escape the 'collective psyche', echoing Stirner's phraseology in depicting this process of individuation as a 'coming to selfhood'. The inability to avoid this collective mental condition was a good thing for individual sanity, he added, reiterating that individuation would inevitably elude the hermit. Citing Jung, Read argued that this process leads to an 'intenser and more universal collective solidarity', a proposition that 'brings us back to Kropotkin and to mutual aid', for the idea that 'individuation must proceed *pari passu* with integration' was 'implicit in Kropotkin's concept'.[166]

Jung was a persistent source of inspiration for Read, but became especially important as he began to adumbrate his mature aesthetic philosophy at the dawn of the 1950s. His adoption of ideas of archetypes and the collective psyche from Jung was also important in highlighting the political edge of this philosophy, particularly given the utility of these concepts in casting light on the relationship between the individual and social groups. There were other reasons for Read's attraction too.

As Jung's personal secretary Aniela Jaffé pointed out, while the psychoanalyst insisted on being 'recognized as an empiricist', there were obvious parallels between 'mysticism and Jungian psychology', especially in its supposed privileged access to an 'originally hidden transcendent reality'.[167] Given Read's agnostic view of science, such 'transcendent' language proved seductive and eminently pliable, evidently more so than the frigidly rational Freud, whose gravitational pull on Read weakened. Jung offered a conceptual lexicon with which to probe the relation between the individual and the community, but as early as 1926 Read had appreciated the value of his work in explaining both the origin of creativity, and the basis of artistic attraction. Jung had missed the 'latent' conclusion of his theory he commented, in his speculative essay 'Psycho-Analysis and Criticism': that the 'poet' is one 'capable of creating phantasies of more than individual use – phantasies... of universal appeal'. Even though he referenced Freud in his 1936 book *Art and Society*, his proposition that from the 'seething cauldron' of the subconscious the artist snatches 'some archetypal form' – forms underlying 'all the casual variations presented by the natural world' – clearly bore the imprimatur of Jung.[168]

An experience that Read later deemed 'apocalyptic' suggests that the importance of Jung's ideas to his own efforts to understand the genesis of creativity only strengthened with time. Taking an interest in children's art while researching *Education Through Art*, Read stumbled across a drawing 'by a girl of five years old which she... called "Snake round the World and a Boat" '. Here, he believed, was Jung's archetype hypothesis confirmed, discerning in these pencil strokes, 'the mandala... a very ancient symbol found in Egypt, and the Far East and throughout Europe in the Middle Ages'.[169] What Jung had apparently shown was that beneath the 'personal unconscious' was a 'collective unconscious' consisting of 'images impressed on the mind from earliest times' or an 'inherited disposition to reaction'. He deemed this a fruitful avenue of enquiry, welcoming investigations like that of Seonaid Robertson, a founder member of the International Society for Education Through Art, into the 'symbolizing activity of children', noting that in their spontaneous daubs they frequently returned to 'two universal archetypes' the 'rosegarden and the labyrinth'.[170] Such an argument also enabled Read to sidestep the relativism that was a potential feature of his aesthetic theory. For if art constituted the only 'certain reality, for reality is what we discover by our senses', the idea of a depository hidden in the mist of the unconscious to which the 'visionary type, in moments of inspiration' gains access, added a universality to the themes that art examined. Changing fashions, fresh techniques, and material innovations influence the specific expression of these images, but both Henry Moore, in his sculptures *Mother and Child* and *The Reclining Figure,* and the child in Cambridgeshire stumbling upon the mandala, supposedly tapped into this gallimaufry of collectively held 'physical imprints of perceptual imagery'.[171]

Such abstract speculation might seem to be some distance from Read's revolutionary politics, but closing *The Politics of the Unpolitical* he moved to unite them. Looking to William Wordsworth's *Preface to the Lyrical Ballads* (1801), he mused on the appositeness of that text given its origins in the poet's growing disenchantment with the French Revolution. The Molotov–Ribbentrop Pact was probably the contemporary 'breaking-point', he reflected, although the Moscow show trials led to a 'realization that the Russian Revolution…followed precisely the same course as the French'. Finding their 'idealism…suddenly dead', poets began to look inwards to discover the truth, but Read suggested they save time and read Wordsworth instead, as he had shown that:

> The artist must…delve below the…crust of conventional thought…into his own unconscious, and into the collective unconscious of his group or race. It is a painful experience: creative work on this level is only done at a cost of mental anguish…The artist is always something of a masochist…He is also an escapist.

It was crucial that the coming social change must guarantee the 'solitude' required by every artist, but as much as Read posed this revolution as the redemption of the individual from the conformity of mass society, this elitism was tempered by a demand for localised democracy. 'Surrender to the state…surrender to mass opinions and mass standards' was one option, the other was that:

> Power must be distributed among the counties, the cities, the villages and the parishes – distributed and broken into human…units. Economic power must be distributed among the guilds and workshops…Productive labour must be recognized as the basic reality, and honoured as such. That is why the poet must be an anarchist. He has no other choice.

Closing his essay, Read observed that this relationship would be dialectical, a perpetual tension between the artist and 'the society which renounces him'. At the same time, the artist cannot reject society, and sit, as the sages had in *The Green Child,* in haughty isolation. Like

Socrates, he concluded, the artist must drink deeply the hemlock in the 'deadly cup' and accept this 'contrary experience'.[172]

As much as Read depicted the artist in aloof terms – complaining in his book with Dahlberg of 'the armies of ignorance' bearing 'down on our slender temples' armed with 'indifference' – it is clear that he still saw a vital symbiosis between the artist and the community. Perhaps seduced in this instance into competing with Dahlberg's magniloquence, Read never saw the artist disentangling themselves from social bonds as possible or preferable. Such a striving for balance led him to reject, in a similar manner to Kropotkin, Stirnerite egoism as justifying 'hedonism... rather than a desirable eudemonism'. Turning his back on this, Read ventured his own moral theory that 'goodness is living beauty – life ordered on the same principles of rhythm and harmony... implicit in a work of art'. But if harmony and balance pervaded an anarchist utopia, he denied that in intellectual matters anarchism was 'egalitarian'. Rather he suggested that in an anarchist society, 'the seer, the visionary, the poet' – words that echoed his description of Kropotkin, 'a seer, a prophet, but above all a scholar' – would be 'respected' as never before.[173] Anxiously insisting that such adoration would not confer any power, Read aimed to show that anarchism, recognising that 'every man is a special kind of artist', would finally appreciate this uniqueness. Uniting Jung and Stirner, he thus turned to Kropotkin:

> [Anarchism's] aim is the fullest development of individuality, combined, in Kropotkin's words, with "the highest development of voluntary association in all its aspects, in all possible degrees, and for all possible purposes; an association that is always changing".[174]

And like Kropotkin, while pointing to a vista of human liberation, he rejected the idea that a golden age of consensus lay ahead. 'Strife' was a promise of utopia, and 'we can venture to say, that the... sharper the conflict – the more vigorous will be the life'. From this maelstrom will emerge fresh prophets with 'acuter points of consciousness' delving into the collective unconscious and revealing precious insights into the nature of life through 'their creative acts of perception'.[175] Anarchism, in other words, would give birth to a richer, fuller, more robust individuality.

Kropotkin, Read, and utopia

Detailing the uneventful retreat of a motley collection of pseudointellectuals and occultists to a country house, Aldous Huxley's first novel, the comic *Crome Yellow* (1921), seems a far cry from his subsequent probing of the dystopian/utopian fault line in *Brave New World* (1932) and *Island* (1962). Beyond lampooning charlatan spiritualists like Mr Barbecue-Smith who, he tells our guide, can write nearly four thousand words of aphorisms a day, even though the exact meaning of his 'very gnomic' utterances sometimes evades him, the logician Mr Scogan points directly to Huxley's later books. Hearing of a soon-to-be slaughtered sow, condemned on account of its flagging fecundity, the eminently practical Scogan ponders the farmyard as a 'model of sound paternal government': 'Make them breed, make them work, and when they're past working or breeding or begetting, slaughter them.' Looking to the future, he longed for a time when the methods of science advanced on 'Eros', replacing 'Nature's hideous system' with 'vast state incubators, rows upon rows of gravid bottles' supplying 'the world with the population it needs'.[176]

For modern readers, the power of such dystopian satires stems in part from a sense that their nightmarish visions came perilously close to realisation. As Huxley's scientists advanced on the mysteries of life, so the Nazis yearned for a eugenic utopia of their own, and as Zamyatin's glass-covered One State allowed every action to be monitored, so the Soviet Union diffused the paranoia of betrayal into neighbours and families. With the line between fact and fiction blurred, there emerged in British intellectual life a coruscating examination of the utopian impulse, coming from thinkers who were often refugees of such projects of celestial rebirth. Berlin and Bauman, Kołakowski and Popper advanced, like Huxley's scientists, on utopianism and detailed its crimes: fixity, conformity, oppression, and monotony. 'Men live tranquilly also in dungeons', wrote Rousseau, 'is that enough to make them contented there?'[177]

For both Kropotkin and Read, the power of utopianism lay in delimiting the possibilities of the present, and thinking creatively about ambitions for the future. As they remained inveterate architects of utopian visions, their thought is vulnerable to this liberal critique. After all, the anti-utopians stressed, however much freedom defined such plans, the inherent inflexibility of seeing a divine path to redemption could warrant supreme brutality in its pursuit. Yet Kropotkin, writing before this assault on utopianism, had addressed similar objections. Hoping to free the communalist project from associations with experiments in commune building in the United States, he moved to offer an image of anarchist society approximating the fluidity he so valued. Localism, purposeful labour, and new techniques to manage productive value-conflict, all suggest that Kropotkin was conscious of the deleterious effects of communal seclusion and stagnation. His was a vision harnessing the power of modern science, convinced of the promise of individual rationality, but also revelling in the romantic possibilities of such a society: individual growth, free expression, and passionate conflict.

Theorising under the weight of both totalitarianism and the intellectual crusade against the utopian mentality, Read echoed Kropotkin's commitments. His anarchist utopianism, built around Kropotkinian precepts and resting on a dialogue with the history of the Soviet Union and Popper's work, insisted on the vitalising quality of utopian speculation. Echoing Kropotkin's fusion of agricultural and industrial space, and similarly cleaving to a belief in the vivifying importance of conflict, Read's primary contribution was to emphasise anarchism's potential to spur cultural renewal. With artistic activity democratised, as creativity becomes a part of daily life, such a utopia, he believed, would also universalise rich aesthetic sensibility. Freed from the strictures of market logic on the one hand, and the demands of the autocratic state on the other, society would finally fully recognise the existential importance of art. And thus its art would also be anarchism's true measure of success.

Conclusion: Inventing a Tradition

George Woodcock's classic history of anarchism opened with an impassioned defence of anarchist thought, and closed with a threnody:

> As a movement, anarchism has failed ... During the past forty years the influence it once established has dwindled, by defeat after defeat and by the slow draining of hope, almost to nothing. Nor is there any reasonable likelihood of a renaissance of anarchism as we have known it ... history suggests that movements which fail to take the chances it offers ... are never born again.[1]

But anarchism, like Jacob Marley, was only dead to begin with. Between the first and second editions of the book, Woodcock found it necessary to amend his dolorous words. By 1986, he spied a resurgence of interest in anarchism occurring on four related planes. Historical distance had pushed 'classic' anarchism far enough into the fog of time that academic historians had begun to show interest, with a spate of works on Kropotkin, Proudhon, and Bakunin. Such attention had, in turn, led to the republication of their works, while scavenging historians had also broadened the anarchist canon, bringing 'lesser but interesting figures like Gustav Landauer, Élisée Reclus, Paul Brousse, and Voltairine de Cleyre' into popular view. Yet Woodcock did not believe that anarchism was simply a curio for the museum cabinet, and perceived this scholarly resurgence fanning the embers of dissenting philosophy in the present. In 'hibernation' throughout the 1950s, the 1960s roused anarchism from its slumber, and gave birth to a new 'originative' politics, based on a critique of 'pie-in-the-sky anarchism' and pursuing concrete change in the present through practical means.[2] Colin Ward and Murray Bookchin were at the forefront of this revival, he noted, and like Paul Klee's *Angelus Novus*, they looked back to the Kropotkinian past for inspiration while the winds of time pushed them into the future.[3]

Although Woodcock noted the continued importance of Kropotkin, he relegated his friend Read to a minor role in the history of anarchism. Indeed, rather immodestly, he put anarchism's somnolence in the 1950s down to the movement losing 'two ... leading figures', the tragic Marie-Louise Berneri who died in childbirth at the age of thirty-one, and 'George Woodcock [who] departed to start a new life in Canada'.[4] What Woodcock missed though, was the extent to which both Ward and Bookchin highlighted the role of Read in shaping their thought. As Ward said, Read was a 'vital influence' and 'struck a vital chord', while Bookchin insisted that, in fact, 'Kropotkin had no influence on my turn from Marxism to anarchism', rather 'it was Herbert Read ... that I found most useful for rooting the views ... I ... developed over the fifties ... in a libertarian pedigree'.[5]

In Woodcock's rendering, the power of this new anarchism lay in its ability to move beyond the limits of the classical tradition. Centrally, this meant jettisoning the unhelpful sense of an 'idealized future', and replacing it with a focus on directing anarchist activities to confront present needs. Yet, in summing up this supposedly new radical vision, Woodcock chose a quotation from Read as the epigraph to his book:

> My understanding of the history of culture has convinced me that the ideal society is a point on a receding horizon. We move steadily towards it but can never reach it. Nevertheless we must engage with passion in the immediate strife.[6]

The citation ended here, but Read continued. 'Such is the nature of things', he wrote, 'and if defeat is inevitable (as it is) we are not excused'. Conceding the charge of fatalism, Read persisted that this did not warrant surrender. Engagement was a human compulsion, and there, in the heat of struggle, while fighting for something new, temporary equilibrium might be reached. As Heraclitus suggested, Read noted, in words that Kropotkin could have written: 'It is in changing ... that things find repose.'[7]

Kropotkin endeavoured to enshrine this notion of transience at the centre of his philosophical system. Looking to modern science, he found sustenance for an ontology defined by continual motion and contention, punctuated by bouts of momentary balance. It was this vision that he tried to bring to his politics, turning to the budding discipline of sociology for support, and conducting a conversation with

Comte and Spencer in particular. Imbibing the irrepressible analytical optimism of positivism, Kropotkin turned from methodological speculation to attempting to understand the totality of human experience. His sociological labours furnished him with a view of human history as one of antagonism, informing a grand philosophy of history in which the clash between the forces of authority and liberty was eternal. An apostle of Darwinian evolutionary theory, albeit with a Lamarckian inflection, Kropotkin's reading of evolution similarly rejected progressive teleology in favour of constant adaptation. His understanding of revolution mirrored this dynamic, seeing this change as a process, and one inevitably assailed by the forces of reaction. Anarchists' success in this conflagration would rest on how well they popularised their message, and how effectively they evolved new systems of distribution, new modes of arbitration, and a new ethic of communality. But even in their victory, Kropotkin's historical sociology warned, defeat was always close at hand.

Read's commitment to this social philosophy developed in tandem with his cultural theory. His prime focus was always the existential importance of art, and an anxiety that the neglect of artistic creativity in capitalist society led to spiritual impoverishment. The spectre of totalitarianism was also important, suggesting to Read that the efforts of autocrats to cloak their crimes in high art was always betrayed by its aesthetic banality, seen in Stalin's Socialist Realism, and the 'slow-witted' Nazis lurching drunkenly to oompah bands.[8] And in those democracies that defined themselves against the state-socialist model, their increasing reliance on the tools of technocratic control – their committees, institutions, and technical reports – betrayed the fact that in terms of the sophistication of their cultural ideas, the distance between the first and second worlds was negligible. Against this mass facileness, Read saw in Kropotkin's politics the roots of a renaissance. His political theory pointed to a kind of social organisation that would recognise the centrality of art to individual wellbeing, democratise the opportunity to take part in creative activity, and allow art to spring naturally from the soil. Developing these ideas through a conversation with both Kropotkin's understanding of mutual aid as an historical force, and his attempts to imagine an anarchist utopia, Read nevertheless diverged from him over the issue of revolution. While subscribing to the general proposition that change must be far-reaching and that such social reorientation would be a process, he remained unmovable on the issue of revolutionary violence. If the sanguinary twentieth century showed anything, for Read it demonstrated the need for battling the state and capitalism with new weapons, and that education was the key.

Kropotkin and Read examined the conceptual resources offered by anarchist political theory to address the political problems confronting them. In doing so, they each embarked on an act of translation: Kropotkin refining a peasant-oriented politics to the most urbanised country in the world, and Read rethinking Kropotkin's political thought for an era of culture wars and the nuclear bomb. At the same time, they were also engaged in the process of outlining a political tradition that was as much invented as it was imagined. If a defining feature of modern nations is their 'invented traditions', encompassing practices possessing 'overtly or tacitly accepted rules' which aim to 'inculcate certain values and norms' and imply 'continuity with the past', then the same applies for political traditions.[9] As Kropotkin and Read both showed, anarchism had its sustaining myths tying it to a long and noble past: from the idea that Lao-Tzu, Zeno, or the Anabaptists were essentially anarchist, to Marx's duplicitous outmanoeuvring of Bakunin in the International, to Spain's flowering anarchism crushed by the commissars and Western indifference. Such history does not, in Tony Judt's words, offer the 'discomforting, even disruptive' narratives of objective analysis, but rather the invention of a memory that 'confirms and reinforces itself'.[10] Such histories enflame hearts with righteous anger, point to the enduring possibilities of the tradition, and freight anarchist theory with historical pedigree.

Of course describing these as myths does not necessarily mean that they are false. Rather, in a Sorelian sense that Read would have appreciated, their power lies in the ability to encourage action and stiffen sinews. The anarchist political culture that Kropotkin and Read inhabited and helped define, was also therefore an 'imagined' community, where in the minds of each individual 'lives the image of their communion' with the rest.[11] Just as modern nations cohered as print-capitalism allowed geographically stratified people to identify with one another, so the ink-smudged paper leaving the desks of anarchist writers as books, pamphlets, letters, newspaper articles, and handbills, allowed this distinctive political culture to construct its community. Similarly, as much as anarchism's Babel-like polyglotism might defy the common language important to national communion, it is not a stretch to see a surrogate for this in the conceptual vocabularies developed by political traditions. After all, comprehension of nomenclature like 'commodity fetishism' and 'direct democracy' is a particularly effective way of defining boundaries, and the multiplicity of meanings attached to terms such as 'liberty' reveals a patchwork of political languages and communities. The erection of these barriers also inevitably descends from theory to practice. Contrary to the popular image, anarchists spend considerable time thinking about how to organise effectively, including on the level of small-scale meetings. In this very local action there is a deep symbolism. In Kropotkin's time, in a room clouded by the fug of cigar smoke and housing a worn printing press, they hoped to build alternatives to the authoritarian decision-making structures of contemporary life. Such efforts show the attempt to define a unique political culture, with its distinct history, language, and methods of action.

This process of invention and imagining is axiomatically larger than the efforts of two intellectuals. But the conversation between Kropotkin and Read across Britain's modern history was marked by an attempt to articulate a distinctive set of theoretical resources that is one aspect of inventing a political tradition. In terms of practical success, the political realist might deem these labours a failure. While paradoxical, there are two clear reasons why Kropotkin's politics failed to take hold in Britain to the extent that he hoped. On the one hand, the fact that Britain had an entrenched language of individual liberty, and a liberal political tradition that was in many ways its mainstream, sapped the power of anarchist critique.[12] At the same time, however, Britain was embarking on a long experiment with state intervention that carried with it a redefinition of liberalism, making anarchism seem anachronistic. This intellectual climate informed Kropotkin's attempts to refine the anarchist message, but Read entered a world in which action through the state was a political orthodoxy – even if important threads of opposition remained, from Social Credit to Guild Socialism. He steadfastly trumpeted the enduring relevance of Kropotkin's ideas, but turned to culture to develop the emancipatory edge of this politics. Read's contribution to anarchism was a richly theoretical aesthetic politics that attempted to theorise a new ground for struggle in artistic practice, while updating Kropotkin's anarchism for the world of totalitarianism. The beauty of Read's contribution was its sophisticated level of philosophical abstraction, and his infusion of his political writing with a poetic voice that stood in contrast to the doggerel of most political polemic. Yet, this was his overwhelming weakness too. Erudite and empyrean, Read was nevertheless poor in outlining an anarchist response to key aspects of the changing nature of the British state: notably universal suffrage, and the broadening of the post-war welfare state.

Despite these limitations, it would be wrong to follow Woodcock and see anarchism in Britain as a feeble sibling of the radical politics that grew in France or Spain. Indeed, while pointing to numerical strength might not be an option, and while anarchists might be resistant to undue focus on the scholarly manifestation of this politics, Kropotkin and Read both rose to prominence in British cultural life in part *because* of their political beliefs. As Kropotkin scribbled on parchment at his desk, and Read thumped into his Corona typewriter, they outlined a shared political tradition that possessed enough intellectual life to remain a guide to action in their diverse contexts. At its heart was the belief that there was a different way for Britain to navigate the industrial age, and that the promise of technology made a new way of life a tantalising possibility. What Tolstoy's rural idyll and Fritz Lang's *Metropolis* masked, for Kropotkin and Read, was that these were not mutually exclusive modes of living, but pointed to a potential synthesis. Reason, Read reflected, was the 'adamantine and invincible' weapon always at his side, ready to be picked up when he 'was compelled to abandon my innocent vision and fight against the despairs of experience'. But counter-balancing reason was a romantic urge: 'creative fictions of the imagination' that clarified and contested the conclusions of the rational mind.[13] Anarchism embodied this balance. Behind the archly scientific carapace of Kropotkin's politics was, nevertheless, a politics of desire: a yearning for unencumbered individuality; a belief in the life-giving qualities of struggle; and a longing for a re-acquaintance with the rhythms of nature. To Read, these were all 'simple ideas', and 'faith' in such simple ideas, he concluded, might just 'have the power to transform the world'.[14]

Notes

Introduction

1. Herbert Read to T.S. Eliot: 1 October 1949: *Herbert Read Archive, University of Victoria* (hereafter *HRAUV*), HR/TSE-170.
2. Herbert Read, *The Contrary Experience: Autobiographies* (London, 1963), 353, 350.
3. Isaiah Berlin, *The Roots of Romanticism* (London, [1965] 2000), 97.
4. For a useful discussion, see: Peter Ryley, *Making Another World Possible: Anarchism, Anti-capitalism and Ecology in Late 19th and Early 20th Century Britain* (New York, 2013); Mark Bevir, *The Making of British Socialism* (Princeton, 2011), 256–277.
5. Martin A. Miller, *Kropotkin* (Chicago, 1976), 166–167; Rodney Barker, *Political Ideas in Modern Britain* (London, 1978), 42 *passim.*
6. H. Oliver, *The International Anarchist Movement in Late Victorian London* (London, 1983), 136; see also: 92, 132–137. For a discussion of the significance of the Congress, see: Davide Turcato, *Making Sense of Anarchism: Errico Malatesta's Experiments with Revolution* (Basingstoke, 2012), 136–139.
7. W. Tcherkesoff, *Let Us Be Just: (An Open Letter to Liebknecht)* (London, 1896), 7.
8. The report offered short biographies of Francesco Merlino, Gustav Landauer, Louise Michel, Amilcare Cipriani, Augustin Hamon, Élisée Reclus, Ferdinand Domela Nieuwenhuis, Bernard Lazare, and Peter Kropotkin. N.A., *Full Report of the Proceedings of the International Workers' Congress, London, July and August, 1896* (London, 1896), 67–72.
9. N.A., *Full Report of the Proceedings*, 21, 17.
10. Matthew S. Adams, 'Herbert Read and the fluid memory of the First World War: Poetry, Prose, and Polemic', *Historical Research* (2014), 1–22; Janet S.K. Watson, *Fighting Different Wars: Experience, Memory, and the First World War in Britain* (Cambridge, 2004), 226.
11. Samuel Hynes, *A War Imagined: The First World War in English Culture* (London, 1990), 353–382.
12. Dan Todman, *The Great War: Myth and Memory* (London, 2011), 88–94.
13. Peter Gay, *Modernism: The Lure of Heresy* (New York, 2008), 3.
14. Allan Antliff, *Anarchist Modernism: Art, Politics, and the First American Avant-Garde* (Chicago, 2001), 1–2.
15. Michael Freeden, *Ideologies and Political Theory: A Conceptual Approach* (Oxford, 2008), 75, 76.
16. Quentin Skinner, *Visions of Politics: Volume 1* (2002), 89 *passim.* For an overview, see: Paul Kelly, 'Rescuing Political Theory from the Tyranny of History', in Jonathan Floyd and Marc Stears (eds) *Political Philosophy versus History?: Contextualism and Real Politics in Contemporary Political Thought* (Cambridge, 2011), 13–37.
17. Quentin Skinner, *The Foundations of Modern Political Thought: Volume 1* (Cambridge, 1978), xi.

18. Keith Michael Baker, *Inventing the French Revolution* (Cambridge, 1994), 19.
19. For an excellent overview of the current state of scholarship on anarchist history, see: Carl Levy, 'Social Histories of Anarchism', *Journal for the Study of Radicalism*, 4:2 (2010), 1–44.
20. George Woodcock, *Anarchism: A History of Libertarian Ideas and Movements* (London, [1962] 1970), 414.
21. Woodcock was not the first to plot the history of anarchism in this manner, but certainly the most influential. For a discussion, see: Matthew S. Adams, 'The Possibilities of Anarchist History: Rethinking the Canon and Writing History', *Anarchist Developments in Cultural Studies* (2013), 33–63.
22. John Quail, *The Slow Burning Fuse* (London, 1978), ix–xv; Oliver, *The International Anarchist Movement*.
23. Peter Marshall, *Demanding the Impossible: A History of Anarchism* (London, 1993), xiii. See also: April Carter, *The Political Theory of Anarchism* (London, 1971); R.B. Fowler, 'The Anarchist Tradition of Political Thought', *The Western Political Quarterly*, 25: 4 (1972), 738–752; Roderick Kedward, *The Anarchists* (New York, 1971); D. Novak, 'The Place of Anarchism in the History of Political Thought', *The Review of Politics*, 20: 3 (1958), 307–329; Quail, *Slow Burning Fuse*; Woodcock, *Anarchism*. On the exclusion of anarchism from histories of socialism, a good example is: Donald Sassoon, *One Hundred Years of Socialism: The West European Left in the Twentieth Century* (London, 2010).
24. Arthur O. Lovejoy, *The Great Chain of Being: A Study of the History of an Idea* (Cambridge, MA, 1961).
25. Skinner, *Visions of Politics*, 72.
26. Consider: Constance Bantman, *The French Anarchists in London: 1880–1914* (Liverpool, 2013); Ryley, *Making Another World Possible*; Michael Schmidt and Lucien van der Walt, *Black Flame: The Revolution Class Politics of Anarchism and Syndicalism* (Edinburgh, 2009).
27. Consider: Ruth Kinna, 'Guy Aldred: Bridging the Gap between Marxism and Anarchism', *Journal of Political Ideologies*, 16:1 (2011), 97–114; Ruth Kinna *Anarchism: A Beginner's Guide* (Oxford, 2005); Carissa Honeywell, 'Bridging the Gaps: Twentieth-Century Anglo-American Anarchist Thought', in Ruth Kinna (ed.) *The Continuum Companion to Anarchism* (London, 2012), 111–139; Benjamin Franks, *Rebel Alliances: The Means and Ends of Contemporary British Anarchisms* (Edinburgh, 2006); Nathan Jun, *Anarchism and Political Modernity* (New York, 2012).
28. For this critique, see: Allan Antliff, 'Anarchy, Power and Post-Structralism', in Duane Rouselle and Süreyyya Evren (eds) *Post-Anarchism: A Reader* (London, 2011), 160–167; Benjamin Franks, 'Post-Anarchism: A Partial Account' in *Post-Anarchism*, 168–180. For works of this nature, see: Saul Newman, *The Politics of Postanarchism* (Edinburgh, 2011); Todd May, *The Political Philosophy of Poststructuralist Anarchism* (Pennsylvania, 1994); Andrew M. Koch, 'Post-Structuralism and the Epistemological Basis of Anarchism', in Duane Rouselle and Süreyyya Evren (eds) *Post-Anarchism: A Reader* (London, 2011), 23–40 (39).
29. For a useful discussion, see: Honeywell, 'Bridging the Gaps', 111–139.
30. Usually 'classical anarchism' refers to the work of Pierre-Joseph Proudhon, Mikhail Bakunin, and Kropotkin. See Jun, *Anarchism*, 111–113.

31. Ruth Kinna, 'Introduction', *Continuum Companion*, 3–38 (17).
32. Carissa Honeywell, *A British Anarchist Tradition: Herbert Read, Alex Comfort and Colin Ward* (London, 2011); Ryley, *Making Another World Possible*. See also: David Goodway. While he is more hesitant about anarchism's claims for 'tradition' status, suggesting that the presence of a 'shared community' of thought is debatable, his book nevertheless suggests that this existed. David Goodway, *Anarchist Seeds Beneath the Snow: Left-Libertarian Thought and British Writers from William Morris to Colin Ward* (Liverpool, 2006), 11–12.
33. Keith Michael Baker, 'Introduction', in Baker (ed.) *The French Revolution and the Creation of Modern Political Culture: Volume 1: The Political Culture of the Old Regime* (Oxford, 1987), xi–xxiv (xii). See also: Wolfgang J. Mommsen, 'History of Political Theory in the Federal Republic of Germany: Strange Death and Slow Recovery', in Dario Castiglione and Iain Hampsher-Monk (eds) *The History of Political Thought in National Context* (Cambridge, 2001), 40–57.
34. Bevir, *Making of British Socialism*, 12.
35. John Dunn, *The History of Political Theory and Other Essays* (Cambridge, 1996), 19.
36. George Crowder, *Classical Anarchism: The Political Thought of Godwin, Bakunin and Kropotkin* (Oxford, 1991); Koch, 'Post-Structuralism and the Epistemological Basis of Anarchism'; May, *Poststructuralist Anarchism*; David Miller, *Anarchism* (London, 1984); Newman, *Politics of Postanarchism*; Richard Sonn, *Anarchism* (New York, 1992).
37. Kropotkin and Read both followed convention in using gendered language. As the rhetorical conversation was a key aspect of their polemical arsenal, in which the use of 'he', 'him', and 'his' abounded, I have opted not to highlight this problematic practice by adding 'sic' after each instance, to avoid cluttering the text.
38. Herbert Read, *Poetry and Anarchism* (London, [1938] 1947), 61.

1 Contexts: Anarchism in British Intellectual History, 1886–1968

1. Percy Wyndham Lewis (ed.) *Blast No.1*, (London, 1914), 36, 39.
2. Edward Wadsworth, 'The Black Country', *Arts and Letter Letters: An Illustrated Quarterly*, 3:1 (1920), 40.
3. Jonathan Black, '"Constructing a Chinese-Puzzle Universe": Industry, National Identity, and Edward Wadsworth's Vorticist Woodcuts of West Yorkshire, 1914–1916', in Mark Antliff et al (eds) *Vorticism: New Perspectives* (Oxford, 2013), 89–99 (98).
4. Peter Kropotkin, 'Western Europe [1924]', from *Memoirs of a Revolutionist* in Marshall S. Shatz (ed.) *The Conquest of Bread and Other Writings* (Cambridge, 1995), 203–232 (204).
5. Peter Kropotkin, *Act for Yourselves: Articles from Freedom: 1886–1907*, Nicolas Walter and Heiner Becker (eds) (London, 1998), 102.
6. Peter Kropotkin, *Fields, Factories and Workshops or Industry Combined with Agriculture and Brain Work with Manual Work* (London, 1912), 77.
7. Alexis de Tocqueville, *Journeys to England and Ireland*, J. P. Mayer (ed.), trans. George Lawrence and K.P. Mayer (New Haven, 1958), 107–108.

8. Herbert Read, *Annals of Innocence and Experience* (London, [1940] 1946), 200.
9. Henry George, *Progress and Poverty: An Inquiry into the Cause of Industrial Depressions and of Increase of Want with Increase of Wealth* (New York, [1876] 1900), 7.
10. Ibid., 297, 312.
11. J. A. Hobson, *Confessions of an Economic Heretic* (London, 1938), 27.
12. Kropotkin, *Act for Yourselves*, 48, 50; Peter Kropotkin, *Memoirs of a Revolutionist* (London, [1899] 1978), 299.
13. Herbert Spencer, *Social Statics: Or, The Conditions Essential to Human Happiness* (London, 1851), 114.
14. Herbert Spencer, *The Man Versus the State* (New York, 1884), 32, 13.
15. Richard Bellamy, 'Introduction', in Bellamy (ed.) *Victorian Liberalism: Nineteenth Century Political Thought and Practice* (London, 1990), 1–14 (2).
16. Michael Bentley, *The Climax of Liberal Politics: British Liberalism in Theory and Practice, 1868–1918* (London, 1987), 49.
17. T. H. Green, 'Lecture on 'Liberal Legislation and Freedom of Contract' ', in R. L. Nettleship (ed.) *Works of Thomas Hill Green: Volume III*, (London, 1888), 365–374 (372, 374).
18. W. H. Greenleaf, *The British Political Tradition: Volume 1* (London, 1983), 15.
19. Freeden, *Ideologies and Political Theory*, 179.
20. Ibid., 187; Martin Pugh, *The Making of Modern British Politics: 1867–1939* (Oxford, 1982), 111.
21. Gregory Claeys, *Citizens and Saints: Politics and Anti-politics in Early British Socialism* (Cambridge, 1989), 2.
22. Michael Freeden, *The New Liberalism: An Ideology of Social Reform* (Oxford, 1978), 25.
23. John Gray, *The Social System: A Treatise on the Principle of Exchange* (Edinburgh, 1831), 369; Claeys, *Citizens and Saints*, 163.
24. Ibid., 101, 99.
25. Frederick Engels, *The Condition of the Working-Class in England in 1844*, trans. Florence Wischnewetzky (London, 1892), 236–237.
26. Claeys, *Citizens and Saints*, 299.
27. H. M. Hyndman, *England for All* (London, 1881), 6, 83.
28. 'Engels to A. Babel, 1883', *Karl Marx and Frederick Engels on Britain* (London, 1953), 515–516 (516).
29. Hyndman, *England for All*, 151, 168 (151).
30. Barker, *Political Ideas in Modern Britain*, 42. It should be noted that there was significant ambiguity surrounding Blatchford's position on imperialism. See: Gregory Claeys, *Imperial Sceptics: British Critics of Empire, 1850–1920* (Cambridge, 2010), 172–180.
31. Robert Blatchford, *Britain for the British* (London, 1907), 84, 143. Original emphasis.
32. Laurence Thompson, *Robert Blatchford: Portrait of an Englishman* (London, 1951), 58, 73, 76.
33. Sidney Webb, 'Historic', *Fabian Essays in Socialism*, G.B. Shaw (ed.) (London, 1889), 30–61 (53, 61).
34. Bevir, *The Making of British Socialism*, 214; Edward Pease, *The History of the Fabian Society* (London, [1918] 1963), 33.
35. Pease, *Fabian Society*, 28, 35.

36. 'The Fabian Course of Lectures' in *Fabian News*, 1:1 (1891), 1; 'The Fabian Course of Lectures' in *Fabian News* 1:2 (1891), 6.
37. Pease, *Fabian Society*, 47.
38. Eric Hobsbawm, *Labouring Men: Studies in the History of Labour* (London, 1964), 250–271.
39. David Howell, *British Workers and the Independent Labour Party, 1888–1906* (Manchester, 1983), 283.
40. Robert Blatchford, *My Eighty Years* (London, 1931), 199.
41. Andrew Thorpe, *A History of the British Labour Party* (New York, 1997), 5–31.
42. J. Keir Hardie, *From Serfdom to Socialism* (London, 1907), 3, 7, 10.
43. *The Manifesto of the Socialist League* (London, 1885), 6, 7, 8.
44. For Morris and his position on anarchism, see: Ruth Kinna, *William Morris: The Art of Socialism* (Cardiff, 2000).
45. Ruth Kinna, 'The Jacobinism and Patriotism of Ernest Belfort Bax', *History of European Ideas*, 30:4 (2004), 463–484 (475).
46. Barker, *Political Ideas*, 83.
47. Kropotkin, *Memoirs*, 299.
48. Ibid., 94. Original emphasis.
49. Ibid., 112, 119.
50. Ibid., 164.
51. Ibid., 172.
52. Marshall S. Shatz, 'Introduction', in Shatz (ed.) *The Conquest of Bread & Other Writings* (Cambridge, 1995), vii–xxiii (xi); Andrezj Walicki, 'Russian Political Thought in the Nineteenth Century', in Gareth Stedman Jones and Gregory Claeys (eds) *The Cambridge History of Nineteenth-Century Political Thought* (Cambridge, 2013), 811–834 (821).
53. Kropotkin, *Memoirs*, 211.
54. Ibid., 194, 196–197.
55. Ibid., 197.
56. James Joll, *The Second International, 1889–1914* (London, 1955), 22.
57. Kropotkin, *Memoirs*, 214, 229.
58. E.H. Carr, *Michael Bakunin* (London, 1937), 220.
59. Kropotkin, *Memoirs*, 250–260.
60. Ibid., 261.
61. Ibid., 264.
62. Ibid., 271. For Kropotkin's time in Switzerland, see also: Dana Ward, 'Alchemy in Clarens: Kropotkin and Reclus, 1877–1881', in Nathan J. Jun and Shane Wahl (eds) *New Perspectives on Anarchism* (Lanham, MD, 2009), 209–226.
63. Ibid., 306.
64. 'The Trial at Lyons', *Daily News*, 10 January 1883, n.p.
65. 'The Trial of Socialists', *The Times*, 20 January 1883, 5.
66. Kropotkin, *Memoirs*, 185.
67. Ibid., 261.
68. 'Prince Krapotkin's Cat', *Chatterbox*, 20 February 1886, 105.
69. Kropotkin, *Memoirs*, 311, 312.
70. For the full list, see: George Woodcock and Ivan Avakumoviæ, *The Anarchist Prince: A Biographical Study of Peter Kropotkin* (New York, 1970), 194.
71. Kropotkin, *Memoirs*, 329.

72. William Morris, '1227: To John Carruthers', in Norman Kelvin (ed.) *The Collected Letters of William Morris: Volume II* (Princeton, 1987), 533–535 (535).
73. Henry Mayers Hyndman, *The Record of an Adventurous Life* (London, 1911), 262; Ernest Belfort Bax, *Reminiscences and Reflexions of a Mid and Late Victorian* (New York, 1920), 42.
74. Walter Crane, *An Artist's Reminiscences* (New York, 1907), 255.
75. Henry W. Nevinson, *Fire of Life* (London, 1935), 53, 54.
76. 'The Gospel According to Krapotkin: By a Sympathizer in Paris', *Pall Mall Gazette*, 1 Mach 1886, 6.
77. 'Prince Kropotkin', *Freeman's Journal and Daily Commercial Advertiser*, 27 October 1887, 5.
78. Peter Kropotkin to May Morris: 23rd February 1889, *British Library Manuscripts Collection* (hereafter *BLMC*), Add. 45346, f.131.
79. See: Oliver, *The International Anarchist Movement*, 42–74.
80. Peter Kropotkin to William Morris, 11th April 1886, *BLMC*, Add. 45345, f.109.
81. Kropotkin, *Fields, Factories and Workshops*, 363.
82. J.B. Priestley, *The Edwardians* (London, 1970), 288.
83. Eric Hobsbawm, *The Age of Empire: 1875–1914* (London, 2002), 100. See also: Walter Kendall, *The Revolutionary Movement in Britain 1900–1921: The Origins of British Communism* (London, 1969), 23–45.
84. Errico Malatesta, *Malatesta: His Life & Ideas* (London, 1984), 260.
85. Peter Kropotkin to J.S. Keltie: 18th August 1916, *Royal Geographical Society Archives, London* [hereafter *RGS*], *RGS* CB8/50.
86. Peter Kropotkin to James Knowles: 6th November 1905, *City of Westminster Archive* [hereafter *CWA*], 716/84/2; Peter Kropotkin to James Knowles: 12th December 1905, *CWA* 716/84/7.
87. Kropotkin wrote a pamphlet concerned with the oppression that followed in the wake of the 1905 Revolution, issued by The Parliamentary Russian Committee, published in 1909. Prince Kropotkin, *The Terror in Russia: An Appeal to the British Nation* (London, 1909).
88. Peter Kropotkin to May Morris: 23rd March 1917, *BLMC*, Add. 45347, ff.167.
89. Paul Avrich, *The Russian Anarchists* (Princeton, 1967), 166.
90. Leon Trotsky, *The History of the Russian Revolution: Volume II*, trans. Max Eastman (Ann Arbor, 1957), 230.
91. Gertrude Himmelfarb, 'The Politics of Democracy: The English Reform Act of 1867', *Journal of British Studies*, 6:1 (1966), 97–138 (97).
92. Peter Kropotkine, *Anarchist Communism: Its Basis and Principles* (London, [1887] 1905), 21.
93. Stanley Baldwin, *This Torch of Freedom: Speeches and Addresses* (London, 1935), 4–5. Although Baldwin usually referred to England, Scotland and Wales also informed his vision. See: G. Ward-Smith, 'Baldwin and Scotland: More than Englishness', *Contemporary British History*, 15:1 (2001), 61–82.
94. Baldwin, *This Torch of Freedom*, 6, 41, 42.
95. Walter Bagehot, *Physics and Politics: or Thoughts on the Application of the Principles of 'Natural Selection' and 'Inheritance' to Political Society* (London, 1881), 201; Baldwin, *This Torch of Freedom*, 42.

96. Stanley Baldwin, *On England and Other Addresses* (London, 1926), 7.
97. Michael Anderson, 'The Social Implications of Demographic Change', in F.M.L. Thompson (ed.) *The Cambridge Social History of Britain: 1750–1950: Volume Two* (Cambridge, 1990), 1–70 (2).
98. Baldwin, *This Torch of Freedom*, 51.
99. Greenleaf, *British Political Tradition: Volume One*, 51.
100. A.J.P. Taylor, *English History: 1914–1945* (Oxford, 1965), 1, 14–15.
101. Communist Party of Great Britain, *Class Against Class: General Election Programme of the Communist Party of Great Britain* (London, 1929), 17.
102. Freeden, *Ideologies and Political Theory*, 76.
103. Alison Light, *Forever England: Femininity, Literature and Conservatism Between the Wars* (London, 1991), 211.
104. Philip Williamson, ' "Safety First": Baldwin, the Conservative Party, and the 1929 General Election', *The Historical Journal*, 25:2 (1982), 385–409.
105. Pugh, *Making of Modern British Politics*, 236.
106. Thorpe, *History of the British Labour Party*, 76; Kevin Morgan, *Ramsey MacDonald* (London, 2006), 73–76.
107. R.H. Tawney, 'The Choice Before the Labour Party', *The Political Quarterly* 3:3 (1932), 323–345 (323, 325,324).
108. Kendall, *The Revolutionary Movement in Britain*, 220.
109. Andrew Thorpe, *The British Communist Party and Moscow: 1920–1943* (Manchester, 2000), 30.
110. Kendall, *Revolutionary Movement*, 218; Thorpe, *British Communist Party*, 29.
111. Ibid., 30.
112. James Klugmann, *History of the Communist Party of Great Britain: Volume One* (London, 1968), 39; Thorpe, *Communist Party*, 30, 41, 45.
113. Thorpe, *Communist Party*, 61, 65, 93.
114. Ibid., 119–120.
115. Kevin Morgan, *Harry Pollitt* (Manchester, 1993), 62.
116. Kevin Morgan, *Against Fascism and War: Ruptures and Continuities in British Communist Politics, 1935–41* (Manchester, 1989), 34.
117. Tom Buchanan, *The Spanish Civil War and the British Labour Movement* (Cambridge, 1991), 37; Thorpe, *British Communist Party*, 231.
118. Morgan, *Against Fascism and War*, 92, 304.
119. William Beveridge, *Social Insurance and Allied Services: Report by Sir William Beveridge* (New York, 1942), 172.
120. Peter Clarke, *Hope and Glory: Britain 1900–2000* (London, 2004), 171.
121. Alan Bold, *MacDiarmid: Christopher Murray Grieve: A Critical Biography* (London, 1988), 83–103.
122. Hugh MacDiarmid, *Lucky Poet: A Self-Study in Literature and Political Ideas* (London, 1943), 26.
123. Hugh MacDiarmid, *Complete Poems: Volume 1*, Michael Grieve and W.R. Aitken (eds) (Manchester, 1993), 551.
124. Ronald Clark, *J.B.S.: The Life and Work of J.B.S. Haldane* (London, 1968), 35–52, 115–119, 166.
125. Mark Mazower, *Dark Continent: Europe's Twentieth Century* (New York, 2000), 120–124.
126. J.B.S. Haldane, *Adventures of a Biologist* (London, 1937), 250, 251.

127. Lancelot Hogben, 'Planning for Human Survival', *What Is Ahead of Us?* (London, 1937), 165–192 (192).
128. Sidney Webb, 'The Future of Soviet Communism', *What Is Ahead of Us?*, 103–132 (130).
129. Richard Overy, *The Twilight Years: The Paradox of Britain Between the Wars* (New York, 2009), 81–83.
130. Kendall, *Revolutionary Movement*, 280–282.
131. Arthur J. Penty, *The Restoration of the Gild System* (London, 1906), n.p. 7, 19.
132. For Read and Leeds, see: Michael Paraskos, 'Herbert Read and Leeds', in Benedict Read and David Thistlewood (eds) *Herbert Read: A British Vision of World Art* (London, 1993), 25–33.
133. Tom Steele, 'The Leeds Art Club: A Provincial Avant-Garde?', *Literature and History*, 14:1 (1988), 91–109.
134. Wallace Martin, *The New Age Under Orage: Chapters in English Cultural History* (Manchester, 1967), 1.
135. G.D.H. Cole, *The World of Labour: A Discussion of the Present and Future of Trade Unionism* (London, 1915), 365, 364.
136. G.D.H. Cole, 'The Genesis of French Syndicalism – and Some Unspoken Morals. – I.', *The New Age*, XIV:14 (1914), 425–427; G.D.H. Cole, 'The Genesis of French Syndicalism – and Some Unspoken Morals', *The New Age*, XIV:16 (1914), 489–490.
137. S.G. Hobson, *National Guilds: An Inquiry Into the Wage System and the Way Out* (London, 1919), 21, 133.
138. G.D.H. Cole, *Guild Socialism Restated* (London, 1920), 39, 122, 123.
139. Hilaire Belloc, *The Servile State* (London, 1912), 187,183.
140. Hilaire Belloc and Cecil Chesterton, *The Party System* (London, 1911), 5, 201.
141. Belloc, *Servile State*, 50, 52. Original emphasis.
142. Victor Serge, *Memoirs of a Revolutionary: 1901–1941*, trans. Peter Sedgwick (Oxford, 1963), 120, 128.
143. These chapters were initially published as *The Innocent Eye* (London, 1933). George Orwell, 'Review of A Coat of Many Colours: Occasional Essays by Herbert Read', in Peter Davinson et al. (eds) *The Complete Works of George Orwell: Volume 17* (London, 1998), 402–405 (405).
144. Read, *Annals*, 125, 67, 68.
145. Ibid., 72.
146. 'Virginia Woolf to Vanessa Bell: 18th May 1929', in Nigel Nicolson (ed.) *A Reflection of the Other Person: The Letters of Virginia Woolf: Volume IV, 1929–1931* (London, 1978), 58–61 (59); Virginia Woolf, *The Diary of Virginia Woolf*, ed. Anne Olivier Bell (London, 1982), 281.
147. Read, *Annals*, 82.
148. Ibid., 86.
149. Claude Lévi-Strauss, *The Savage Mind* (Chicago, 1962), 16–18. I am grateful to Dr Michael Sanders for alerting me to this reference.
150. James King, *The Last Modern: A Life of Herbert Read* (New York, 1990), 33. For a useful overview, see: Michael Paraskos, 'Imagination Seizes Power: A Brief Introduction', in Paraskos (ed.) *Rereading Read* (London, 2007), 8–17.
151. Read, *Annals*, 137.

152. Herbert Read, *The Cult of Sincerity* (London, 1968), 54.
153. Read, *Annals*, 83.
154. The diary was in fact letters from Read to his first wife Evelyn. As Abbs has noted, as the 'War Diary' is comprised of edited letters, the originals of which were destroyed, it is likely that Read excised sexual and sentimental sections, thus giving the diary its tone of 'business-like despatch'. See: Peter Abbs, 'Herbert Read as an Autobiographer' in David Goodway (ed.) *Herbert Read Reassessed* (Liverpool, 1998) 83–99 (95).
155. Read, *The Contrary Experience*, 96.
156. Herbert Read, 'The World and the Guild Idea – I. The Natural Basis', *The Guildsman: a Journal of Social and Industrial Emancipation*, 5 (1917), 6.
157. Read, *Annals*, 97, 98. Original emphasis.
158. Herbert Read, 'Sir Herbert Read', in Alister Kershaw et al (eds) *Richard Aldington: An Intimate Portrait* (Carbondale, 1965), 123; Read, *Annals*, 101.
159. King, *Last Modern*, 47.
160. Herbert Read, 'The Curfew' and 'The Pond', *Arts and Letters: An Illustrated Quarterly*, 1:1 (1917), 2.
161. Walter Sicket, 'Study' and Harold Gilman, 'Mrs. Mounter', *Arts and Letters* 1:1, 5, 29; H. Gaudier-Brzeska, 'Animal Study', *Arts and Letters: An Illustrated Quarterly*, 1:2 (1917), 35; C.R.W. Nevinson, 'Woodcut' and Paul Nash, 'Black Park Lake', *Arts and Letters: An Illustrated Quarterly*, 1:3 (1918), 75, 97.
162. Osbert Sitwell, *Laughter in the Next Room: Being the Fourth Volume of Left Hand, Right Hand!* (London, 1950), 31, 29.
163. Read, *Contrary Experience*, 137.
164. Read, *Annals*, 190; Read, *Cult of Sincerity*, 55.
165. Read, *Annals*, 191, 193.
166. Siegfried Sassoon to Herbert Read: 28th March 1919, *HRAUV*: HR/SS-2.
167. Read, *Annals*, 203.
168. John Middleton Murry, 'Reason and Criticism', *The Times Literary Supplement*, 8 July 1926, 453.
169. Alan Porter, 'Prose', *The Spectator*, 21 July 1928, 40–41 (41).
170. John Cann Bailey, 'Two Books on Wordsworth', *The Times Literary Supplement*, 18 December 1930, 1073.
171. Herbert Read, *The Meaning of Art* (London, 1931), 202–224.
172. David Gascoyne, 'The Significance of English Art', *New English Weekly*, 11 January 1934, 306–307 (306); Percy Wyndham Lewis, *The Demon of Progress in the Arts* (London, 1954), 50, 53.
173. Herbert Read, *Art Now: an Introduction to the Theory of Modern Painting and Sculpture* (London [1933] 1960), 21, 42.
174. Herbert Read, *Art and Society* (London, [1936] 1967), 43, 129.
175. Herbert Read, 'Introduction', in Read (ed.) *Surrealism* (London, 1936), 19–91 (22, 26). See: Herbert Read, *The Philosophy of Modern Art: Collected Essays* (London, 1954), 105–144.
176. Read, 'Introduction', *Surrealism*, 89, 90.
177. *Authors Take Sides on the Spanish War* (London, N.D.), n.p.
178. Herbert Read, *Essential Communism* (London, 1935), 11, 20.
179. A.R. Orage, *Selected Essays and Critical Writings*, Herbert Read and Denis Saurat (eds) (London, 1935).

180. Herbert Read, *In Defence of Shelley & Other Essays* (New York, [1936] 1968), 282.
181. For an overview of Read's politics, see: Dana Ward, 'Art and Anarchy: Herbert Read's Aesthetic Politics', in Michael Paraskos (ed.) *Rereading Read*, 20–33.
182. Read, *Poetry and Anarchism*, 9.
183. Herbert Read, *A Coat of Many Colours: Occasional Essays* (London, 1947), 65.
184. *Kropotkin: Selections from his Writings*, Herbert Read (ed.) (London, 1942).
185. Read, *Cult of Sincerity*, 90.
186. King, *Last Modern*, 166, 297.
187. 'Freedom Defence Committee Constitution', *HRAUV*, 7:11.
188. Richard Taylor, *Against the Bomb: The British Peace Movement: 1958–1965* (Oxford, 1988), 61–75.
189. Maurice Cranston, 'Metaphysical Rebellion', *The Manchester Guardian*, 20 April 1954, 4.
190. Goodway, *Anarchist Seeds*, 183; George Woodcock, *Herbert Read: The Stream and the Source* (London, 1972), 117.
191. Michael De-la-Noy, 'Obituary: Professor Maurice Cranston', *The Independent*, 8 November 1993, 12.
192. Herbert Read, *A Concise History of Modern Painting* (London, 1968), 279, 280.
193. Read, *Cult of Sincerity*, 48, 49.
194. Thomas Hardy, *The Mayor of Casterbridge* (London, 1902), 66.
195. Herbert Read, 'Preface', *To Hell With Culture* (London, 1963), ix–xii (xii).

2 Foundations: System-Building Philosophy

1. John Stuart Mill, *Autobiography* (London, [1873] 1989), 112, 129.
2. Nicholas Capaldi, *John Stuart Mill: A Biography* (Cambridge, 2004), 164.
3. Mill, *Autobiography*, 132.
4. Robert C. Solomon, *Continental Philosophy Since 1750: The Rise and Fall of the Self* (Oxford, 1988), 73; J. W. Burrow, *The Crisis of Reason: European Thought, 1848–1914* (London, 2000), 67.
5. Friedrich Nietzsche, *Beyond Good and Evil*, trans. Helen Zimmern (New York, [1886] 1954), 4.
6. Burrow, *Crisis of Reason*, 234; Arthur P. Mendel, *Michael Bakunin: Roots of Apocalypse* (New York, 1981), 419.
7. James Joll, *The Anarchists* (London, 1979), 112, 110.
8. H. Stuart Hughes, *Consciousness and Society* (New York, 1958), 29.
9. Jean-Francois Lyotard, *The Postmodern Condition* (Manchester, 1984), 38; Lewis Call, *Postmodern Anarchism* (Oxford, 2002), 16.
10. Peter Kropotkin, 'Modern Science and Anarchism [1912]', in George Woodcock (ed.) *Evolution and Environment* (Montréal, 1995), 15–107 (21, 29).
11. See: Malatesta, *Malatesta*, 257–268; Errico Malatesta, *The Anarchist Revolution: Polemical Articles, 1924–1931* (London, 1995), 45–52.
12. Miller, *Anarchism*, 75.
13. Brian Morris, *Kropotkin: The Politics of Community* (New York, 2004), 113.
14. Kropotkin, *Memoirs*, 29, 81.

15. Kropotkin, *Memoirs*, 93.
16. Voltaire, *Philosophical Letters*, trans. Ernest Dilworth (Indianapolis, 1961), 79.
17. Johan Heilbron, *The Rise of Social Theory*, trans. Sheila Gogol (Minneapolis, 1995), 81; Charles de Secondat de Montesquieu, *The Spirit of the Laws*, trans. Thomas Nugent (N.P., 1748), 10.
18. Heilbron, *Social Theory*, 7.
19. P. A. Kropotkin, *The Great French Revolution: 1789–1793* (London, 1909), 243.
20. Prince Kropotkin, *Ethics: Origin and Development*, trans. Louis Friedland (New York, 1924), 196.
21. See also: C. Alexander McKinley, *Illegitimate Children of the Enlightenment: Anarchists and the French Revolution 1880–1914* (New York, 2008), 83–113.
22. Kropotkin, 'Modern Science', 32.
23. Ibid., 33. Original emphasis.
24. Kropotkin, *Ethics*, 249.
25. H. S. Jones, 'Introduction', *Auguste Comte: Early Political Writings* (Cambridge, 1998), vi–xxviii (xv).
26. David Wiltshire, *The Social and Political Thought of Herbert Spencer* (Oxford, 1978), 77.
27. Kropotkin, *Memoirs*, 262.
28. See: Matthew S. Adams, 'Formulating an Anarchist Sociology: Peter Kropotkin's Reading of Herbert Spencer', *Journal of the History of Ideas* – forthcoming.
29. Kropotkin, 'Modern Science', 43; 'Notes: Herbert Spencer', *Freedom: A Journal of Anarchist Communism* (January1904), 2.
30. Herbert Spencer, 'Reasons for Dissenting from the Philosophy of M. Comte', *Essays: Scientific, Political, and Speculative: Vol. III* (London, [1864] 1874), 57–80.
31. Kropotkin, 'Modern Science', 34, 42.
32. Kropotkin, 'Modern Science', 42; P. Kropotkin, 'Herbert Spencer III: Continued', *Freedom: A Journal of Anarchist Communism* (August, 1904), 31; Kropotkin, 'Modern Science', 43.
33. P. A. K., 'Anarchism' in *Encyclopaedia Britannica: Eleventh Edition* (Cambridge, 1910), 914–919 (918).
34. P. Kropotkin, 'Hebert Spencer II', *Freedom: A Journal of Anarchist Communism* (April–May, 1904), 15.
35. P. Kropotkin, 'Herbert Spencer III', *Freedom: A Journal of Anarchism Communism* (June, 1904), 23.
36. Kropotkin, 'Herbert Spencer III', 23. Original emphasis.
37. Kropotkin, *Words of a Rebel*, 57.
38. P. Kropotkin, 'Herbert Spencer III: Continued', *Freedom: A Journal of Anarchist Communism* (September, 1904), 35.
39. Kropotkin, 'Modern Science', 33, 44.
40. Kropotkin, 'Modern Science', 51.
41. Saul Newman, 'Postanarchism: A Politics of Anti-Politics,' *Journal of Political Ideologies*, 16:3 (2011), 313–327; May, *Poststructuralist Anarchism*, 63; Saul Newman, 'Post-Anarchism and Radical Politics Today', in Duane Rousselle and Sureyyya Evren (eds) *Post-Anarchism: A Reader* (London, 2012), 46–69, 61.

42. Morris, *Kropotkin*, 113.
43. Crowder, *Classical Anarchism*, 34–6; Miller, *Anarchism*, 75; Sonn, *Anarchism*, 37.
44. Peter Kropotkin, *Anarchism: Its Philosophy and Ideal* (London, 1897), 2.
45. Kropotkin, *Anarchism: Its Philosophy*, 7.
46. Kropotkin, *Anarchism: Its Philosophy*, 14.
47. Kropotkin, 'Modern Science', 53, 41.
48. Peter Kropotkin, *The Coming Revival of Socialism* (London, 1904), 6.
49. Kropotkin, 'Western Europe', 221; 'Modern Science', 53.
50. Durkheim deemed 'evolutionist' social theory one of these intellectual fashions. Émile Durkheim, *The Rules of Sociological Method*, trans. W.D. Halls (Basingstoke, 1982), 159.
51. P. Kropotkin, 'The Theory of Evolution and Mutual Aid', *The Nineteenth Century and After* (January 1910), 86–107 (88). On Spencer, see: 97, 98.
52. Kropotkin, *Anarchism: Its Philosophy*, 2–3, 4, 3, 6.
53. Kropotkin, *Anarchism: Its Philosophy*, 3; Pierre Kropotkin, *The Place of Anarchism in Socialistic Evolution* (New York, [1886] 1973), 18.
54. Kropotkin, *Ethics*, 209.
55. Graham Purchase, *Evolution and Revolution: an Introduction to the life and thought of Peter Kropotkin* (Sydney, 1996), 133–4; Schmidt and van der Walt, *Black Flame*, 52, 87; Woodcock, *Anarchist Prince*, 321. Morris is more sensitive to the subtleties of this relationship, but at times follows suit: Morris, *Kropotkin*, 90, 130.
56. Knud Haakonssen, 'Introduction', in Haakonssen (ed.) *The Cambridge Companion to Adam Smith* (Cambridge, 2006), 1–21 (2).
57. Norman Barry, *An Introduction to Modern Political Theory* (Basingstoke, 2000), 79–80.
58. Adam Smith, *The Theory of Moral Sentiments* (London, [1759] 1853), 264; Adam Smith, *An Inquiry Into the Nature and Causes of the Wealth of Nations: Volume One* (London, [1776] 1921), 456.
59. Adam Smith, *An Inquiry into the Nature and Causes of the Wealth of Nations: Volume Two* (London, [1776] 1921), 206.
60. Smith, *Moral Sentiments*, 265.
61. Kropotkin, *Words of a Rebel*, 78.
62. Nietzsche, *Beyond Good and Evil*, 189–9.
63. Antonio Gramsci, *Pre-prison Writings*, Richard Bellamy (ed.) (Cambridge, [1918]1994), 54, 43.
64. J. Stalin, *Dialectical and Historical Materialism* (Moscow, 1939), 18.
65. Herbert Read, *A One-Man Manifesto and Other Writings for Freedom Press*, David Goodway (ed.) (London, 1994), 124.
66. Goodway, *Anarchist Seeds*, 191; Marshall, *Demanding the Impossible*, 592.
67. H. W. Häusermann, 'The Development of Herbert Read', in Henry Treece (ed.) *Herbert Read: An Introduction to His Work by Various Hands* (London, 1944), 52–80 (79).
68. Read, *Annals*, 111–112.
69. Read, *Annals*, 125, 128.
70. Herbert Read, *Design and Tradition: The Design Oration* (Hemingford Grey, 1962), 5.
71. Herbert Read to Edward Dahlberg: 26th December 1959, *HRAUV*,HR/ED-415: Encls.026.

72. Read, *Annals*, 130–2; Herbert Read, *Anarchy and Order: Essays in Politics* (London, 1954), 26; Read, *One-Man Manifesto*, 106–111.
73. Herbert Read to George Woodcock: 12th January 1965, *HRAUV*, 62.29.18; Herbert Read to George Woodcock: 3rd August 1966, *HRAUV*, 62.29.20.
74. Lévi-Strauss, *Savage Mind*, 17.
75. Herbert Read, *Tenth Muse: Essays in Criticism* (London, 1957), 175.
76. Read, *Tenth Muse*, 176.
77. Read, *Annals*, 111.
78. Read, *Contrary Experience*, 70, 71.
79. Read, *Tenth Muse*, 178.
80. Read, *Tenth Muse*, 4, 3.
81. Herbert Read to Francis Berry: 10th April 1953, *HRAUV*, 61/20/9.
82. Read, *Anarchy and Order*, 9.
83. Read, *Annals*, 225.
84. e.g. Herbert Read, *Art and Industry: The Principles of Industrial Design* (London, [1934] 1944), 55; Read, *Anarchy and Order*, 220.
85. Michael Paraskos, 'Introduction', Herbert Read, *To Hell With Culture* (London, 2002), ix–xxiii (xv). See also: Allan Antliff, 'Biocentrism and anarchy: Herbert Read's Modernism', in Oliver A.I. Botar and Isabel Wünsche (eds) *Biocentrism and Modernism* (Farnham, 2011), 153–160.
86. Herbert Read, *Reason and Romanticism: Essays in Literary Criticism* (London, 1926), 104.
87. Read, *Forms of Things Unknown*, 76, 92.
88. Read, *Anarchy and Order*, 24; Herbert Read, *Art and Alienation: The Role of the Artist in Society* (New York, 1967), 137.
89. Herbert Read, *The Politics of the Unpolitical* (London, 1943), 124; Read, *Art and Society*, 2.
90. Read, *Art and Society*, 112.
91. Read, *Art and Industry*, 7.
92. Ibid., 54, 55.
93. Herbert Read, *Education Through Art* (London, 1943), 297.
94. Read, *Cult of Sincerity*, 90.
95. George Woodcock, 'Anarchism and the Role of Art: Review of Education Through Art', *The Nation*, 12 October 1974, 341–3 (341).
96. Herbert Read to Edward Dahlberg: 20th April 1956, *HRAUV*, 228: Encl.08; Edward Dahlberg, *The Confessions of Edward Dahlberg* (New York, 1971), 222.
97. Herbert Read, *The Knapsack: A Pocket-Book of Prose and Verse* (London, 1939), v.
98. Read, *Cult of Sincerity*, 165, 178, 182.
99. Read, *Tenth Muse*, 53, 89.
100. Read, *Cult of Sincerity*, 112.
101. Read, *Tenth Muse*, 90, 93, 96. Original emphasis.
102. 'A Conversation with Herbert Read', *Art Education*, 20:9 (1967), 32–35 (34).
103. Read, *To Hell With Culture* (2002), 167.
104. Alexandra Harris, *Romantic Moderns* (London, 2010), 11.
105. Jay Winter, *Sites of Memory, Sites of Mourning: The Great War in European Cultural History* (Cambridge, 1995), 58.

106. Honeywell, *British Anarchist Tradition*, 54.
107. Herbert Read, *Existentialism, Marxism and Anarchism* (London, 1949), 28, 29.
108. Herbert Read, 'Introduction', *Kropotkin: Selections from his Writings* (London, 1942), 7–16 (15).
109. Read, *Art and Society*, 112; Read, *Art Now*, 38; Herbert Read, *Form in Modern Poetry: An Essay in Aesthetics* (London, 1948), 7.
110. Read, *Reason and Romanticism*, 83–106. e.g. Read, *Education through Art*, 84–6, 179–85; Read, *Cult of Sincerity*, 86–91.
111. Alex Comfort, *Authority and Delinquency: A Study in the Psychology of Power* (London, [1950] 1970), 13.
112. Read, *Anarchy and Order*, 15.
113. *The Times*, 9 December 1903, 9.
114. Gay, *Modernism*, 381.

3 Statism: The Power of History

1. James Mavor, *My Windows on the Street of the World: Volume 2* (London, 1923), 91–93.
2. 'Kropotkin Says State Socialism is Thriving in the U.S.', *Boston Daily Advertiser*, 23 November 1897, n.p.
3. Miller, *Anarchism*, 3; Freeden, *Ideologies*, 311–312.
4. Benj. R. Tucker, *Instead of a Book: By a Man Too Busy to Write One: A Fragmentary Exposition of Philosophical Anarchism* (New York, [1897] 1972), 404.
5. P.A.K., 'Anarchism', 917; Kropotkin, 'Modern Science', 64.
6. Tucker, *Instead of a Book*, 389, 390.
7. Kinna, *Anarchism*, 44–81.
8. 'Prefatory Note', *English Historical Review*, 1:1 (1886), 1–6 (2, 3).
9. Peter Kropotkin, 'The State: Its Historic Role [1896]', in George Woodcock (ed.) *Fugitive Writings* (Montréal, 1993), 159–201 (197).
10. 'A Teacher of Anarchy', *The North American*, 27 October 1897, 1; 'Justice, Morality', *Boston Daily Advertiser*, 8 November 1897, 3.
11. Rowland Kenney, *Westering: An Autobiography* (London, 1939), 245; 'Fields, Factories and Workshops', *Daily News*, 10 April 1889, 3; 'Lectures by Prince Kropotkin', *Glasgow Herald*, 5 March 1897; 'Prince Kropotkin on Economics', *Glasgow Herald*, 18 February 1899, 4; 'Untitled', *Aberdeen Weekly Journal*, 26 March 1889, 4.
12. Woodcock, *Anarchist Prince*, 171–205.
13. Crowder, *Classical Anarchism*, 168; Miller, *Anarchism*, 84; Newman, 'Post-Anarchism and Radical Politics', 61.
14. Martin Buber, *Paths in Utopia* (London, 1949), 38.
15. Pierre Kropotkine, *Law and Authority: An Anarchist Essay* (London, 1886), 17, 3, 17, 6,7.
16. P. Kropotkin, *The Conquest of Bread* (New York, 1907), vi.
17. Kropotkin, *French Revolution*, 373, 489.
18. Miller, *Anarchism*, 94; Kropotkin, *French Revolution*, 491.
19. Ibid., 362.

20. G.D.H. Cole, *A History of Socialist Thought: Volume 1* (London, 1953), 7; Leszek Kołakowsi, *Main Currents of Marxism: The Forerunners, The Golden Age, The Breakdown*, trans. P.S. Falla (New York, 2007), 175–176.
21. Kropotkin, *Conquest of Bread*, viii.
22. Kropotkin, 'Modern Science', 28–29.
23. Kropotkin, *Conquest of Bread*, ix.
24. Robert Owen, *The Life of Robert Owen* (London, 1920), 132.
25. 'Motion Respecting Mr. Owen's Plan' 16th December 1819, *The Parliamentary Debates from the Year 1803 to the Present Time: Volume 41* (London, 1820), 1189–1216 (1189, 1216).
26. Kropotkin, 'Modern Science', 19.
27. Kropotkin, 'Modern Science', 18.
28. P. Kropotkin, *Mutual Aid: A Factor of Evolution* (London, [1902] 1939), 1.
29. Kropotkin, *French Revolution*, 582.
30. Kropotkin, *Place of Anarchism in Socialistic Evolution*, 7.
31. Kropotkin, 'Modern Science', 35, 39, 65.
32. Kropotkin, 'Modern Science', 66, 70.
33. Kropotkin, *Conquest of Bread*, ix.
34. Kropotkin, *Words of a Rebel*, 91.
35. Beverley Southgate, 'Humani nil alienum: The Quest for "Human Nature" ', in Keith Jenkins (ed.) *Manifestos for History* (Oxford, 2007), 67–76 (69).
36. Thomas Babington Macaulay, *Macaulay's History of England: From the Accession of James II: Vol. 1* (London, 1953), 1.
37. John Burrow, *A History of Histories: Epics, Chronicles, Romances and Inquiries from Herodotus and Thucydides to the Twentieth Century* (New York, 2008), 346–348.
38. Macaulay, *England*, 1, 154.
39. Karl Marx, *Capital: A Critique of Political Economy* (Chicago, [1867] 1906), 788 n1.
40. Kropotkin, 'Modern Science', 61, 62, 70–72.
41. H. Butterfield, *The Whig Interpretation of History* (London, 1950), v.
42. Miller, *Anarchism*, 75; Crowder, *Classical Anarchism*, 168; Sonn, *Anarchism*, 37.
43. Peter Kropotkin, *Socialism and Politics* (London, 1903), 15.
44. It is worth noting that while Kropotkin followed convention in using terms like 'barbarian' and 'savage' he was actively seeking to deny the pejorative connotations apparent in such terms. Kropotkin, *Mutual Aid*, 118, 83.
45. Kropotkin, 'The State', 160.
46. Kropotkin, *Mutual Aid*, 109, 135, 175, 178.
47. Ibid., 114, 132, 118.
48. Ibid., 118, 130.
49. Ibid., 131.
50. Kropotkin, 'The State', 170; Kropotkin, *Mutual Aid*, 101.
51. Ibid., 135.
52. Kropotkin, 'The State', 171; Kropotkin, *Mutual Aid*, 147.
53. Ibid., 149.
54. Kropotkin, 'The State', 173; Kropotkin, *Mutual Aid*, 140.
55. Kropotkin, *Mutual Aid*, 142.
56. Kropotkin, 'The State', 174, 175.

57. James E. Thorold Rogers, *The Economic Interpretation of History* (London, [1888] 1909), 306; Kropotkin, *Mutual Aid*, 159.
58. A. Dwight Culler, *The Victorian Mirror of History* (London, 1985), 155.
59. Bertrand Russell, *Why I am Not a Christian and Other Essays* (London, 1957), 128.
60. William Chester Jordan, *Europe in the High Middle Ages* (London, 2001), 188; Kropotkin, *Mutual Aid*, 136.
61. Kropotkin, *Mutual Aid*, 143.
62. Carol Lansing, *The Florentine Magnates: Lineage and Faction in a Medieval Commune* (Princeton, 1991), 167.
63. Kropotkin, *Words a Rebel*, 85.
64. Karl Marx and Friedrich Engels, *The Communist Manifesto* (London, [1888] 2002), 224.
65. Kropotkin, *Mutual Aid*, 177.
66. Kropotkin, 'The State', 173, Kropotkin, *Mutual Aid*, 174.
67. Kropotkin, *Mutual Aid*, 138.
68. Ibid., 175.
69. Ibid., 177.
70. Ibid., 178.
71. Ibid., 182.
72. Jean-Jacques Rousseau, *The Social Contract or Principles of Political Right*, trans. Henry J. Tozer (New York, [1762] 1898), 197; Kropotkin, 'The State', 188.
73. Read, *Philosophy of Modern Art*, 13.
74. The ascendency of Marxism within in the academy, especially in art and cultural studies, is a persuasive explanation for Read's eclipse from intellectual life after his death. See: Michael Paraskos, 'The Curse of King Bomba: Or How Marxism Stole Modernism', in Paraskos (ed.) *Rereading Read*, 44–57.
75. Tom Steele, 'Circles of Modernism: Herbert Read, Arnold Hauser and the Emergence of Art History in Leeds', in Michael Paraskos (ed.) *Rereading Read*, 112–119.
76. Herbert Read, 'Introduction', in F.D. Kingender, *Goya in the Democratic Tradition* (London, 1968), vii.
77. John Berger to Herbert Read: 29th December 1961, *HRAUV*, HR/JB-20; Cutting of review of 'The Grass Roots of Art' in *The Tribune*, *HRAUV*, HR/JB-2.
78. Read, *Meaning of Art*, 116.
79. For an invaluable discussion of this work, see: David Thistlewood, 'Herbert Read's Organic Aesthetic [II] 1950–1968', *Herbert Read Reassessed*, 233–247 (238–241).
80. Herbert Read to Stephen Spender: 22nd February 1955', *HRAUV*, 49/28/1.
81. Herbert Read, *Icon & Idea: The Function of Art in the Development of the Human Consciousness* (New York, [1955] 1965), 32.
82. Ibid., 31.
83. Read, *Anarchy and Order*, 220.
84. Read, *Icon & Idea*, 17, 1,
85. Ibid., 70, 75–76, 82.
86. Ibid., 27; Herbert Read, *The Origins of Form in Art* (London, 1965), 78.
87. Read, *Icon & Idea*, 38, 42.

88. Ibid., 42. Original emphasis.
89. Ibid., 38–39.
90. On modernism as a critique of modernity, see: Stephen Ross, 'Introduction: The missing link', in Ross (ed.) *Modernism and Theory: A Critical Debate* (London, 2009), 1–17. On 'primitivism', see: Tim Armstrong, *Modernism: A Cultural History* (Cambridge, 2005), 140.
91. Read, *Coat of Many Colours*, 129.
92. Read, *The Tenth Muse*, 304, 305, 310.
93. Read, *Icon & Idea*, 53, 59.
94. Ibid., 60, 75, 78, 82.
95. Ibid., 87.
96. Edgar Wind, 'Ideas and Images', *Times Literary Supplement*, 11 May 1956, 277–278 (278).
97. Read, *Politics of the Unpolitical*, 47.
98. Read, *Coat of Many Colours*, 6.
99. Read, *Icon & Idea*, 86.
100. Read, *Art and Alienation*, 73.
101. Read, *Politics of the Unpolitical*, 99.
102. Herbert Read, *The Forms of Things Unknown: Essays Towards an Aesthetic Philosophy* (London, 1960), 195, 204.
103. Read, *Icon & Idea*, 137.
104. Ibid., 21; Read, *Art Now*, 85; Read, *Art and Alienation*, 7.
105. Read, *Icon & Idea*, 37.
106. Read, *Forms of Things Unknown*, 142.
107. Read, *Kropotkin*, 15.
108. Andrew Causey, 'Herbert Read and Contemporary Art', *Hebert Read Reassessed*, 123–144 (125–126, 136–138). Read, *Icon & Idea*, 1; Read, *Philosophy of Modern Art*, 7.
109. Read, *Art and Alienation*, 126; Read, *Philosophy of Modern Art*, 27.
110. Read, *Icon & Idea*, 92.
111. Kropotkin, *Mutual Aid*, 171.
112. Read, *Anarchy and Order*, 222; Herbert Read, *The Philosophy of Anarchism* (London, 1940), 11.
113. Read, *Art and Alienation*, 17.
114. Read, *Anarchy and Order*, 225.
115. Read, *Coat of Many Colours*, 65.
116. Read, *Icon & Idea*, 138.
117. Theodor Adorno, 'The Schema of Mass Culture', in J.M. Bernstein (ed.) *The Culture Industry: Selected Essays on Mass Culture* (London, 1991), 61–97 (96).
118. Read, *Tenth Muse*, 142.
119. Herbert Read, *The Grass Roots of Art: Lectures on the Social Aspects of Art in an Industrial Age* (London, 1955), 127.
120. Herbert Read to Victor Gollancz: 24th December 1948, *HRAUV*, B7:11; Edward Dahlberg to Herbert Read: 15th November 1951, *HRAUV*, HR/ED-75.
121. Herbert Read to John Berger: 31st July 1955, *HRAUVI*, HR/JB: Encl.02.
122. J.B. Priestley, *Letter to a Returning Serviceman* (London, 1945), 31; Richard Hoggart, *Mass Media in a Mass Society* (London, 2004), 128.
123. Read, *Politics of the Unpolitical*, 107.

124. Peter Hennessy, *Never Again: Britain 1954–51* (London, 2006), 430.
125. Read, *Philosophy of Modern Art*, 60, 61, 69.
126. Read, *Coat of Many Colours*, 114.
127. Kropotkin, *Selected Writings*, 144–145. Original emphasis.

4 Revolution: The Journey to Communism

1. *Punch, Or the London Charivari*, 26 April 1922, 327.
2. A. Fenner Brockway, *Socialism for Pacifists* (Manchester, 1916), 50.
3. 'Heir to Austrian Throne, Archduke Ferdinand, and Wife Slain by Assassin', *Washington Post*, 29 June 1914, 1.
4. 'Germany the Aggressor', *The Times*, 24 October 1916, 9.
5. Read, *Annals*, 138.
6. Herbert Read, *A World Within a War* (London, 1944), 22.
7. George Woodcock, *Letters to the Past: An Autobiography* (Toronto, 1982), 306.
8. Peter Kropotkin, *Wars and Capitalism* (London, 1914), 3.
9. Peter Kropotkine, *Revolutionary Studies* (London, 1892), 18.
10. Prince Kropotkin, 'War or Peace [1896]', *Report of Proceedings of the International Workers' Congress*,75–82 (77).
11. Ibid., 26.
12. Kropotkin, *Act for Yourselves*, (120).
13. P. Kropotkin, 'Herbert Spencer [III]', *Freedom: A Journal of Anarchist Communism*, (February 1904), 7–8 (7).
14. Kropotkin, 'War or Peace?', 76.
15. Ibid.; Kropotkin, *Wars and Capitalism*, 13.
16. Kropotkin, 'War or Peace?', 76; Kropotkin, *Wars and Capitalism*, 13.
17. Peter Kropotkin, 'Anarchist Morality [1892]', in George Woodcock (ed.) *Fugitive Writings* Montréal, 1993), 127–153 (127); Kropotkin, *Mutual Aid*, 178.
18. Kropotkine, *Revolutionary Studies*, 27.
19. Peter Kropotkin, *Words of a Rebel*, trans. George Woodcock (Montréal, [1885] 1992), 101–102; Kropotkin, *Act for Yourselves*, 117.
20. Bevir, *British Socialism*, 276.
21. Woodcock, *Anarchist Prince*, 408, 415–416, 426–427, 429–430; Miller, *Anarchism*, 75, 194 n40.
22. 'Prince Krapotkin [sic] on Socialism', *Aberdeen Weekly Journal*, 2 November 1886, 2; 'Prince Krapotkin [sic] in Leeds', *The Leeds Mercury*, 24 March 1887, 3; 'Prince Krapotkin [sic]', *The Dundee Courier & Argus*, 6 December 1886, n.p.; 'Prince Krapotkin [sic]' in Bradford', *The Leeds Mercury*, 24 March 1887, 3; 'Prince Kropotkine on the Nationalisation of Land', *Edinburgh Evening News*, 11 November 1886, 3; 'Prince Krapotkin [sic] in Ancoats', *Manchester Times*, 20 October 1888, 2; 'Woodcock, *Anarchist Prince*, 245.
23. Kropotkin, *Words of a Rebel*, 33.
24. 'Fields, Factories and Workshops', *Daily News*, 10 April 1899, n.p.
25. Ruth Kinna, 'Fields of Vision: Kropotkin and Revolutionary Change', *SubStance*, 36:2 (2007), 67–86 (76–77).
26. Kropotkin, *Act for Yourselves*, 120, 121.
27. Miller, *Anarchism*, 74.

28. Sonn, *Anarchism*, 37; George V. Plekhanov, *Fundamental Problems of Marxism* (New York, 1975), 141.
29. Nicolas Walter, *The Anarchist Past & Other Essays*, David Goodway (ed.) (Nottingham, 2009), 113. See also: May, *Poststructuralist Anarchism*, 60; Saul Newman, 'Anarchism, Utopianism and the Politics of Emancipation', in Laurance Davis and Ruth Kinna (eds) *Anarchism and Utopianism* (Manchester, 2009), 207–220 (213).
30. Kropotkin, *Ethics*, 3.
31. Kropotkin, *Words of a Rebel*, 29.
32. Kropotkin, *Conquest of Bread*, 154.
33. Kropotkin, 'Modern Science', 93, 31, 21. Original emphasis.
34. Kropotkin, *Ethics*, 49; *Mutual Aid*, 232; Kropotkin '*Anarchist Commuism: Its Basis and Principles*', 4.
35. Kropotkin, *Ethics*, 14, 18.
36. See also: Matthew S. Adams, 'Kropotkin: Evolution, Revolutionary Change and the End of History', *Anarchist Studies*, 19:1 (2011), 54–81.
37. Kropotkin, *French Revolution*, 576.
38. Kropotkin, *Anarchism: Its Philosophy and Ideal*, 27.
39. Kropotkin, *Revolutionary Studies*, 9.
40. Peter Kropotkin to W. Wray Skilbeck: 16th November 1909, *CWA*, 716/84/23; Peter Kropotkin to W. Wray Skilbeck: 14th April 1010, *CWA*, 716/84/39.
41. Kropotkin, 'Theory of Evolution and Mutual Aid', 86–107.
42. P. Kropotkin, 'The Direct Action of Environment of Plants', *The Nineteenth Century and After* (July, 1910), 58–77 (59). Original emphasis.
43. For more on this see: Adams, 'Formulating an Anarchist Sociology'.
44. Kropotkin, *Mutual Aid*, 76.
45. Stefan Collini, Donald Winch, and John Burrow, *That Noble Science of Politics: A Study in Nineteenth Century Intellectual History* (Cambridge, 1987), 146.
46. Krishan Kumar, 'Maine and the Theory of Progress', *The Victorian Achievement of Sir Henry Maine: A Centennial Reappraisal* (Cambridge, 1991), 76–87 (76–77).
47. Henry Sumner Maine, *Village-Communities in the East and West* (London, 1871); Henry Sumner Maine, *Ancient Law* (London, [1861] 1931), 2.
48. *Derby Daily Telegraph*, 31 December 1891, 3; *The Nottingham Evening Post*, 31 December 1891, 3; *The Yorkshire Herald*, 1 January 1892, 7; *Citizen*, 7 January 1892, 4.
49. Walter, *The Anarchist Past*, 114; Quail, *Slow Burning Fuse*, 52.
50. Kropotkin, *Revolutionary Studies*, 27.
51. Kropotkin, *Coming Revival of Socialism*, 23.
52. Peter Kropotkin, 'Preface', in Émile Pataud and Émile Pouget, *How We Shall Bring About the Revolution* (London, [1913] 1990), xxxi–xxxvii (xxxi, xxxii).
53. Kropotkin, *Conquest of Bread*, 23, 24, 25.
54. Ibid., 28. Original emphasis.
55. Kropotkin, *Act for Yourselves*, 32. Original emphasis.
56. Kropotkin, *Words of a Rebel*, 171.
57. Kropotkin, *Conquest of Bread*, 57, 54, 58.

58. Ibid., 64.
59. Ibid., 68, 69, 85.
60. Kropotkin, *Fields, Factories and Workshops*, 21, 22.
61. Ibid., 22; Adam Smith, *The Wealth of Nations: Books IV-V* (London, [1776] 1999), 368.
62. Hobsbawm, *Age of Empire*, 271.
63. Kropotkin, *Fields, Factories and Workshops*, 327.
64. Ibid., 83–98.
65. Ibid., 158, 136, 233.
66. Ibid., 159.
67. Kropotkin, *Act for Yourselves*, 58, 59, 72.
68. Kropotkin, *Conquest of Bread*, x, 72, 75.
69. Kropotkin, *Act for Yourselves*, 69.
70. Kropotkin, *Conquest of Bread*, 77.
71. Kropotkin, *Words of a Rebel*, 182, 33, 90.
72. Ibid., 72.
73. Kropotkin, *Conquest of Bread*, 73.
74. Kropotkin, *French Revolution*, 64.
75. Ibid., 58.
76. Fred Morrow Fling, 'The Great French Revolution, 1789–1793', *American Historical Review*, 15:3 (1910), 601–602 (602).
77. 'Histories of the Autumn', *The Times Literary Supplement*, 7 December 1909, 472.
78. Kropotkin, *Act for Yourselves*, 35, 36.
79. Kropotkin, *Revolutionary Studies*, 5.
80. Kropotkin, *French Revolution*, 181; Kropotkin, *Revolutionary Studies*, 4.
81. Kropotkin, *French Revolution*, 385; George Woodcock, 'An Introduction', in Peter Kropotkin, *The Great French Revolution* (Montréal, 1989), x–xxviii (xxvi–xxviii).
82. Kropotkin, *French Revolution*, 335.
83. Maximilien Robespierre, 'On the Conduct to be Pursued', in H. Morse Stephens (ed.) *Orators of the French Revolution: Volume II* (Oxford, 1892), 357–366 (366).
84. Kropotkin, *French Revolution*, 380, 462, 297.
85. P.A. Kropotkin, 'To Steffen', *Selected Writings on Anarchism and Revolution* (London, [1914] 1970), 308–319 (310).
86. Hagen Schulze, *States, Nations and Nationalism: From the Middle Ages to the Present* (Oxford, 1996), 233.
87. Kropotkin, *French Revolution*, 253.
88. Ibid., 253.
89. Uri Gordon, *Anarchy Alive! Anti-authoritarian Politics from Practise to Theory* (London, 2008), 98–100; P. Kropotkine, *In Russian and French Prisons* (London, 1887), 338–371.
90. François Furet, 'The French Revolution Revisited', in Gary Kates (ed.) *The French Revolution: Recent Debates and New Controversies* (London, 1998), 71–90 (80).
91. Emmanuel Joseph Sieyès, 'What Is the Third Estate?', in Michael Sonenscher (ed.) *Sieyès: Political Writings* (Indianapolis, 2003), 92–162.
92. Kropotkin, *Words of a Rebel*, 75.

93. Orwell, 'Review of *A Coat of Many Colours*', 402–405; Goodway, *Anarchist Seeds*, 193.
94. 'The New Year Honours', *The Times* 1 January 1953, 2.
95. Albert Meltzer, *I Couldn't Paint Golden Angels: Sixty Years of Commonplace Life and Anarchist Agitation* (Edinburgh, 1996), 126.
96. 'The Honours List', *The Manchester Guardian*, 1 January 1953, 4.
97. Read, *One-Man Manifesto*, 204.
98. Colin Ward, 'Herbert Read: The Anarchist Knight', *Peace News*, 21 June 1968, 2.
99. Herbert Read, 'Drawings by Augustus John', *The Burlington Magazine for Connoisseurs*, 78:454 (1941), 28; Michael Holroyd, *Augustus John: A Biography* (London, 1976), 685, 769; Read, *One-Man Manifesto*, 204.
100. Robert Irwin, *Memoirs of a Dervish: Sufis, Mystics and the Sixties* (London, 2011), n.p.
101. Woodcock, *Stream and the Source*, 245; George Woodcock, *Taking it to the Letter* (Ontario, 1981), 46.
102. Herbert Read to George Woodcock: 12th April 1953, *HRAUV*, 62.29.12.
103. Herbert Read to Margaret Gardiner: 12th December 1965, *BLMC*, Add.71607, ff.107.
104. King, *Last Modern*, 263–264.
105. Geoffrey Grigson, *Recollections: Mainly of Writers & Artists* (London, 1984), 57, 59.
106. P.N. Purbank, *E.M. Forster: A Life: Volume One* (London, 1977), 24.
107. Read, *One-Man Manifesto*, 205; Herbert Read to George Woodcock: 25th December 1952, *HRAUV*, 62.29.12.
108. Stephen Spender, *The Thirties and After: Poetry, Politics, People* (Glasgow, 1978), 174, 175, 251.
109. C.P. Snow, *The Two Cultures and the Scientific Revolution* (Cambridge, 1959), 21, 24.
110. Snow, *Two Cultures*; Herbert Read, 'Mood of the Month – X', *The London Magazine*, 6:8 (1959), 39–43 (41).
111. Ibid., 41.
112. C.P. Snow, 'Correspondence', *The London Magazine*, 16:10 (1959), 57–59 (57); Read, 'Introduction', *Surrealism*, 60; Read, *Philosophy of Modern Art*, 127.
113. Snow, 'Correspondence', 57.
114. Herbert Read, 'Correspondence', *The London Magazine*, 16:11 (1959), 73–74 (73).
115. Herbert Read, 'Art and the Revolutionary Attitude', *The Southern Review*, 1 (1935), 239–252 (248); Read, *Poetry and Anarchism*, 55.
116. Read, *Anarchy and Order*, 16, 17.
117. David Sachs, '*The Rebel*. By Albert Camus', *The Philosophical Review*, 64:1 (1955), 150–152 (152).
118. Hebert Read, 'Foreword', in Albert Camus, *The Rebel: An Essay on Man in Revolt* (New York, 1956), n.p.
119. Read, *Cult of Sincerity*, 92, 93.
120. Herbert Read, 'Pragmatic Anarchism', *Encounter*, 30:1 (1968), 54–61 (61,60). Leonard Krimerman and Lewis Perry (eds) *Patterns of Anarchy: A Collection of Writings on the Anarchist Tradition* (New York, 1966).

121. For a discussion, see: Matthew S. Adams, 'Art, Education, and Revolution: Herbert Read and the Reorientation of British Anarchism', *History of European Ideas*, 39:5 (2013) 709–728.
122. David Stafford, 'Anarchists in Britain Today', in David E. Apter and James Joll (eds) *Anarchism Today* (London, 1971), 84–104 (92); Landauer cited in Eugene Lunn, *Prophet of Community: The Romantic Socialism of Gustav Landauer* (Berkley, CA, 1973), 3.
123. Colin Ward, *Anarchy in Action* (London, 2008), 10, 23.
124. King, *Last Modern*, 202.
125. Read, *Education Through Art*, 65, 296, 297, 221, 275.
126. Herbert Read, *The Education of Free Men* (London, 1944), 6, 15, 24.
127. Ibid., 31.
128. Honeywell, *A British Anarchist Tradition*, 62.
129. David Thistlewood, 'Herbert Read', *Prospects*, 24:1–2 (1994), 375–390 (376).
130. Read, *Education through Art*, 233.
131. Herbert Read, *Education for Peace* (London, 1950), 44, 46. Original emphasis.
132. Ibid., 47.
133. Read, *Cult of Sincerity*, 92.
134. Read, *Education for Peace*, 46.
135. Ibid., 47.
136. Ibid., 48, 49, 50, 58.
137. Read, *One-Man Manifesto*, 124, 125.
138. Read, *Education for Peace*, 56.
139. Edward Dahlberg to Herbert Read: 15th November 1951, *HRAUV*, HR/ED-75; Herbert Read to Edward Dahlberg: 19th November 1951, *HRAUV*, HR/ED-77.
140. Read, *Education for Peace*, 54.
141. Vernon Richards, *Lessons of the Spanish Revolution* (London, [1955] 1995), 201, 204.
142. Bart de Ligt, *The Conquest of Violence: An Essay on War and Revolution* (London, 1989), 201.
143. Sean Scalmer, *Gandhi in the West: The Mahatma and the Rise of Radical Protest* (Cambridge, 2011), 116. For Read's copies of de Light's and Gregg's books: *Herbert Read Collection, Brotherton Special Collections, University of Leeds* [hereafter: *HRCUL*]: MS20c and C3016.
144. Nicolas Walter, 'Remembering Herbert Read', *Anarchy*, 91 (1968), 287–288 (288).
145. Read, *Poetry and Anarchism*, 75.
146. Martin Ceadel, *Pacifism in Britain 1914–1945: The Defining of a Faith* (Oxford, 1980), 3–5.
147. A.J.P. Taylor, *The Trouble Makers: Dissent Over Foreign Policy 1729–1939* (London, [1957] 1993), 51n.
148. Modris Eksteins, 'All Quiet on the Western Front and the Fate of a War', *Journal of Contemporary History*, 15:2 (1980), 345–366.
149. Erich Maria Remarque to Herbert Read: 18th May 1929, *HRAUV*, HR-EMR-8; Erich Maria Remarque: 5th February 1929, *HRAUV*, HR-EMR-3: Encl.01. I am indebted to Timo Schaefer for translating these letters.
150. Watson, *Fighting Different Wars*, 187.

151. Read, *Poetry and Anarchism*, 63, 68, 72, 73, 74, 75.
152. Read, *One-Man Manifesto*, 33, 34, 37.
153. Read, *Annals*, 130, 131.
154. Read, *One-Man Manifesto*, 34.
155. Read, *Cult of Sincerity*, 92; Herbert Read, *The Sense of Glory: Essays in Criticism* (Cambridge, 1929), 43.
156. Read, *Annals*, 132; Herbert Read, *Freedom: Is It a Crime?* (London, 1945), 6.
157. Ibid., 10, 12.
158. Ibid., 10.
159. Goodway, *Anarchist Seeds*, 190.
160. Herbert Read, 'The War as Seen by British Artists', in Monroe Wheeler (ed.) *Britain at War* (New York, [1941] 1972), 11–12 (12).
161. Read, *Freedom*, 7.
162. Mazower, *Dark Continent*, 237.
163. Herbert Read, 'What is Freedom?', *The New Statesman*, 26th August 1944, 137.
164. It should be noted, however, that Read's interest in the relationship between art and education existed before the Second World War. In his inaugural address at the University of Edinburgh, he longed for a time when 'art should so dominate our lives that we might say: there are no longer works of art, but art only', and hinted at the moralising attributes of the cultivation of 'sensibility'. See: 'Appendix D: The Place of Art in a University [1931]' in *Education through Art*, 258, 253.
165. E.M. Foster to Herbert Read: 15th February 1945', *HRAUV*, 48.41.
166. 'Freedom Defence Committee Constitution', *HRAUV*, 7:11:50/1.
167. Herbert Read to Victor Gollancz, 24th December 1948, *HRAUV*, 7:11: Unnumbered.
168. Kenneth O. Morgan, *The People's Peace: British History: 1945–1990* (Oxford, 1992), 167–168.
169. Herbert Read, 'Gandhi's 'Autobiography', *The Listener*, (21 July 1949), 121.
170. Herbert Read, 'Three Page Statement', *HRAUV*, 49/17/4; Herbert Read to Arthur Koestler, George Mikes and Stephen Spender, N.D. [circa 1956]: 49/17/7.
171. 'Sir Herbert Read Joins Sit-Down', *Peace News*, 6 January 1961, 1–2; Herbert Read, 'Disobedience Against Polaris', *Peace News*, 20 January 1961, 1.
172. Taylor, *Against the Bomb*, 193.
173. Herbert Read to Margaret Gardiner: 11th October 1967, *BLMC*, Add.71607, f.110; Frantz Fanon, *The Wretched of the Earth*, trans. Constance Farrington (New York, 1961), 315, 316.
174. Herbert Read to Margaret Gardiner: 16th October 1967, *BLMC*, Add.71607, f.110.
175. Hugh Gaitskell cited in Alan Sinfield, *Literature, Politics, and Culture in Postwar Britain* (Berkeley, 1989), 254.
176. Herbert Read to Margaret Gardiner: 16th October 1967.
177. Sir Herbert Read, 'Anarchism in the Affluent Society', *Underground* (1966), 1–11 (9, 8).
178. Jack London, *The Iron Heel* (New York, 1908), xi, 353, xii, xiv.
179. Herbert Read to Francis Berry: 10th April 1953, *HRAUV*, 61/20/9.

5 Utopia: Imagining Post-capitalist Society

1. Karl Marx and Frederick Engels, *Collected Works: Volume 35* (London, 1986), 12–23 (17).
2. Marx and Engels, *Communist Manifesto*, 255, 256.
3. Isaiah Berlin, *The Crooked Timber of Humanity*, ed. Henry Hardy (London, 2003), 48; Henry Hardy, 'Editor's Preface', *The Crooked Timber*, ix–xii (xi–xii).
4. Berlin, *Crooked Timber*, 12, 46, 211.
5. Karl Marx, *The Eighteenth Brumaire of Louis Bonaparte*, trans. Daniel De Leon (Chicago, 1907), 5.
6. Yevgeny Zamyatin, *We*, trans. Michael Glenny (London, [1924] 1984), 19.
7. Isaiah Berlin, *Liberty* (Oxford, 2002), 112.
8. Leszek Kołakowski, *Modernity on Endless Trial* (London, 1990), 142.
9. Zygmunt Bauman, *Modernity and the Holocaust* (Ithaca, NY, 1989), 113.
10. Barbara Goodwin and Keith Taylor, *The Politics of Utopia: A Study in Theory and Practise* (London, 1982), 93.
11. Berlin, *Crooked Timber*, 211.
12. Aileen Kelly, *Mikhail Bakunin: A Study in the Psychology and Politics of Utopianism* (Oxford, 1982), 198, 292, 291–293.
13. H.M. Hyndman, *The Historical Basis of Socialism in England* (London, 1883), 424, 425.
14. P. Kropotkin, 'Bakunin', *Freedom: A Journal of Anarchist Communism* (June–July 1905), 18–19 (18).
15. Peter Kropotkin, 'Le Vingtième Siècle', *La Révolte*, 30 November 1889, 1; Edward Bellamy, *Looking Backward: 2000–1887* (New York, [1888] 1917), 146, 99, 100; Peter Kropotkin, 'Le Vingtième Siècle II', *La Révolte*, 14 December 1889), 1.
16. Richard Jefferies, *After London; or, Wild England* (London, [1885] 1886), 33; Ignatius Donnelly, *Caesar's Column: A Story of the Twentieth Century* (Chicago, 1890), 38.
17. Kropotkin, *Act for Yourselves*, 91; P. Kropotkin, 'Past and Future: A Speech Delivered by P. Kropotkin at South Place Chapel at the Commemoration of the Paris Commune', *Freedom: A Journal of Anarchist Communism* (April, 1889), 17–18 (18).
18. Peter Kropotkin, 'Must We Occupy Ourselves with an Examination of the Ideal of a Future System?', *Fugitive Writings*, 13–68 (13, 14).
19. Alexander Herzen, *From the Other Side and the Russian People and Socialism* (London, [1851] 1956), 189.
20. Michel Bakounine, *Oeuvres: Tome II* (Paris, 1907), 93; Michael Bakunin, *Statism and Anarchy* (Cambridge, [1873] 2005), 209.
21. Kropotkin, *Conquest of Bread*, x, 26, 64, 98, 211.
22. Kropotkine, *Anarchist Communism: Its Basis and Principles*, 21.
23. P. Kropotkin, 'Herbert Spencer: III', *Freedom: A Journal of Anarchist Communism* (September, 1904), 35–36 (35).
24. Webb, 'Historic', 52, 53.
25. Kropotkin, *Act for Yourselves*, 93, 94, 95.
26. Kropotkin, *Conquest of Bread*, 21–22.
27. Ibid., 37, 158, 159, 163, 164.
28. Kropotkin, *Mutual Aid*, 141. Original emphasis.

29. Kropotkine, *Anarchist Communism: Its Basis and Principles*, 8.
30. Kropotkin, *Anarchism: Its Philosophy and Ideal*, 8.
31. John Stuart Mill, *On Liberty and Other Writings* (Cambridge, [1859] 1989), 8; Alexis de Tocqueville, *Democracy in America* (London, [1835] 2003), 292–300.
32. P. Kropotkine, 'Advice to Those About the Emigrate', *Freedom: A Journal of Anarchist Communism* (March, 1893), 14.
33. P. Kropotkine, 'Communism and Anarchy', *Freedom: A Journal of Anarchist Communism* (July, 1901), 30–31 (31); Peter Kropotkin, 'Proposed Communist Settlement: A New Colony for Tyneside or Wearside', *The Newcastle Daily Chronicle*, 20 February 1895, 4.
34. Kropotkin, *Words of a Rebel*, 88.
35. Kropotkin, *Conquest of Bread*, 106.
36. Kropotkin, 'Communism and Anarchy', 31.
37. Max Nettlau, 'Anarchism: Individualist or Communist? – Both', *Anarchy! An Anthology of Emma Goldman's Mother Earth* (New York, [1914] 2000), 79–83 (80).
38. P.A.K., 'Anarchism', *Encyclopaedia Britannica*, 916, 917, 914. Original emphasis.
39. Freeden, *Ideologies and Political Theory*, 82–85; Alan Ritter, *Anarchism: A Theoretical Analysis* (Cambridge, 1980), 26.
40. Kinna, 'Fields of Vision', 70.
41. Kropotkin, *Anarchism: Its Philosophy and Ideal*, 7.
42. Kropotkin, *Conquest of Bread*, 126.
43. Matthew S. Adams, 'Rejecting the American Model: Peter Kropotkin's Radical Communalism', *History of Political Thought*, 35:1, 147–173 (162); Carl J. Guarneri, *The Utopian Alternative: Fourierism in Nineteenth Century America* (London, 1991).
44. Eugene Kamenka, 'Community and the Socialist Ideal', in Kamenka (ed.) *Community as a Social Ideal* (London, 1982), 3–26 (6).
45. Berlin, *Crooked Timber*, 46; Kołakowski, *Modernity*, 138.
46. Nathaniel Hawthorne, *Blithedale Romance* (Boston, 1852), 46.
47. Kropotkin, *Fields, Factories and Workshops*, 19–23.
48. Ibid., 32, 77. Original emphasis.
49. Kropotkin, *Memoirs*, 95; *Fields, Factories and Workshops*, 350. See also: William Morris, 'How We Live and How We Might Live', in A.L. Morton (ed.) *Political Writings of William Morris* (London, 1973), 134–158 (152).
50. Kropotkin, 'The State', 178; Kropotkin, *Words of a Rebel*, 85.
51. Martin Jay, *The Dialectical Imagination: A History of the Frankfurt School* (California, 1996), 57; Kropotkin, *Fields, Factories and Workshops*, 151, 355.
52. Peter Kropotkin, 'Forewords by Prince Kropotkin', in Thomas Smith, *French Gardening* (London, 1909), v–x (ix).
53. Kropotkin, *Fields, Factories and Workshops*, 125, 266, 243; Kropotkin, *Conquest of Bread*, x.
54. Kropotkin, *Fields, Factories and Workshops*, 18, 340.
55. Frederick Engels, 'Refugee Literature [1874]', Karl Marx and Frederick Engels, *Collected Works: Volume 24* (London, 1989), 3–73 (45, 46).
56. Kropotkin, *Words of a Rebel*, 88.

57. Kropotkin, *Fields, Factories and Workshops*, 22.
58. Kropotkin, *Conquest of Bread*, 150; Kropotkin, *Fields, Factories and Workshops*, 350.
59. Ibid., 38, 363, 364, 382. See also: Peter Kropotkin, 'What Geography Ought to Be', *The Nineteenth Century*, 18 (1885), 940–956.
60. Kropotkin, *Fields, Factories and Workshops*, 176.
61. Kropotkin, *Conquest of Bread*, 139, 140.
62. Ibid., 141, 142.
63. Burrow, *Crisis of Reason*, 183.
64. J.G.A. Pocock, 'Between Machiavelli and Hume: Gibbon as Civic Humanist and Philosophical Historian', *Daedalus*, 105:3 (1976), 153–169. Although Gibbon retained faith in the possibly limitless potential of European rationalism. For competing views of Gibbon's progressive narrative, see: Peter Gay, *The Enlightenment: An Interpretation* (London, 1996), 98–99; Burrow, *History of Histories*, 335–336.
65. Kropotkin, *Words of a Rebel*, 53.
66. Peter Kropotkin, *Russian Literature: Ideals and Realities* (Montréal, [1905] 1991), 90.
67. Kropotkin, *Words of a Rebel*, 54.
68. Burrow, *Crisis of Reason*, 183.
69. Bauman, *Modernity*, 13.
70. Michael Freeden, 'Eugenics and Progressive Thought: A Study in Ideological Affinity', *The Historical Journal*, 22:3 (1979), 645–671.
71. Karl Pearson, *National Life from the Standpoint of Science: An Address Delivered at Newcastle* (London, 1901), 44, 60, 61–62.
72. Donald MacKenzie, 'Eugenics in Britain', *Social Studies of Science*, 6:3/4 (1976), 499–532 (515–516).
73. Kropotkin 'Theory of Evolution and Mutual Aid', 136, 137.
74. 'First International Eugenics Conference', *British Medical Journal*, 2:2692 (3, 1912), 253–255 (253).
75. P. Kropotkin, 'The Sterilisation of the Unfit', *Freedom: A Journal of Anarchist Communism* (October, 1912), 77–78 (77).
76. Kropotkine, *Russian and French Prisons*, 347, 348, 350.
77. Kropotkin, 'Sterilisation', 78.
78. Berlin, *Roots of Romanticism*, 21–22; *Historical Inevitability* (Oxford, 1954), 68–69.
79. Berlin, *Crooked Timber*, 12.
80. Ruth Kinna, 'Anarchism and the Politics of Utopia', in Laurence Davis and Ruth Kinna (eds) *Anarchism and Utopianism* (Manchester, 2009), 221–240 (226).
81. Jonathan Wolff, *An Introduction to Political Philosophy* (London, 1996), 33; David Morland, *Demanding the Impossible?: Human Nature and Politics in the Nineteenth Century Social Anarchism* (London, 1997), 17.
82. Kropotkin, 'Herbert Spencer (III) Continued', 31; Lee Alan Dugatkin, *The Altruism Equation* (Princeton, 2006), 31.
83. Kołakowski, *Main Currents of Marxism*, 370.
84. Kropotkin, *Mutual Aid*, xv, xvi. Original emphasis.
85. For useful contextual discussions, see: Ruth Kinna, 'Kropotkin and Huxley', *Politics*, 12:2 (1992), 41–47; and Ruth Kinna, 'Kropotkin's Theory of Mutual

Aid in Historical Context', *International Review of Social History* 40 (1995), 259–283.

86. Kropotkin, *Memoirs*, 336.
87. Thomas H. Huxley, 'The Struggle for Existence in Human Society [1888]', *Evolution and Ethics and Other Essays* (New York, 1897), 195–236.
88. Kropotkin, *Mutual Aid*, 4, 3, 78.
89. Ibid., 5.
90. Ibid., 293.
91. Ibid., 295, 297.
92. Ibid., 174, 181, 186, 197.
93. Michael Bakunin, 'Revolutionary Catechism: 1866', in Sam Dolgoff (ed.) *Bakunin on Anarchism* (Montréal, 1989), 76–97 (80); Kropotkin, 'Must We Occupy', 26.
94. Kropotkin, *Conquest of Bread*, 178, 179, 192, 193, 196.
95. Kropotkin, *Mutual Aid*, 143.
96. Dante Alighieri, *The Inferno of Dante*, trans. Charles Rogers (London, 1782), 110; Trevor Dean, 'Marriage and Mutilation: Vendetta in Late Medieval Italy', *Past & Present*, 157 (1997), 3–36 (3).
97. Kropotkin, *Words of Rebel*, 158.
98. Kropotkin, *Russian and French Prisons*, 361, 369, 370.
99. Ibid., 353; Kropotkin, *Place of Anarchism*, 20–21.
100. Kropotkin, 'Anarchist Morality', 146.
101. Michel Foucault, *Madness and Civilization: A History of Insanity in the Age of Reason*, trans. Richard Howard (New York, 1988), 242.
102. Kropotkin, *Anarchism: Its Philosophy and Ideal*, 28. Original emphasis.
103. Read, *Philosophy of Anarchism*, 31.
104. Herbert Read, 'A Nest of Gentle Artists', *Apollo*, XXXVI:7 (1962), 537–538 (537).
105. Noel Perrin, 'Eden Under the Earth', *The Washington Post Book World*, 19 August 1984, 215.
106. Orlando Cyprian Williams, 'A Philosophical Romance', *Times Literary Supplement*, 11 February 1935, 693.
107. A.L. Morton, *The English Utopia* (London, 1969), 161.
108. Goodway, *Anarchist Seeds*, 177; Richard E. Brown, 'Worlds of Darkness, Light and Half-Light in *The Green Child*', *Extrapolation*, 31:2 (1990), 170–186 (170).
109. Brown, 'Worlds of Darkness'; Leena Kore Schröder, '"Rumbling in the Depths": "The Green Child" and the Uncanny', *ReReading Read*, 188–206.
110. Graham Greene, 'Introduction', in Herbert Read, *The Green Child* (London, [1935] 1947), v–viii.
111. William of Newburgh, *The Church Historians of England: Vol. IV – Part II*, trans. Joseph Stevenson (London, 1856), 436.
112. Herbert Read, *English Prose Style* (London, 1932), 140. On the broader significance of the story, see: Jeffrey Jerome Cohen, 'Green Children from Another World, or the Archipelago in England', in Cohen (ed.) *Cultural Diversity in the British Middle Ages: Archipelago, Island, England* (Basingstoke, 2008), 75–94.
113. Read, *Green Child*, 57, 105.
114. Read, *Green Child*, 149, 150.

115. Read, *Green Child*, 159, 170, 181, 194.
116. Lyman Tower Sargent, 'Is There Only One Utopian Tradition?', *Journal of the History of Ideas*, 43:4 (1982), 681–689 (682).
117. Read, *Anarchy and Order*, 22, 23.
118. H.G. Wells, *An Englishman Looks at the World* (London, 1914), 202, 204.
119. Read, *English Prose*, 146.
120. Read, *Contrary Experience*, 89.
121. Barker, *Political Ideas*, 50.
122. H.G. Wells, *The Way the World Is Going: Guesses & Forecasts of the Years Ahead* (London, 1928), 66, 67, 70; Philip Coupland, 'H.G. Wells's "Liberal Fascism"', *Journal of Contemporary History*, 35:4 (2000), 541–558 (543). H.G. Wells, *Democracy Under Revision: A Lecture Delivered at the Sorbonne on March 15th, 1927* (London, 1927): *HRCUL*, D5102.
123. Wells, *The Way the World Is Going*, 70.
124. H.G. Wells, *Anticipations: of the Reaction of Mechanical and Scientific Progress Upon Human Life and Thought* (London, 1902), 298, 311.
125. H.G. Wells, *A Modern Utopia* (London, 1905), 278.
126. H.G. Wells, *An Experiment in Autobiography: Discoveries and Conclusions of a Very Ordinary Brain: Volume II* (London, 1934), 658–659.
127. J.D. Bernal, *The Social Function of Science* (London, [1939] 1967), 398.
128. Dimitri Mirsky, *The Intelligentsia of Great Britain* (London, 1935), 75.
129. H.G. Wells, 'Letters to the Editor: War Aims', *The Times*, 26 September 1939, 4; H.G. Wells, 'Letters to the Editor: War Aims: The Rights of Man', *The Times*, 25 October 1939, 6; H.G. Wells, *The Rights of Man, or What are We Fighting For?* (London, 1940); H.G. Wells (ed.) *The Rights of Man: An Essay in Collective Definition* (Brighton, 1943).
130. Herbert Read to H.G. Wells: 28th July 1943, *HRAUV*, HR/HGW-7: Encl.02.
131. Read, 'Anarchism in the Affluent Society', 8.
132. Read, *Green Child*, 137, 139.
133. Ibid., 149, 150.
134. Wells, *Experiment in Autobiography*, 649.
135. Read, *Green Child*, 174, 175.
136. Ibid., 182.
137. Richard Wasson, 'The Green Child: Herbert Read's Ironic Fantasy', *PMLA*, 77:5 (1962), 645–651.
138. Herbert Read to Edward Dahlberg: 6th March 1949, *HRAUV*, HR/ED-40: Encl.03.
139. Dick Whitty to Herbert Read: 13th June 1946, *HRAUV*, 61.223; Herbert Read to Dick Whitty, 25th October 1948, *HRAUV*, 61.223. I am grateful to Huw Wahl for alerting me to these letters.
140. Read, *Anarchy and Order*, 19, 20; Read, *Cult of Sincerity*, 46.
141. Read, *Anarchy and Order*, 20, 21, 22.
142. Marie-Louise Berneri, *Journey Through Utopia* (New York, 1969), 2.
143. Read, *One-Man Manifesto*, 150, 151.
144. Read, *Anarchy and Order*, 19.
145. Read, *One-Man Manifesto*, 152.
146. Read, *Politics of Unpolitical*, 133, 134.
147. 'Paris Ready for Gay Summer With Exposition Opening in May', *Washington Post*, 14 March 1937, 5; Sibilla Skidelsky, 'Paris Exposition Does Little For

Architecture: German and Russian Pavilions Draw Attention', *Washington Post*, 19 September 1947, 7.
148. Read, *Politics of Unpolitical*, 135.
149. Read, *Politics of the Unpolitical*, 136, 138, 139.
150. Jean Baudrillard, *The Illusion of the End*, trans. Chris Turner (Cambridge, 1992), 45.
151. Read, *Politics of the Unpolitical*, 140, 143.
152. Read, *Poetry and Anarchism*, 8.
153. Read, *Coat of Many Colours*, 323.
154. Read, *Poetry and Anarchism*, 24; Read, *Coat of Many Colours*, 65.
155. Orwell, 'Review of *A Coat of Many Colours*', 403, 404, 406.
156. G. Bernard Shaw, 'Use of Land: Russian Theories and Practise', *The Times*, 1 October 1940, 6.
157. Read, *One-Man Manifesto*, 54, 55.
158. Read, *Contrary Experience*, 342, 343; Woodcock, *Stream and the Source*, 260.
159. Woodcock, *The Stream and the Source*, 234.
160. Herbert Read, 'Letters From China, 1959', *A Tribute to Herbert Read 1893–1968* (Bradford, 1975), 43–49 (45, 47, 49).
161. Sam Dolgoff, *Fragments: A Memoir* (London, 1986), 179–182.
162. Donald D. Egbert, *Social Radicalism and the Arts* (New York, 1970), 559.
163. On this 'synthesis', see: Ward, 'Art and Anarchy', 32–33.
164. Read, *Forms of Things Unknown*, 173; Stirner cited in Read, *Tenth Muse*, 80.
165. Read, *Forms of Things Unknown*, 174; Read, *Education through Art*, 5.
166. Read, *Cult of Sincerity*, 89, 90, 91.
167. Aniela Jaffé, *Was C.G. Jung a Mystic? And Other Essays* (Einsiedeln, 1989), 1.
168. Read, *Reason and Romanticism*, 90; Read, *Art and Society*, 94, 125.
169. Read, *Cult of Sincerity*, 44, 45.
170. Read, *Education through Art*, 180, 181; Herbert Read, 'Introduction', in Seonaid M. Robertson, *Rosegarden and Labyrinth: A Study in Art Education* (New York, 1963), xiii–xiv (xiii).
171. Herbert Read, *A Letter to a Young Painter* (New York, 1962), 254; Read, *Art and Alienation*, 135; Read, *Icon & Idea*, 31.
172. Read, *Politics of the Unpolitical*, 156, 158, 159, 160.
173. Herbert Read and Edward Dahlberg, *Truth Is More Sacred: A Critical Exchange on Modern Literature* (London, 1961), 22; Read, *Poetry and Anarchism*, 55; Read, *Kropotkin*, 16.
174. Read, *Education Through Art*, 302; Read, 'Anarchism in the Affluent Society', 8.
175. Read, *Education of Free Men*, 18; Read, *Anarchy and Order*, 24.
176. Aldous Huxley, *Crome Yellow* (London, [1921] 2001), 19, 22, 29.
177. Rousseau, *Social Contract*, 104.

Conclusion: Inventing a Tradition

1. Woodcock, *Anarchism*, 443.
2. George Woodcock, *Anarchism: A History of Libertarian Ideas and Movements* (London, 1986), 410, 411, 420.
3. Walter Benjamin, *Illuminations*, trans. Harry Zohn (New York, 2007), 257–258.

4. Woodcock, *Anarchism* (1986), 385.
5. Colin Ward and David Goodway, *Talking Anarchy* (Nottingham, 2003), 99; Murray Bookchin, 'Deep Ecology, Anarchosyndicalism, and the Future of Anarchist Thought', in Bookchin et al. (eds) *Deep Ecology & Anarchism: A Polemic* (London, 1997), 47–58 (53).
6. Read quoted in Woodcock, *Anarchism* (1986), 422.
7. Read, *The Cult of Sincerity*, 57.
8. Herbert Read, *To Hell With Culture: Democratic Values are New Values* (London, 1941), 12.
9. Eric Hobsbawm, 'Introduction: Inventing Traditions', in Hobsbawm and Terence Ranger (eds) *The Invention of Tradition* (Cambridge, 1983), 1–14 (1, 2).
10. Tony Judt, *Postwar: A History of Europe Since 1945* (London, 2005), 830.
11. Benedict Anderson, *Imagined Communities: Reflections on the Origin and Spread of Nationalism* (London, 1983), 15.
12. Goodway, *Anarchist Seeds*, 4.
13. Read, *Contrary Experience*, 352.
14. Read, *Cult of Sincerity*, 49.

Bibliography

Archival collections

British Library Manuscripts Collection, London (BLMC)
City of Westminster Archive, London (CWA)
Herbert Read Archive, MacPherson Library, University of Victoria, Canada (HRAUV)
Herbert Read Collection, Brotherton Special Collections, University of Leeds (HRCUL)
Royal Geographical Society Archives, London (RGS)

Newspapers

Aberdeen Weekly Journal
Boston Daily Advertiser
Chatterbox
Citizen
Daily News
Derby Daily Telegraph
The Dundee Courier & Argus
Edinburgh Evening News
Fabian News
Freedom: A Journal of Anarchist Communism
Freeman's Journal and Daily Commercial Advertiser
Glasgow Herald
The Leeds Mercury
The Manchester Guardian
Manchester Times
The North American
The Nottingham Evening Post
Pall Mall Gazette
Peace News
Punch, Or the London Charivari
The Times
The Times Literary Supplement
Washington Post
The Yorkshire Herald

Kropotkin

Kropotkin, Peter, 'Must We Occupy Ourselves with an Examination of the Ideal of a Future System?', in George Woodcock (ed.) *Fugitive Writings* (Montréal, [1873] 1993), 13–68

——, 'What Geography Ought to Be', *The Nineteenth Century*, 18 (1885), 940–956
——, *Words of a Rebel*, trans. George Woodcock (Montréal, [1885] 1992)
——, 'Past and Future: A Speech Delivered by P. Kropotkin at South Place Chapel at the Commemoration of the Paris Commune', *Freedom: A Journal of Anarchist Communism* (April, 1889), 17–18
——, 'Anarchist Morality [1892]', in George Woodcock (ed.) *Fugitive Writings* (Montréal, 1993), 127–153
——, 'Proposed Communist Settlement: A New Colony for Tyneside or Wearside', *The Newcastle Daily Chronicle*, 20 February 1895, 4
——, 'The State: Its Historic Role [1896]', in George Woodcock (ed.) *Fugitive Writings* (Montréal, 1993), 159–201
——, *Anarchism: Its Philosophy and Ideal* (London, 1897)
——, *Memoirs of a Revolutionist* (London, [1899] 1978)
——, *Mutual Aid: A Factor of Evolution* (London, [1902] 1939)
——, *Socialism and Politics* (London, 1903)
——, *The Coming Revival of Socialism* (London, 1904)
——, 'Herbert Spencer', *Freedom: A Journal of Anarchist Communism* (February 1904), 7–8
——, 'Hebert Spencer II', *Freedom: A Journal of Anarchist Communism* (April–May, 1904), 15
——, 'Herbert Spencer III', *Freedom: A Journal of Anarchism Communism* (June, 1904), 23.
——, 'Herbert Spencer III: Continued', *Freedom: A Journal of Anarchist Communism* (August, 1904), 31
——, 'Herbert Spencer III: Continued', *Freedom: A Journal of Anarchist Communism* (September, 1904), 35–36
——, 'Bakunin', *Freedom: A Journal of Anarchist Communism* (June–July, 1905), 18–19
——, *Russian Literature: Ideals and Realities* (Montréal, [1905] 1991)
——, *The Conquest of Bread* (New York, 1907)
——, 'Forewords by Prince Kropotkin', in Thomas Smith (eds), *French Gardening* (London, 1909), v–x
——, *The Great French Revolution: 1789–1793* (London, 1909)
——, 'The Theory of Evolution and Mutual Aid', *The Nineteenth Century and After* (January 1910), 86–107
——, 'The Direct Action of Environment of Plants', *The Nineteenth Century and After* (July, 1910), 58–77
——, *Fields Factories and Workshops or Industry Combined with Agriculture and Brain Work with Manual Work* (London, 1912)
——, 'Modern Science and Anarchism [1912]', in George Woodcock (ed.) *Evolution and Environment* (Montréal, 1995), 15–107
——, 'The Sterilisation of the Unfit', *Freedom: A Journal of Anarchist Communism* (October, 1912), 77–78
——, 'Preface', in Émile Pataud and Émile Pouget, *How We Shall Bring About the Revolution* (London, [1913] 1990), xxxi–xxxvii
——, *Wars and Capitalism* (London, 1914)
——, 'To Steffen', *Selected Writings on Anarchism and Revolution* (London, [1914] 1970), 308–319

——, '"Western Europe", from Memoirs of a Revolutionist', in Marshall S. Shatz (ed.) *The Conquest of Bread and Other Writings* (Cambridge, [1924] 1995), 203–232

——, *Act for Yourselves: Articles from Freedom: 1886–1907*, Nicolas Walter and Heiner Becker (eds) (London, 1998)

Prince Kropotkin, 'War or Peace', *Full Report of the Proceedings of the International Workers' Congress, London, July and August, 1896* (London, 1896), 75–82

——, *The Terror in Russia: An Appeal to the British Nation* (London, 1909)

——, *Ethics: Origin and Development*, trans. Louis Friedland (New York, 1924)

——, *Kropotkin: Selections from his Writings*, in Herbert Read (ed.) (London, 1942)

Kropotkine, P., *Law and Authority: An Anarchist Essay* (London, 1886)

——, *The Place of Anarchism in Socialistic Evolution* (New York, [1886] 1973)

——, *Anarchist Communism: Its Basis and Principles* (London, [1887] 1905)

——, *In Russian and French Prisons* (London, 1887)

——, 'Le Vingtième Siècle', La Révolte, 30 November 1889, 1

——, 'Le Vingtième Siècle II', La Révolte, 14 December 1889, 1

——, *Revolutionary Studies* (London, 1892)

——, 'Advice to Those About the Emigrate', *Freedom: A Journal of Anarchist Communism* (March, 1893), 14

——, 'Communism and Anarchy', *Freedom: A Journal of Anarchist Communism* (July, 1901), 30–31

P.A.K., 'Anarchism' in *Encyclopaedia Britannica: Eleventh Edition* (Cambridge, 1910), 914–919

Read

Herbert Read, 'The World and the Guild Idea – I. The Natural Basis' *in The Guildsman: A Journal of Social and Industrial Emancipation*, 5 (1917), 6

——, 'The Curfew' and 'The Pond', *Arts and Letters: An Illustrated Quarterly*, 1:1 (1917), 2

——, *Reason and Romanticism: Essays in Literary Criticism* (London, 1926)

——, *The Sense of Glory: Essays in Criticism* (Cambridge, 1929)

——, *The Meaning of Art* (London, 1931)

——, *English Prose Style* (London, 1932)

——, *Art Now: An Introduction to the Theory of Modern Painting and Sculpture* (London [1933] 1960)

——, *The Innocent Eye* (London, 1933)

——, *Art and Industry: The Principles of Industrial Design* (London, [1934] 1944)

——, 'Art and the Revolutionary Attitude', *The Southern Review*, 1 (1935), 239–252

——, *Essential Communism* (London, 1935)

——, *The Green Child* (London, [1935] 1947)

——, *Art and Society* (London, [1936] 1967)

——, *In Defence of Shelley & Other Essays* (New York, [1936] 1968)

——, 'Introduction', in Read (ed.) *Surrealism* (London, 1936), 19–91

——, *Poetry and Anarchism* (London, [1938] 1947)

——, *The Knapsack: A Pocket-Book of Prose and Verse* (London, 1939)

——, *Annals of Innocence and Experience* (London, [1940] 1946)
——, *The Philosophy of Anarchism* (London, 1940)
——, 'Drawings by Augustus John', *The Burlington Magazine for Connoisseurs*, 78:454 (1941), 28
——, 'The War as Seen by British Artists', in Monroe Wheeler (ed.) *Britain at War* (New York, [1941] 1972), 11–12
——, *To Hell With Culture: Democratic Values are New Value* (London, 1941)
——, 'Introduction', *Kropotkin: Selections from His Writings* (London, 1942), 7–16
——, *Education Through Art* (London, 1943)
——, *The Politics of the Unpolitical* (London, 1943)
——, *A World Within a War* (London, 1944)
——, *The Education of Free Men* (London, 1944)
——, 'What Is Freedom?', *The New Statesman*, 26 August 1944, 137
——, *Freedom: Is It a Crime?* (London, 1945)
——, *A Coat of Many Colours: Occasional Essays* (London, 1947)
——, *The Grass Roots of Art: Lectures on the Social Aspects of Art in an Industrial Age* (London, [1947] 1955)
——, *Form in Modern Poetry: An Essay in Aesthetics* (London, 1948)
——, *Existentialism, Marxism and Anarchism* (London, 1949)
——, 'Gandhi's 'Autobiography', *The Listener*, (21 July 1949), 121
——, *Education for Peace* (London, 1950)
——, *Anarchy and Order: Essays in Politics* (London, 1954)
——, *The Philosophy of Modern Art: Collected Essays* (London, 1954)
——, *Icon & Idea: The Function of Art in the Development of the Human Consciousness* (New York, [1955] 1965)
——, 'Foreword', *The Rebel: An Essay on Man in Revolt* (New York, 1956)
——, *The Tenth Muse: Essays in Criticism* (London, 1957)
——, 'Letters from China, 1959', *A Tribute to Herbert Read 1893–1968* (Bradford, [1959] 1975), 43–9
——, 'Correspondence', *The London Magazine*, 16:11 (1959), 73–74
——, 'Mood of the Month – X', *The London Magazine*, 6:8 (1959), 39–43
——, *The Forms of Things Unknown: Essays Towards an Aesthetic Philosophy* (London, 1960)
——, 'Disobedience Against Polaris', *Peace News*, 20 January 1961, 1
——, and Edward Dahlberg, *Truth Is More Sacred: A Critical Exchange on Modern Literature* (London, 1961)
——, *A Letter to a Young Painter* (New York, 1962)
——, 'A Nest of Gentle Artists', *Apollo*, XXXVI:7 (1962), 537–538
——, *Design and Tradition: The Design Oration* (Hemingford Grey, 1962)
——, 'Introduction', in Seonaid M. Robertson (ed.), *Rosegarden and Labyrinth: A Study in Art Education* (New York, 1963), xiii–xiv
——, *The Contrary Experience: Autobiographies* (London, 1963)
——, 'Preface', *To Hell With Culture* (London, 1963), ix–xii
——, *The Origins of Form in Art* (London, 1965)
——, 'Sir Herbert Read', in Alister Kershaw and F.J. Temple (eds) *Richard Aldington: An Intimate Portrait* (Carbondale, 1965)
——, 'Anarchism in the Affluent Society', *Underground* (1966), 1–11
——, *Art and Alienation: The Role of the Artist in Society* (New York, 1967)
——, 'A Conversation with Herbert Read', *Art Education*, 20:9 (1967), 32–35

——, *A Concise History of Modern Painting* (London, 1968)
——, 'Introduction', in F.D. Kingender (ed), *Goya in the Democratic Tradition* (London, 1968), vii
——, 'Pragmatic Anarchism', *Encounter*, 30:1 (1968), 54–61
——, *The Cult of Sincerity* (London, 1968)
——, 'Letters from China, 1959', *A Tribute to Herbert Read 1893–1968* (Bradford, 1975), 43–49
——, *A One-Man Manifesto and Other Writings for Freedom Press*, in David Goodway (ed.) (London, 1994)
——, *To Hell With Culture*, in Michael Paraskos (ed.) (London, 2002)

Other Sources

'Motion Respecting Mr. Owen's Plan' 16 December 1819, *The Parliamentary Debates from the Year 1803 to the Present Time: Volume 41* (London, 1820), 1189–1216
The Manifesto of the Socialist League (London, 1885)
'Prefatory Note', *English Historical Review*, 1:1 (1886), 1–6
Full Report of the Proceedings of the International Workers' Congress, London, July and August, 1896 (London, 1896)
'Notes: Herbert Spencer', *Freedom: A Journal of Anarchist Communism* (January, 1904), 2
'Histories of the Autumn', *The Times Literary Supplement*, 7 December 1909, 472
'First International Eugenics Conference', *British Medical Journal*, 2:2692 (1912), 253–255
'Paris Ready for Gay Summer With Exposition Opening in May', *Washington Post*, 14 March 1937, 5
'Sir Herbert Read Joins Sit-Down', *Peace News*, 6 January 1961, 1–2
Authors Take Sides on the Spanish War (London, N.D.)
Abbs, Peter, 'Herbert Read as an Autobiographer' in David Goodway (ed.) *Read Reassessed* (Liverpool, 1998) 83–99
Adams, Matthew S., 'Kropotkin: Evolution, Revolutionary Change and the End of History', *Anarchist Studies*, 19:1 (2011), 54–81
——, 'Art, Education, and Revolution: Herbert Read and the Reorientation of British Anarchism', *History of European Ideas*, 39:5 (2013), 709–728
——, 'The Possibilities of Anarchist History: Rethinking the Canon and Writing History', *Anarchist Developments in Cultural Studies* (2013), 33–63
——, 'Herbert Read and the Fluid Memory of the First World War: Poetry, Prose, and Polemic', *Historical Research* (2014), 1–22
——, 'Rejecting the American Model: Peter Kropotkin's Radical Communalism', *History of Political Thought*, 35:1 (2014), 147–173
——, 'Formulating an Anarchist Sociology: Peter Kropotkin's Reading of Herbert Spencer', *Journal of the History of Ideas*, forthcoming
Adorno, Theodor, 'The Schema of Mass Culture', in J.M. Bernstein (ed.) *The Culture Industry: Selected Essays on Mass Culture* (London, 1991), 61–97
Alighieri, Dante, *The Inferno of Dante*, trans. Charles Rogers (London, 1782)

Anderson, Benedict, *Imagined Communities: Reflections on the Origin and Spread of Nationalism* (London, 1983)
Anderson, Michael, 'The Social Implications of Demographic Change', in F.M.L. Thompson (ed.) *The Cambridge Social History of Britain: 1750–1950: Volume 2* (Cambridge, 1990), 1–70
Antliff, Allan, 'Anarchy, Power and Post-Structralism', in Duane Rouselle and Süreyyya Evren (eds) *Post-Anarchism: A Reader* (London, 2011), 160–167
——, 'Biocentrism and Anarchy: Herbert Read's Modernism', in Oliver Botar and Isabel Wünsche (eds) *Biocentrism and Modernism* (Farnham, 2011), 153–160
——, *Anarchist Modernism: Art, Politics, and the First American Avant-Garde* (Chicago, 2001)
Armstrong, Tim, *Modernism: A Cultural History* (Cambridge, 2005)
Avrich, Paul, *The Russian Anarchists* (Princeton, 1967)
Bagehot, Walter, *Physics and Politics: or Thoughts on the Application of the Principles of 'Natural Selection' and 'Inheritance' to Political Society* (London, 1881)
Bailey, John Cann, 'Two Books on Wordsworth', *The Times Literary Supplement*, 18 December 1930, 1073
Baker, Keith Michael, 'Introduction', in Baker (ed.) *The French Revolution and the Creation of Modern Political Culture: Volume 1: The Political Culture of the Old Regime* (Oxford, 1987), xi–xxiv
——, *Inventing the French Revolution* (Cambridge, 1994)
Bakounine, Michel, *Oeuvres: Tome II* (Paris, 1907)
Bakunin, Michael, 'Revolutionary Catechism: 1866', in Sam Dolgoff (ed.) *Bakunin on Anarchism* (Montréal, 1989), 76–97
——, *Statism and Anarchy* (Cambridge, [1873] 2005)
Baldwin, Stanley, *On England and Other Addresses* (London, 1926)
——, *This Torch of Freedom: Speeches and Addresses* (London, 1935)
Bantman, Constance, *The French Anarchists in London: 1880–1914* (Liverpool, 2013)
Barker, Rodney, *Political Ideas in Modern Britain* (London, 1978)
Barry, Norman, *An Introduction to Modern Political Theory* (Basingstoke, 2000)
Baudrillard, Jean, *The Illusion of the End*, trans. Chris Turner (Cambridge, 1992)
Bauman, Zygmunt, *Modernity and the Holocaust* (Ithaca, NY, 1989)
Bax, Ernest Belfort, *Reminiscences and Reflexions of a Mid and Late Victorian* (New York, 1920)
Bellamy, Edward, *Looking Backward: 2000–1887* (New York, [1888] 1917)
Bellamy, Richard, 'Introduction', in Bellamy (ed.) *Victorian Liberalism: Nineteenth-Century Political Thought and Practice* (London, 1990), 1–14
Belloc, Hilaire, and Cecil Chesterton, *The Party System* (London, 1911)
Belloc, Hilaire, *The Servile State* (London, 1912)
Benjamin, Walter, *Illuminations*, trans. Harry Zohn (New York, 2007)
Bentley, Michael, *The Climax of Liberal Politics: British Liberalism in Theory and Practice, 1868–1918* (London, 1987)
Berlin, Isaiah, *Historical Inevitability* (Oxford, 1954)
——, *The Roots of Romanticism* (London, [1965] 2000)
——, *Liberty* (Oxford, 2002)
——, *The Crooked Timber of Humanity*, Henry Hardy (ed.) (London, 2003)
Bernal, J.D., *The Social Function of Science* (London, [1939] 1967)
Berneri, Marie-Louise, *Journey Through Utopia* (New York, 1969)

Beveridge, William, *Social Insurance and Allied Services: Report by Sir William Beveridge* (New York, 1942)
Bevir, Mark, *The Making of British Socialism* (Princeton, 2011)
Black, Jonathan, '"Constructing a Chinese-Puzzle Universe": Industry, National Identity, and Edward Wadsworth's Vorticist Woodcuts of West Yorkshire, 1914–1916', in Mark Antliff and Scott W. Klein (eds) *Vorticism: New Perspectives* (Oxford, 2013), 89–99
Blatchford, Robert, *Britain for the British* (London, 1907)
——, *My Eighty Years* (London, 1931)
Bold, Alan, *MacDiarmid: Christopher Murray Grieve: A Critical Biography* (London, 1988)
Brockway, A. Fenner, *Socialism for Pacifists* (Manchester, 1916)
Bookchin, Murray, 'Deep Ecology, Anarchosyndicalism, and the Future of Anarchist Thought', in Bookchin et al. (eds) *Deep Ecology & Anarchism: A Polemic* (London, 1997), 47–58
Brown, Richard E., 'Worlds of Darkness, Light and Half-Light in The Green Child', *Extrapolation*, 31:2 (1990), 170–186
Buber, Martin, *Paths in Utopia* (London, 1949)
Buchanan, Tom, *The Spanish Civil War and the British Labour Movement* (Cambridge, 1991)
Burrow, John, *A History of Histories: Epics, Chronicles, Romances and Inquiries From Herodotus and Thucydides to the Twentieth Century* (New York, 2008)
Burrow, J.W., *The Crisis of Reason: European Thought, 1848–1914* (London, 2000)
Butterfield, H., *The Whig Interpretation of History* (London, 1950)
Call, Lewis, *Postmodern Anarchism* (Oxford, 2002)
Capaldi, Nicholas, *John Stuart Mill: A Biography* (Cambridge, 2004)
Carr, E.H., *Michael Bakunin* (London, 1937)
Carter, April, *The Political Theory of Anarchism* (London, 1971)
Causey, Andrew, 'Herbert Read and Contemporary Art', in David Goodway (ed.) *Hebert Read Reassessed* (Liverpool, 1998), 123–144
Ceadel, Martin, *Pacifism in Britain 1914–1945: The Defining of a Faith* (Oxford, 1980)
Claeys, Gregory, *Citizens and Saints: Politics and Anti-politics in Early British Socialism* (Cambridge, 1989)
——, *Imperial Sceptics: British Critics of Empire, 1850–1920* (Cambridge, 2010)
Clark, Ronald, *J.B.S.: The Life and Work of J.B.S. Haldane* (London, 1968)
Clarke, Peter, *Hope and Glory: Britain 1900–2000* (London, 2004)
Cohen, Jeffrey Jerome, 'Green Children from Another World, or the Archipelago in England', in Cohen (ed.) *Cultural Diversity in the British Middle Ages: Archipelago, Island, England* (Basingstoke, 2008), 75–94
Cole, G.D.H., 'The Genesis of French Syndicalism – and Some Unspoken Morals – I.', *The New Age*, XIV:14 (Febuary1914), 425–427
——, 'The Genesis of French Syndicalism – and Some Unspoken Morals', *The New Age*, XIV:16 (1914), 489–490
——, *The World of Labour: A Discussion of the Present and Future of Trade Unionism* (London, 1915)
——, *Guild Socialism Restated* (London, 1920)
——, *A History of Socialist Thought: Volume 1* (London, 1953)

Collini, Stefan, Donald Winch and J.W. Burrow, *That Noble Science of Politics: A Study in Nineteenth Century Intellectual History* (Cambridge, 1987)
Comfort, Alex, *Authority and Delinquency: A Study in the Psychology of Power* (London, [1950] 1970)
Communist Party of Great Britain, *Class Against Class: General Election Programme of the Communist Party of Great Britain* (London, 1929)
Coupland, Philip, 'H.G. Wells's "Liberal Fascism"', *Journal of Contemporary History*, 35:4 (2000), 541–558
Crane, Walter, *An Artist's Reminiscences* (New York, 1907)
Cranston, Maurice, 'Metaphysical Rebellion', *The Manchester Guardian*, 20 April 1954, 4
Crowder, George, *Classical Anarchism: The Political Thought of Godwin, Bakunin and Kropotkin* (Oxford, 1991)
Culler, A. Dwight, *The Victorian Mirror of History* (London, 1985)
Dahlberg, Edward, *The Confessions of Edward Dahlberg* (New York, 1971)De-la-Noy, Michael, 'Obituary: Professor Maurice Cranston', *The Independent*, 8 November 1993, 12
Dean, Trevor, 'Marriage and Mutilation: Vendetta in Late Medieval Italy', *Past & Present*, 157 (1997), 3–36
Dolgoff, Sam, *Fragments: A Memoir* (London, 1986)
Donnelly, Ignatius, *Caesar's Column: A Story of the Twentieth Century* (Chicago, 1890)
Dugatkin, Lee Alan, *The Altruism Equation* (Princeton, 2006)
Dunn, John, *The History of Political Theory and Other Essays* (Cambridge, 1996)
Durkheim, Émile, *The Rules of Sociological Method*, trans. W.D. Halls (Basingstoke, 1982)
Eksteins, Modrisk 'All Quiet on the Western Front and the Fate of a War', *Journal of Contemporary History*, 15:2 (1980), 345–366
Egbert, Donald D., *Social Radicalism and the Arts* (New York, 1970)
Engels, Friedrich, 'Engels to A. Babel, 1883', *Karl Marx and Frederick Engels on Britain* (London, 1953), 515–516
Engels, Frederick, *The Condition of the Working-Class in England in 1844*, trans. Florence Wischnewetzky (London, 1892)
——, 'Refugee Literature [1874]', Karl Marx and Frederick Engels, *Collected Works: Volume 24* (London, 1989), 3–73
Fanon, Frantz, *The Wretched of the Earth*, trans. Constance Farrington (New York, 1961)
Fling, Fred Morrow, 'The Great French Revolution, 1789–1793', *American Historical Review*, 15:3 (1910), 601–602
Foucault, Michel, *Madness and Civilization: A History of Insanity in the Age of Reason*, trans. Richard Howard (New York, 1988)
Fowler, R.B., 'The Anarchist Tradition of Political Thought', *The Western Political Quarterly*, 25:4 (1972), 738–752
Franks, Benjamin, 'Post-Anarchism: A Partial Account' in Duane Rouselle and Süreyyya Evren (eds) *Post-Anarchism: A Reader* (London, 2011), 168–180
——, *Rebel Alliances: The Means and Ends of Contemporary British Anarchisms* (Edinburgh, 2006)
Freeden, Michael, *The New Liberalism: An Ideology of Social Reform* (Oxford, 1978)

——, 'Eugenics and Progressive Thought: A Study in Ideological Affinity', *The Historical Journal*, 22:3 (1979), 645–671
——, *Ideologies and Political Theory: A Conceptual Approach* (Oxford, 2008)
Furet, François, 'The French Revolution Revisited', in Gary Kates (ed.) *The French Revolution: Recent Debates and New Controversies* (London, 1998), 71–90
Gascoyne, David, 'The Significance of English Art', *New English Weekly*, 11 January 1934, 306–307
Gay, Peter, *The Enlightenment: An Interpretation* (London, 1996)
——, *Modernism: The Lure of Heresy* (New York, 2008)
George, Henry, *Progress and Poverty: An Inquiry into the Cause of Industrial Depressions and of Increase of Want with Increase of Wealth* (New York, [1876] 1900)
Goodway, David, *Anarchist Seeds Beneath the Snow: Left-Libertarian Thought and British Writers from William Morris to Colin Ward* (Liverpool, 2006)
Goodwin, Barbara, and Keith Taylor, *The Politics of Utopia: A Study in Theory and Practise* (London, 1982)
Gordon, Uri, *Anarchy Alive! Anti-authoritarian Politics from Practise to Theory* (London, 2008)
Gramsci, Antonio, *Pre-prison Writings*, in Richard Bellamy (ed.) (Cambridge, [1918] 1994)
Gray, John, *The Social System: A Treatise on the Principle of Exchange* (Edinburgh, 1831)
Green, T.H., 'Lecture on 'Liberal Legislation and Freedom of Contract'', in R.L. Nettleship (ed.) *Works of Thomas Hill Green: Volume III* (London, 1888), 365–386
Greene, Graham, 'Introduction' in Herbert Read (ed.), *The Green Child* (London, [1935] 1947), v–viii
Greenleaf, W.H., *The British Political Tradition: Volume 1* (London, 1983)
Grigson, Geoffrey, *Recollections: Mainly of Writers & Artists* (London, 1984)
Guarneri, Carl J., *The Utopian Alternative: Fourierism in Nineteenth-Century America* (London, 1991)
Haakonssen, Knud, 'Introduction', in Haakonssen (ed.) *The Cambridge Companion to Adam Smith* (Cambridge, 2006), 1–21
Haldane, J.B.S., *Adventures of a Biologist* (London, 1937)
Hardie, J. Keir, *From Serfdom to Socialism* (London, 1907)
Hardy, Henry, 'Editor's Preface' to *The Crooked Timber* (London, 2003), ix–xii
Hardy, Thomas, *The Mayor of Casterbridge* (London, 1902)
Harris, Alexandra, *Romantic Moderns* (London, 2010)
Häusermann, H.W., 'The Development of Herbert Read', in Henry Treece (ed.) *Herbert Read: An Introduction to His Work by Various Hands* (London, 1944), 52–80
Hawthorne, Nathaniel, *Blithedale Romance* (Boston, 1852)
Heilbron, Johan, *The Rise of Social Theory*, trans. Sheila Gogol (Minneapolis, 1995)
Hennessy, Peter, *Never Again: Britain 1945–51* (London, 2006)
Herzen, Alexander, *From the Other Side and the Russian People and Socialism* (London, [1851] 1956)
Himmelfarb, Gertrude, 'The Politics of Democracy: The English Reform Act of 1867', *Journal of British Studies*, 6:1 (1966), 97–138

Hobsbawm, Eric, *Labouring Men: Studies in the History of Labour* (London, 1964)

——, 'Introduction: Inventing Traditions', in Hobsbawm and Terence Ranger (eds) *The Invention of Tradition* (Cambridge, 1983), 1–14

——, *The Age of Empire: 1875–1914* (London, 2002)

Hobson, J.A., *Confessions of an Economic Heretic* (London, 1938)

Hobson, S.G., *National Guilds: An Inquiry Into the Wage System and the Way Out* (London, 1919)

Hogben, Lancelot, 'Planning for Human Survival', *What Is Ahead of Us?* (London, 1937), 165–192

Hoggart, Richard, *Mass Media in a Mass Society* (London, 2004)

Holroyd, Michael, *Augustus John: A Biography* (London, 1976)

Honeywell, Carissa, *A British Anarchist Tradition: Herbert Read, Alex Comfort and Colin Ward* (London, 2011)

——, 'Bridging the Gaps: Twentieth-Century Anglo-American Anarchist Thought', in Ruth Kinna (ed.) *The Continuum Companion to Anarchism* (London, 2012), 111–139

Howell, David, *British Workers and the Independent Labour Party, 1888–1906* (Manchester, 1983)

Hughes, H. Stuart, *Consciousness and Society* (New York, 1958)

Huxley, Aldous, *Crome Yellow* (London, [1921] 2001)

Huxley, Thomas H., 'The Struggle for Existence in Human Society [1888]', *Evolution and Ethics and Other Essays* (New York, 1897), 195–236

Hyndman, H.M., *England for All* (London, 1881)

——, *The Historical Basis of Socialism in England* (London, 1883)

——, *The Record of an Adventurous Life* (London, 1911)

Hynes, Samuel, *A War Imagined: The First World War in English Culture* (London, 1990)

Irwin, Robert, *Memoirs of a Dervish: Sufis, Mystics and the Sixties* (London, 2011)

Jaffé, Aniela, *Was C.G. Jung a Mystic? And Other Essays* (Einsiedeln, 1989)

Jay, Martin, *The Dialectical Imagination: A History of the Frankfurt School* (California, 1996)

Jefferies, Richard, *After London; or, Wild England* (London, [1885] 1886)

Joll, James, *The Second International, 1889–1914* (London, 1955)

——, *The Anarchists* (London, 1979)

Jones, H.S., *Victorian Political Thought* (Basingstoke, 2000)

——, 'Introduction' to *Auguste Comte: Early Political Writings* (Cambridge, 1998), vi–xxviii

Jordan, William Chester, *Europe in the High Middle Ages* (London, 2001)

Joyce, Patrick, *The Rule of Freedom: Liberalism and the Modern City* (London, 2003)

Judt, Tony, *Postwar: A History of Europe Since 1945* (London, 2005)

Jun, Nathan, *Anarchism and Political Modernity* (New York, 2012)

Kamenka, Eugene, 'Community and the Socialist Ideal', in Kamenka (ed.) *Community as a Social Ideal* (London, 1982), 3–26

Kedward, Roderick, *The Anarchists* (New York, 1971)

Kelly, Aileen, *Mikhail Bakunin: A Study in the Psychology and Politics of Utopianism* (Oxford, 1982)

Kelly, Paul, 'Rescuing political theory from the tyranny of history', in Jonathan Floyd and Marc Stears (eds) *Political Philosophy versus History?: Contextualism and Real Politics in Contemporary Political Thought* (Cambridge, 2011), 13–37

Kendall, Walter, *The Revolutionary Movement in Britain 1900–1921: The Origins of British Communism* (London, 1969)

Kenney, Rowland, *Westering: An Autobiography* (London, 1939)

King, James, *The Last Modern: A Life of Herbert Read* (New York, 1990)

Kinna, Ruth, 'Kropotkin and Huxley', *Politics*, 12:2 (1992), 41–47

——, 'Kropotkin's Theory of Mutual Aid in Historical Context', *International Review of Social History* 40 (1995), 259–283

——, *William Morris: The Art of Socialism* (Cardiff, 2000)

——, 'The Jacobinism and Patriotism of Ernest Belfort Bax', *History of European Ideas*, 30:4 (2004), 463–484

——, *Anarchism: A Beginners Guide* (Oxford, 2005)

——, 'Fields of Vision: Kropotkin and Revolutionary Change', *Substance*, 36:2 (2007), 67–86

——, 'Anarchism and the Politics of Utopia', in Laurence Davis and Ruth Kinna (eds) *Anarchism and Utopianism* (Manchester, 2009), 221–240

——, 'Guy Aldred: Bridging the Gap Between Marxism and Anarchism', *Journal of Political Ideologies*, 16:1 (2011), 97–114

——, 'Introduction', in Kinna (ed.) *Continuum Companion to Anarchism* (London, 2012), 3–38

Klugmann, James, *History of the Communist Party of Great Britain: Volume 1* (London, 1968)

Koch, Andrew M., 'Post-Structuralism and the Epistemological Basis of Anarchism', in Duane Rouselle and Süreyyya Evren (eds) *Post-Anarchism: A Reader* (London, 2011), 23–40

Kołakowsi, Leszek, *Modernity on Endless Trial* (London, 1990)

——, *Main Currents of Marxism: The Forerunners, The Golden Age, The Breakdown*, trans. P.S. Falla (New York, 2007)

Krimerman, Leonard and Lewis Parry, *Patterns of Anarchy: A collection of Writings on the Anarchist Tradition* (New York, 1966)

Kumar, Krishan, 'Maine and the Theory of Progress', *The Victorian Achievement of Sir Henry Maine: A Centennial Reappraisal* (Cambridge, 1991), 76–87

Lansing, Carol, *The Florentine Magnates: Lineage and Faction in a Medieval Commune* (Princeton, 1991)

Lévi-Strauss, Claude, *The Savage Mind* (Chicago, 1962)

Levy, Carl, 'Social Histories of Anarchism', *Journal for the Study of Radicalism*, 4:2 (2010), 1–44

Lewis, Percy Wyndham (ed) *Blast No.1* (London, 1914)

——, *The Demon of Progress in the Arts* (London, 1954)

Light, Alison, *Forever England: Femininity, Literature and Conservatism Between the Wars* (London, 1991)

Ligt, Bart de, *The Conquest of Violence: An Essay on War and Revolution* (London, 1989)

London, Jack, *The Iron Heel* (New York, 1908)

Lovejoy, Arthur O., *The Great Chain of Being: A Study of the History of an Idea* (Cambridge, MA, 1961)

Lunn, Eugene, *Prophet of Community: The Romantic Socialism of Gustav Landauer* (Berkley, CA, 1973)

Lyotard, Jean-Francois, *The Postmodern Condition* (Manchester, 1984)
Macaulay, Thomas Babington, *Macaulay's History of England: From the Accession of James II: Volume 1* (London, 1953)
MacDiarmid, Hugh, *Lucky Poet: A Self-Study in Literature and Political Ideas* (London, 1943)
——, *Complete Poems: Volume 1*, Michael Grieve and W.R. Aitken (eds) (Manchester, 1993)
MacKenzie, Donald, 'Eugenics in Britain', *Social Studies of Science*, 6:3–4 (1976), 499–532
Maine, Henry Sumner, *Village-Communities in the East and West* (London, 1871)
——, *Ancient Law* (London, [1861] 1931)
Malatesta, Errico, *Malatesta: His Life & Ideas* (London, 1984)
——, *The Anarchist Revolution: Polemical Articles, 1924–1931* (London, 1995)
Marshall, Peter, *Demanding the Impossible: A History of Anarchism* (London, 1993)
Martin, Wallace, *The New Age Under Orage: Chapters in English Cultural History* (Manchester, 1967)
Marx, Karl, *Capital: A Critique of Political Economy* (Chicago, [1867] 1906)
——, *The Eighteenth Brumaire of Louis Bonaparte*, trans. Daniel De Leon (Chicago, [1852] 1907)
——, and Friedrich Engels, *The Communist Manifesto*, (London, [1888] 2002)
——, *Collected Works: Volume 35* (London, 1986), 12–23
Mavor, James, *My Windows on the Street of the World: Volume 2* (London, 1923)
May, Todd, *The Political Philosophy of Poststructuralist Anarchism* (Pennsylvania, 1994)
Mazower, Mark, *Dark Continent: Europe's Twentieth Century* (New York, 2000)
McKinley, C. Alexander, *Illegitimate Children of the Enlightenment: Anarchists and the French Revolution 1880–1914* (New York, 2008)
Meltzer, Albert, *I Couldn't Paint Golden Angels: Sixty Years of Commonplace Life and Anarchist Agitation* (Edinburgh, 1996)
Mendel, Arthur P., *Michael Bakunin: Roots of Apocalypse* (New York, 1981)
Mill, John Stuart, *Autobiography* (London, [1873] 1989)
——, *On Liberty and Other Writings* (Cambridge, [1859] 1989)
Miller, David, *Anarchism* (London, 1984)
Miller, Martin A., *Kropotkin* (Chicago, 1976)
Mirsky, Dimitri, *The Intelligentsia of Great Britain* (London, 1935)
Mommsen, Wolfgang J., 'History of Political Theory in the Federal Republic of Germany: Strange Death and Slow Recovery', in Dario Castiglione and Iain Hampsher-Monk (eds) *The History of Political Thought in National Context* (Cambridge, 2001), 40–57
Montesquieu, Charles de Secondat de, *The Spirit of the Laws*, trans. Thomas Nugent (N.D., 1748), 10
Morgan, Kenneth O., *The People's Peace: British History: 1945–1990* (Oxford, 1992)
Morgan, Kevin, *Against Fascism and War: Ruptures and Continuities in British Communist Politics, 1935–1941* (Manchester, 1989)
——, *Harry Pollitt* (Manchester, 1993)
——, *Ramsey MacDonald* (London, 2006)
Morland, David, *Demanding the Impossible?: Human Nature and Politics in the Nineteenth-Century Social Anarchism* (London, 1997)
Morris, Brian, *Kropotkin: The Politics of Community* (New York, 2004)

Morris, William, 'How We Live and How We Might Live', in A.L. Morton (ed.) *Political Writings of William Morris* (London, 1973), 134–158
——, '1227: To John Carruthers', in Norman Kelvin (ed.) *The Collected Letters of William Morris: Volume II* (Princeton, 1987), 533–535
Morton, A.L., *The English Utopia* (London, 1969)
Murry, John Middleton, 'Reason and Criticism', *The Times Literary Supplement*, 8 July 1926, 453
Nettlau, Max, 'Anarchism: Individualist or Communist? – Both', Anarchy!' *An Anthology of Emma Goldman's Mother Earth* (New York, [1914] 2000), 79–83
Nevinson, Henry W., *Fire of Life* (London, 1935)
Newburgh, William of, *The Church Historians of England: Volume IV – Part II*, trans. Joseph Stevenson (London, 1856)
Newman, Saul, 'Anarchism, Utopianism and the Politics of Emancipation', in Laurnce Davis and Ruth Kinna (eds) *Anarchism and Utopianism* (Manchester, 2009), 207–220
——, 'Postanarchism: A Politics of Anti-politics,' *Journal of Political Ideologies*, 16:3 (2011), 313–327
——, *The Politics of Postanarchism* (Edinburgh, 2011)
Nietzsche, Friedrich, *Beyond Good and Evil*, trans. Helen Zimmern (New York, [1886] 1954)
Novak, D., 'The Place of Anarchism in the History of Political Thought', *The Review of Politics*, 20:3 (1958), 307–329
Oliver, H., *The International Anarchist Movement in Late Victorian London* (London, 1983)
Orage, A.R., *Selected Essays and Critical Writings*, Herbert Read and Denis Saurat (eds) (London, 1935)
Orwell, George, 'Review of A Coat of Many Colours: Occasional Essays by Herbert Read', in Peter Davinson et al. (eds) *The Complete Works of George Orwell: Volume 17* (London, 1998), 402–405
Overy, Richard, *The Twilight Years: The Paradox of Britain Between the Wars* (New York, 2009)
Owen, Robert, *The Life of Robert Owen* (London, 1920)
Paraskos, Michael, 'Herbert Read and Leeds', in Benedict Read and David Thistlewood (eds) *Herbert Read: A British Vision of World Art* (London, 1993), 25–33
——, 'Introduction' to Read, *To Hell With Culture* (London, 2002), ix–xxiii
——, 'Imagination Seizes Power: A Brief Introduction', in Michael Paraskos (ed.) *Rereading Read* (London, 2007), 8–17
——, 'The Curse of King Bomba: Or How Marxism Stole Modernism', in Michael Paraskos (ed.) *Rereading Read* (London, 2007), 44–57
Pearson, Karl, *National Life from the Standpoint of Science: An Address Delivered at Newcastle* (London, 1901)
Pease, Edward, *The History of the Fabian Society* (London, [1918] 1963)
Penty, Arthur J., *The Restoration of the Gild System* (London, 1906)
Perrin, Noel, 'Eden Under the Earth', *The Washington Post Book World*, 19 August 1984, 215
Plekhanov, George V., *Fundamental Problems of Marxism* (New York, 1975)
Pocock, J.G.A., 'Between Machiavelli and Hume: Gibbon as Civic Humanist and Philosophical Historian', *Daedalus*, 105:3 (1976), 153–169

Porter, Alan, 'Prose', *The Spectator*, 21 July 1928, 40–1
Priestley, J.B., *Letter to a Returning Serviceman* (London, 1945)
——, *The Edwardians* (London, 1970)
Pugh, Martin, *The Making of Modern British Politics: 1867–1939* (Oxford, 1982)
Purbank, P.N., *E.M. Forster: A Life: Volume 1* (London, 1977)
Purchase, Graham, *Evolution and Revolution: An Introduction to the Life and Thought of Peter Kropotkin* (Sydney, 1996)
Quail, John, *The Slow Burning Fuse* (London, 1978)
Richards, Vernon, *Lessons of the Spanish Revolution* (London, [1955] 1995)
Ritter, Alan, *Anarchism: A Theoretical Analysis* (Cambridge, 1980)
Robespierre, Maximilien, 'On the Conduct to be Pursued', in H. Morse Stephens (ed.) *Orators of the French Revolution: Volume II* (Oxford, 1892), 357–366
Rogers, James E. Thorold, *The Economic Interpretation of History* (London, [1888] 1909)
Ross, Stephen, 'Introduction: The missing link', in Ross (ed.) *Modernism and Theory: A Critical Debate* (London, 2009), 1–17
Rousseau, Jean Jacques, *The Social Contract or Principles of Political Right*, trans. Henry J. Tozer (New York, [1762] 1898)
Russell, Bertrand, *Why I am Not a Christian and Other Essays* (London, 1957)
Ryley, Peter, *Making Another World Possible: Anarchism, Anti-Capitalism and Ecology in Late 19th and Early 20th Century Britain* (New York, 2013)
Sachs, David, 'The Rebel. By Albert Camus', *The Philosophical Review*, 64:1 (1955), 150–152
Sargent, Lyman Tower, 'Is There Only One Utopian Tradition?', *Journal of the History of Ideas*, 43:4 (1982), 681–689
Sassoon, Donald, *One Hundred Years of Socialism: The West European Left in the Twentieth Century* (London, 2010)
Scalmer, Sean, *Gandhi in the West: The Mahatma and the Rise of Radical Protest* (Cambridge, 2011)
Schmidt, Michel, and Lucien van der Walt, *Black Flame: The Revolution Class Politics of Anarchism and Syndicalism* (Edinburgh, 2009)
Schulze, Hagen, *States, Nations and Nationalism: From the Middle Ages to the Present* (Oxford, 1996)
Serge, Victor, *Memoirs of a Revolutionary: 1901–1941*, trans. Peter Sedgwick (Oxford, 1963)
Shatz, Marshall S., 'Introduction', in Shatz (ed.) *The Conquest of Bread & Other Writings* (Cambridge, 1995), vii–xxiii
Shaw, G. Bernard, 'Use of Land: Russian Theories and Practise', *The Times*, 1 October 1940, 6
Sieyès, Emmanuel Joseph, 'What is the Third Estate?', in Michael Sonenscher (ed.) *Sieyès: Political Writings* (Indianapolis, 2003), 92–162
Sinfield, Alan, *Literature, Politics, and Culture in Postwar Britain* (Berkeley, 1989)
Sitwell, Osbert, *Laughter in the Next Room: Being the Fourth Volume of Left Hand, Right Hand!* (London, 1950)
Skidelsky, Sibilla, 'Paris Exposition Does Little for Architecture: German and Russian Pavilions Draw Attention', *Washington Post*, 19 September 1947, 7
Skinner, Quentin. *The Foundations of Modern Political Thought: Volume 1* (Cambridge, 1978)

——, *Visions of Politics: Volume 1* (2002)
Smith, Adam, *An Inquiry into the Nature and Causes of the Wealth of Nations: Volume 1* (London, [1776] 1921)
——, *An Inquiry into the Nature and Causes of the Wealth of Nations: Volume 2* (London, [1776] 1921)
——, *An Inquiry into the Nature and Causes of the Wealth of Nations: Books IV–V* (London, [1776] 1999)
——, *The Theory of Moral Sentiments* (London, [1759] 1853)
Snow, C.P., *The Two Cultures and the Scientific Revolution* (Cambridge, 1959)
——, 'Correspondence', *The London Magazine*, 16:10 (1959), 57–59
Solomon, Robert C., *Continental Philosophy Since 1750: The Rise and Fall of the Self* (Oxford, 1988)
Sonn, Richard, *Anarchism* (New York, 1992)
Southgate, Beverley, 'Humani nil alienum: The Quest for "Human Nature" ', in Keith Jenkins (ed.) *Manifestos for History* (Oxford, 2007), 67–76
Spencer, Herbert, *Social Statics: Or, The Conditions Essential to Human Happiness* (London, 1851),
——, 'Reasons for Dissenting from the Philosophy of M. Comte', *Essays: Scientific, Political, and Speculative: Volume III* (London, [1864] 1874), 57–80
——, *The Man Versus the State* (New York, 1884)
Spender, Stephen, *The Thirties and After: Poetry, Politics, People* (Glasgow, 1978)
Stafford, David, 'Anarchists in Britain Today', in David E. Apter and James Joll (eds) *Anarchism Today* (London, 1971), 84–104
Stalin, J., *Dialectical and Historical Materialism* (Moscow, 1939)
Steele, Tom, 'The Leeds Art Club: A Provincial Avant-Garde?', *Literature and History*, 14:1 (1988), 91–109
——, 'Circles of Modernism: Herbert Read, Arnold Hauser and the Emergence of Art History in Leeds', in Michael Paraskos (ed.) *Rereading Read* (London, 2007), 112–119
Taylor, A.J.P., *The Trouble Makers: Dissent Over Foreign Policy 1729–1939* (London, [1957] 1993)
——,*English History: 1914–1945* (Oxford, 1965)
Taylor, Richard, *Against the Bomb: The British Peace Movement: 1958–1965* (Oxford, 1988)
Tawney, R.H., 'The Choice Before the Labour Party', *The Political Quarterly*, 3:3 (1932), 323–345
Tcherkesoff, W., *Let Us Be Just: (An Open Letter to Liebknecht)* (London, 1896)
Thistlewood, David, 'Herbert Read', *Prospects*, 24:1–2 (1994), 375–390
——, 'Herbert Read's Organic Aesthetic [II] 1950–1968', in David Goodway (ed.) *Herbert Read Reassessed* (Liverpool, 1998), 233–247
Thompson, Laurence, *Robert Blatchford: Portrait of an Englishman* (London, 1951)
Thorpe, Andrew, *A History of the British Labour Party* (New York, 1997)
——, *The British Communist Party and Moscow: 1920–1943* (Manchester, 2000)
Tocqueville, Alexis de, *Journeys to England and Ireland*, J.P. Mayer (ed.), trans. George Lawrence and K.P. Mayer (New Haven, 1958)
——, *Democracy in America* (London, [1835] 2003)
Todman, Dan, *The Great War: Myth and Memory* (London, 2011)
Trotsky, Leon, *The History of the Russian Revolution: Volume II*, trans. Max Eastman (Ann Arbor, 1957)

Tucker, Benj. R., *Instead of a Book: By a Man Too Busy to Write One: A Fragmentary Exposition of Philosophical Anarchism* (New York, [1897] 1972)
Turcato, Davide, *Making Sense of Anarchism: Errico Malatesta's Experiments With Revolution* (Basingstoke, 2012)
Voltaire, *Philosophical Letters*, trans. Ernest Dilworth (Indianapolis, 1961)
Walicki, Andrezj, 'Russian Political Thought in the Nineteenth Century', in Gareth Stedman Jones and Gregory Claeys (eds) *The Cambridge History of Nineteenth-Century Political Thought* (Cambridge, 2013), 811–834
Walter, Nicolas, 'Remembering Herbert Read', *Anarchy 91* (1968), 287–288
——, *The Anarchist Past & Other Essays*, David Goodway (ed.) (Nottingham, 2009)
Ward, Colin and David Goodway, *Talking Anarchy* (Nottingham, 2003)
Ward, Colin, 'Herbert Read: The Anarchist Knight', *Peace News*, 21 June 1968, 2
——, *Anarchy in Action* (London, 2008)
Ward, Dana, 'Art and Anarchy: Herbert Read's Aesthetic Politics', in Michael Paraskos (ed.) *Rereading Read* (London, 2007), 20–33
——, 'Alchemy in Clarens: Kropotkin and Reclus, 1877–1881', in Nathan J. Jun and Shane Wahl (eds) *New Perspectives on Anarchism* (Lanham, MD, 2009), 209–226
Ward-Smith, G., 'Baldwin and Scotland: More than Englishness', *Contemporary British History*, 15:1 (2001), 61–82
Wasson, Richard, 'The Green Child: Herbert Read's Ironic Fantasy', *PMLA*, 77:5 (1962), 645–651
Watson, Janet S.K., *Fighting Different Wars: Experience, Memory, and the First World War in Britain* (Cambridge, 2004)
Webb, Sidney, 'Historic', in G.B. Shaw (ed.) *Fabian Essays in Socialism*, (London, 1889), 30–61
——, 'The Future of Soviet Communism', *What Is Ahead of Us?* (London, 1937), 103–132
Wells, H.G., *Anticipations: Of the Reaction of Mechanical and Scientific Progress Upon Human Life and Thought* (London, 1902)
——, *A Modern Utopia* (London, 1905)
——, *An Englishman Looks at the World* (London, 1914)
——, *Democracy Under Revision: A Lecture Delivered at the Sorbonne on March 15th, 1927* (London, 1927)
——, *The Way the World is Going: Guesses & Forecasts of the Years Ahead* (London, 1928)
——, *An Experiment in Autobiography: Discoveries and Conclusions of a Very Ordinary Brain: Volume II* (London, 1934)
——, 'Letters to the Editor: War Aims: The Rights of Man', *The Times*, 25 October 1939, 6
——, 'Letters to the Editor: War Aims', *The Times*, 26 September 1939, 4
——, *The Rights of Man, or What Are We Fighting For?* (London, 1940)
——, (ed.) *The Rights of Man: An Essay in Collective Definition* (Brighton, 1943)
Williams, Orlando Cyprian, 'A Philosophical Romance', *Times Literary Supplement*, 11 February 1935, 693
Williamson, Philip, ' "Safety First": Baldwin, the Conservative Party, and the 1929 General Election', *The Historical Journal*, 25:2 (1982), 385–409
Wiltshire, David, *The Social and Political Thought of Herbert Spencer* (Oxford, 1978)
Wind, Edgar, 'Ideas and Images', *Times Literary Supplement*, 11 May 1956, 277–278

Winter, Jay, *Sites of Memory, Sites of Mourning: The Great War in European Cultural History* (Cambridge, 1995)
Wolff, Jonathan, *An Introduction to Political Philosophy* (London, 1996)
Woodcock, George, and Ivan Avakumović, *The Anarchist Prince: A Biographical Study of Peter Kropotkin* (New York, 1970)
Woodcock, George, *Anarchism: A History of Libertarian Ideas and Movements* (London, [1962] 1970)
——, *Herbert Read: The Stream and the Source* (London, 1972)
——, 'Anarchism and the Role of Art: Review of Education Through Art', *The Nation*, 12 October 1974, 341–3
——, *Taking It to the Letter* (Ontario, 1981)
——, *Letters to the Past: An Autobiography* (Toronto, 1982)
——, *Anarchism: A History of Libertarian Ideas and Movements* (London, 1986)
——, 'An Introduction' to Peter Kropotkin, *The Great French Revolution* (Montréal, 1989), x–xxviii
Woolf, Virginia, 'Virginia Woolf to Vanessa Bell: 18th May 1929' in Nigel Nicolson (ed.) *A Reflection of the Other Person: The Letters of Virginia Woolf: Volume IV, 1929–1931* (London, 1978), 58–61
——, *The Diary of Virginia Woolf*, Anne Olivier Bell (ed.) (London, 1982)
Zamyatin, Yevgeny, *We*, trans. Michael Glenny (London, [1924] 1984)

Index

Note: Locators followed by the letter 'n' refer to notes.

Printed and bound in Great Britain by
CPI Group (UK) Ltd, Croydon, CR0 4YY